BLOOD RELATIONS

BLOOD RELATIONS

Christian and Jew
in *The Merchant of Venice*

JANET ADELMAN

THE UNIVERSITY OF CHICAGO PRESS

CHICAGO AND LONDON

JANET ADELMAN is professor of English at the University of California at Berkeley. She is the author of *Suffocating Mothers: Fantasies of Maternal Origin in Shakespeare's Plays, "Hamlet" to "The Tempest"* (1992) and *The Common Liar: An Essay on "Antony and Cleopatra"* (1973) and the editor of *Twentieth Century Interpretations of "King Lear": A Collection of Critical Essays* (1978).

The University of Chicago Press, Chicago 60637
The University of Chicago Press, Ltd., London
© 2008 by The University of Chicago
All rights reserved. Published 2008
Printed in the United States of America

17 16 15 14 13 12 11 10 09 08   1 2 3 4 5

ISBN-13: 978-0-226-00681-9 (cloth)
ISBN-10: 0-226-00681-6 (cloth)

An early version of chapter 3 appeared in an article entitled "Her Father's Blood: Race, Conversion, and Nation in *The Merchant of Venice*" in *Representations* 81 (Winter 2003): 4–30. Copyright © 2003 by the Regents of the University of California.

Library of Congress Cataloging-in-Publication Data
Adelman, Janet.
    Blood relations : Christian and Jew in the Merchant of Venice / Janet Adelman.
        p. cm.
    Includes bibliographical references (p.) and index.
    ISBN-13: 978-0-226-00681-9 (cloth : alk. paper)
    ISBN-10: 0-226-00681-6 (cloth : alk. paper) 1. Shakespeare, William, 1564–1616. Merchant of Venice. 2. Shakespeare, William, 1564–1616—Characters—Jews. 3. Shakespeare, William, 1564–1616—Characters—Antonio. 4. Religion and literature—England—History—16th century. 5. Religion and literature—England—History—17th century. 6. Shylock (Fictitious character) 7. Christians in literature. 8. Jews in literature. 9. Antisemitism in literature. 10. Religion in literature. I. Title.
    PR2825.A36 2008
    822.3'3—dc22

                                                                2007023707

CONTENTS

ACKNOWLEDGMENTS

This book has had a very long germination period. The first references to Shylock as a figment of Antonio's desire start turning up in my lecture notes around 1990, and I first went public with a version of that idea in 1991, in a paper for Marjorie Garber's MLA Shakespeare Forum on Character Assassination. Part of the delay was due to routine causes, but part I think came from the personal difficulty I had in confronting this most painful of plays. As a consequence, the debts that I want to acknowledge here are as much personal as intellectual and institutional (in fact, the personal and the intellectual have been unusually hard to separate in this instance).

Let me begin with the institutional. I first understood that I was working on a book rather than an essay while I was at the Bellagio Study Center in 1998, when I found myself writing a too-long chunk on Lancelot's attempt to leave Shylock; I am very grateful to the Rockefeller Foundation for providing me with just the right balance of undisturbed time, serenity in beautiful surroundings, and good company at dinner to enable me to see the shape that this work would take. A residential stay at the Liguria Study Center in 2003, provided by the Bogliasco Foundation, similarly provided me with essential work time and space at a later stage of the project. My own home institution, the University of California, Berkeley, has generously supported this project with annual research grants, sabbatical leaves, and a Humanities Research Fellowship. But its support has extended far beyond the fiscal. Berkeley has been a wonderful place to spend my working life, and I still—after thirty-nine years—count myself extraordinarily lucky to have been here, in a university and a department of such intellectual richness, where faculty are encouraged to go their own way and good work of all kinds is supported and recognized, and where students at all levels are a constant source of stimulation and pleasure. (I am particularly grateful to those graduate students who have served as my research assistants on this project: Michael Farry, Jennifer Shoffeit, and Elisabeth Lampert Thompson.) It's always hard to imagine who one might have become had one been elsewhere; but I am in every sense deeply grateful to have been here.

For much of the time, the writing of this book has felt like a private obsession, but an obsession sustained by crucial ventures into a more public world. A very early version of the book (while I still thought of it as a too-long essay) was greeted with enthusiasm and helpful comments by my writing group in the early 1990s—Elizabeth Abel, Marilyn Fabe, Gayle Greene, Claire Kahane, and Madelon Sprengnether—and also by Richard Wheeler; friendships with these people have continued to sustain it, and me, over the intervening years. I presented versions of the book to the Ohio Shakespeare Conference on Shakespeare and Multiculturalism in 1996, to the Bay Area Early Modern Group in 1999, to the Renaissance Society of America, the Renaissance Colloquium at Harvard University (once again at the gracious invitation of Marjorie Garber), and the Australian/New Zealand Shakespeare Conference organized by Michael Neill, all in 2000, and to the New Orleans meeting of the Shakespeare Association of America in 2004, as part of a panel organized by Heather James. The warm reception given these various trial balloons, especially by Michael Neill, Heather James, Ralph Hexter, Patricia Parker, Coppélia Kahn, Gail Paster, Meredith Skura, Peter Stallybrass, and (most of all) David Bevington, gave me the courage and the motivation to continue. I am also very grateful to the anonymous reviewers for the University of Chicago Press, who responded to the initial manuscript with the perfect mix of generosity and helpful criticism.

Ralph Hexter needs repeated mention here: as dean of Arts and Humanities while I was chair of the English Department, he provided the kinds of intellectual sustenance and comradeship that helped me to retain the conviction that I still had an intellectual life and something worth saying. Wonderful conversations with Steven Justice and Marcia Cavell served much the same purpose during the same period and afterward. Catherine Gallagher solicited an early version of chapter 3 for *Representations*; her faith in this project, and her friendly insistence that I not go on revising it forever, have helped to bring it to completion. My beloved friend Nick Howe did not live long enough to see it published, but his continual nudging before his death also helped me to let go of the book, as well as (by his own capacious example) to imagine other sorts of writing that I might want to do once I was no longer enmeshed in this project. Much in Daniel Boyarin's work—as well as his friendship and his conviction that anything is fair game for thought—has provided important support for my own thinking. And at the crucial final stages of this project, extraordinarily generous readings by Steven Goldsmith and Susan Schweik—two of its most ideal non-Shakespearean readers—have made me feel less abashed at having taken so long to trace the workings of this obsession.

My last set of debts are harder to specify but at least equally important. Kehilla Community Synagogue has for many years made available to me a form of Judaism that I could embrace and thus enabled me finally to be able to write about *The Merchant of Venice* from my perspective as a Jew; I am deeply grateful to its spiritual leaders and especially to the members of my chavurah, comrades all, who have sustained me in this project without ever having read a word of it. And I am most of all grateful to my children, Brian Osserman and Stephen Osserman, continual sources of wonder and delight, and to my husband, Bob Osserman, who graciously agreed to have his life bent out of shape by this project for many years and who provides a foundation and a safe haven for my life in all ways.

All unspecified references to Shakespeare's works are to the *Norton Shakespeare* (general editor, Stephen Greenblatt); Katharine Eisaman Maus is the editor of *The Merchant of Venice* for that edition. Unless otherwise noted, all citations of the Bible are to *The Geneva Bible: A Facsimile of the 1560* Edition. Bibliographic details for both are given in the Works Cited section. Except when I cite works familiar in modern editions, I have generally used early modern editions; in order to preserve the sense of strangeness and the immediacy of these texts, I have reproduced their original spelling, punctuation, and capitalization. I have thus retained the initial *v* for *u* (e.g., "vnto"), the medial *u* for *v* (e.g., "saue"), and the *i* for *j* (e.g., "iudgment" or "Iew"). But I have silently altered unfamiliar contractions, abbreviations, and orthographic forms that might make my text too forbidding to a contemporary reader.

CHAPTER ONE

Introduction: Strangers within Christianity

At the beginning of my career, in 1968, just when I had come to Berkeley and was attempting to manage the transition from graduate student to full-fledged Shakespearean, a senior Renaissance scholar told me that Jews shouldn't be allowed to teach Renaissance literature because Renaissance literature was Christian literature. I think that he would, if queried now, disown his comment as facetious, but I don't think that it was facetious; I think that it was provoked by the spectacle of yet another Jew—and a woman to boot—coming to teach *his* literature in a department already littered with Jews. In 1968, Berkeley included among its Renaissance scholars Jonas Barish, Don Friedman, Norman Rabkin, Stephen Orgel, Stanley Fish, and Paul Alpers, though not yet Stephen Greenblatt or Joel Fineman, both of whom came within a few years—in fact an extraordinary collection of Jews working in the Renaissance, and my interlocutor was right to be worried. Though there were still major universities where Jewish faculty members were welcomed cautiously, if at all, at least at Berkeley Jews had entered what was then the inner sanctum of literature and were converting this holy of holies to their own uses, developing a set of critical practices that read obliquely, against the grain, and permanently changing the map of Renaissance studies in the process.

Perhaps no one would now say aloud what my interlocutor said in 1968. But as recently as 1992, in the course of a book attacking bardolatry and the belief that Shakespeare wrote "Shakespeare," Elliott Baker had this to say on the subject of Jews and the study of Shakespeare:

Maybe people are only "chosen" to interpret and perform; a possible explanation of why, in our grubby world of takeovers, the violins [stereotypically carried by "good little Jewish boys" in "the good old days"] have been replaced by facsimiles of the First Folio and the new Shakespearean authorities while predominantly American are also disproportionately Jewish.

Pioneer, Oh Pioneer! In this case, Sidney Lee (nee Solomon Lazarus) won himself a knighthood from Queen Victoria for his *A Life of William Shakespeare* and the signal went out that the promised land could be along the banks of the Avon. . . . But the big Shakespeare takeover has been comparatively recent.

If Yeshiva University had a football team, the lineup could read pretty much the same: Adelman, Fineman, Goldberg, Greenblatt, Kahn, Schwartz, plus a few ringers from inter-marriages.[1]

The same moneygrubbing Jews in charge of corporate takeovers have (Baker suggests) taken over the green heart of England, converting "the banks of the Avon" to their grubby new promised land. But despite the concern with a debased commercial culture registered in his incipient pun on "banks," Baker is less worried about the contamination of Shakespeare—after all, he claims not to believe in "Shakespeare"—than he is about place-shifting Jews who refuse to stay in the cultural positions previously allotted them, Jews who have climbed up into the cultural center: "Greenblatt and Levi, once a good masthead for a clothing store. But things change, things change. Stephen Greenblatt is Professor of English Literature at the University of California and Peter Levi occupies a similar cushion at Oxford." In fact, Baker is willing to attribute the taint of the Jew to Shakespeare himself in the interest of maintaining his anti-Stratfordian argument. In his opening chapter ("The Schlock and the Sodomite"), Baker defines schlock as "one of those noises that came out of a ram's horn" and then poses Shakespeare as its anachronistic embodiment, by nature the opposite of the sodomite who wrote the sonnets: he is a social-climbing "rising schlock," a "schlock opera-tor" whose only hand in the works that bear his name was as a "schlock play broker" who took advantage of the work of others, the first of an "ignoble breed" recognizable to anyone familiar with "Shangri-Sinai (also known as Hollywood)."[2]

Like my interlocutor in 1968, Baker wants to protect the terrain of Eng-lish literature from the Jews; unlike him, he would count Shakespeare him-self among them. But Shakespeare's "Jewishness" is a shifty signifier for Baker's anti-Stratfordian purposes: although he makes Shakespeare Jewish here in order to distinguish him from the sodomite who wrote the sonnets, when he explicitly poses the question in his next chapter—entitled "Was Shakespeare Jewish?"—he answers it in the negative, this time in order to

seduce his Jewish Shakespeareans away from devotion to the man they worship because they mistakenly believe him to be a fellow Jew. His premise
is that only a sense of kinship would make a Jew into a Shakespearean; and
because he assumes that Jews recognize a "lanzman" in Shylock's apparently
philo-Semitic "Hath not a Jew eyes?" speech, he creates a bizarre historical
fantasy in which Queen Elizabeth writes the speech and forces Shakespeare
to include it, thus demonstrating that Shakespeare is not Jewish after all and
that Jews are therefore "worshipping at the wrong shrine."[3] And with that
issue settled, Baker can happily look forward to his own version of the conversion of the Jews, this time to the camp of the anti-Stratfordians.[4]

I begin with these odd interlocutors because they haunt the edges of this
book. First of all, they eerily replicate some of the anxieties that drive *The
Merchant of Venice*: my senior scholar in 1968 imagined English Renaissance literature as a kind of Christian Belmont where no Jewish foreigners
need apply; Baker imagines it as already contaminated at its source, salvage-
able only by a latter-day conversion that would repudiate its Jewishness.
And if on the one hand both demonstrate that certain aspects of my subject
in this book are alive and well (though sometimes forced to live under an
assumed name), on the other hand both induce a certain self-consciousness
about my own position as its author. Both assume that my Jewishness must
matter to my reading of Shakespeare: my interlocutor in 1968 that my status as a Jew would necessarily interfere with my reading of "Christian"
Shakespeare; Baker that no Jew could be drawn to study Shakespeare without construing Shakespeare as somehow "Jewish." The question raised by
these assumptions—and sometimes echoed by Jews who ask with irritation
why I am devoting my time to the author of so manifestly anti-Semitic a
play—stands obliquely behind the writing of this book. For what is a Jewish
Shakespearean to make of *The Merchant of Venice* if she wishes neither to
convert Shakespeare by making him a kinsman or partisan of Shylock nor
to convert herself into the normative Christian reader my interlocutor en-
visioned in 1968?[5]

One option would be to ignore the theology of the play altogether, but
this option seems to me to ignore much of what is most compelling in the
play. *Merchant*'s representation of its Jews begins and ends with the issue
of conversion, and its most dramatic scene threatens to replay the killing of
Christ, the theological event that for Christians defined the relation between
Christian and Jew: how can one not take its Christian supersessionist theology seriously? My own solution—and the implicit answer to the question I
pose above—has been to take that theology very seriously indeed, without
entirely endorsing a Christian triumphalist reading of it. For despite the se-

rene triumph that some critics attribute both to the doctrine and to the play as a document in "Christian apologetics,"[6] Christian supersessionist theology seems to me to carry its own residue of anxiety with it, anxiety that *Merchant* traces back to the vexed familial relations between Judaism and Christianity: to Christianity's simultaneous dependence on its literal and theological lineage in Judaism and its guilty disavowal of that inheritance, to its chronic need both to claim and to repudiate the Jew.[7] My own position as a Jew writing on this Christian text has, I think, made me particularly sensitive to this anxiety, as—at an earlier stage in my career—my position as a woman made me particularly sensitive to anxieties about the ways in which masculine identity in Shakespeare is compromised by its female origins. Despite its ostentatious theological triumphalism, *The Merchant of Venice* persistently troubles the distinction between Christian and Jew, and not only in the domain of the economic, where the distinction between usurer and merchant was increasingly difficult to maintain:[8] theologically, the knowledge that *Merchant* simultaneously gestures toward and defends against is that the Jew is not the stranger outside Christianity but the original stranger within it.

Let me begin to approach these issues via those literal strangers within English Christianity, the conversos in London. The promise—or threat—of Jewish conversion that is at the heart of *Merchant* is a primary site of the anxieties I have just described, not only insofar as conversion threatens to unmake the crucial distinction between Christian and Jew but also insofar as it reiterates Christianity's originary act of disavowal, with all its attendant guilt; and the presence of Jewish converts in Shakespeare's London may have served as a kind of local irritant, uncomfortably reminding his audiences of these anxieties.[9] But apparently the presence of the conversos in London could not be "known" in the Shakespearean mainstream until Jewish scholars themselves had made it into the Shakespearean mainstream and became comfortable enough there to address explicitly "Jewish" topics.[10] It should have been known.[11] Although England had expelled its Jews in 1290, London had a "House of Converts" all through the period of exile,[12] and individuals and small groups of converted Jews had been living in England off and on since the expulsion.[13] Anglo-Jewish historians had been writing specifically about the presence of a small Sephardic community in Shakespeare's London since the late nineteenth century; and even before Lucien Wolf's massive essay listing its members was published in *Transactions of the Jewish*

Historical Society of England in 1926, much of S. L. Lee's early account of that community had been reproduced in the 1888 Variorum edition of *The Merchant of Venice*.[14] Together with the Variorum, C. J. Sisson's unambiguously titled "A Colony of Jews in Shakespeare's London"—written by a well-known Shakespearean and published in 1938 by a major academic press at the cultural center—should have moved knowledge of this community from the periphery to the Shakespearean mainstream. Scholars since Lee had cited the case of its most prominent member—Rodrigo Lopez, personal physician to the queen, accused and convicted of plotting to poison her in 1594—as part of the context for *The Merchant of Venice* and probably an impetus for the 1594 revival of *The Jew of Malta*; and in 1955 John Russell Brown's introduction to his Arden edition of *Merchant* (hardly a text on the cultural margins) had called attention to the presence of what he calls "real Jews" in Shakespeare's London.[15]

Why, then, did so astute a scholar as G. K. Hunter maintain in 1964—in an essay which cites Sisson's account of the converso community—not only that Judaism was for Tudor England a theological, rather than a racial, category but also that England was "a country bare of racial Jews,"[16] and why was his claim so readily accepted at the time? Though Hunter himself cautioned scholars against the ways in which contemporary concerns may inappropriately impinge on scholarship, it is likely that he was responding at least in part to the Nazis' deadly racialization of the Jews with what was then politically correct doctrine; certainly, the mantra of my youth was "Judaism is a religion, not a race."[17] But despite the official tenets of a Christian universalism that welcomed converts as equal participants in the church, Shakespeare's contemporaries were far less sure than Hunter that Judaism was a theological, rather than a racial, category. Jerome may have said that "Christians are made, not born," and Christianity may be hypothetically open to all, but the suspicion that a troubling Jewish "residue" remained in Jewish converts to Christianity was at least as old as the thirteenth century.[18] And whatever his intention, the effect of Hunter's foundational essay was to erase the presence of that residue in England, shoring up the fantasy of England as a purely "Christian" domain that so captivated my 1968 interlocutor and rendering both the issue of Jewish "race" and the converted Jews of London invisible, along with the questions that their presence might have provoked.

I find it both moving and intriguing to contemplate these precariously situated converted Jews in England. What were their lives like? The men who left traces in the historical record were for the most part physicians and merchants; one—Francis Añes—served as a secret agent for Drake in the

Azores and later commanded an English garrison in Ireland. (Records for the
women are harder to come by, but there are historical traces of at least one
remarkable woman earlier in the century: Beatriz Fernandes, whose household was apparently at the center of the Sephardic community in Bristol,
and who was instrumental in converting at least one young converso back
to Judaism, if we can trust testimony provided to the Inquisition.)[19] But in
what sense were the conversos in Shakespeare's London attempting to live
lives as Jews despite their perhaps-nominal Christianity? A deposition given
to the Inquisition in Madrid in 1588 alleges of them that "it is public and
notorious in London, that by race they are all Jews, and it is notorious that
in their own homes they live as such observing their Jewish rites." Since
the Inquisition presumably got what it wanted to hear from this witness, his
testimony about their observance of Jewish rites may be less than entirely
reliable. But Edward Barton, the English ambassador to Constantinople, and
presumably a more reliable source, corroborates this testimony: he complains in a letter to Burghley that the envoy of the Jewish Duke of Metilli
(himself a former converso with many ties to the English conversos) openly
held Jewish services with some members of the community in London in
1592 ("he and all his trayne used publickely the Jewes rytes in prayinge, ac-
companyed with divers secrett Jewes resident in London").[20] Closer to home,
a court case from 1596 relied on servants to pry into the interior of converso
households to discover their inhabitants' secret Jewish practices; Sisson's
account of the case concludes that the servants' garbled description of what
went on behind the conversos' closed curtains "is, in fact, reliable enough"
and gives us "a record of a Jewish household practicing its observances in
secret."[21] According to Sisson, one member of this colony of secret Jews "in
his will proclaims himself a Jew" despite having been "for twenty-five years
at least . . . an observing Christian in his parish-church." There is, moreover,
evidence that several members of the community—Rodrigo Lopez among
them—contributed to the synagogue at Antwerp; and according to a document (dated February 16, 1594) in the State Archives in Florence, Lopez
himself "paid a visit to the Ghetto in Venice"—Shylock's ghetto—"in the
company of his brothers and wife."[22]

But whether or not some of the conversos continued to consider themselves Jews, to what extent did Shakespeare's contemporaries consider them
Jews and how was their "Jewishness" received? The conversos were troubling partly because they demonstrated the impossibility of knowing what
is within. It is clear that at least some of their contemporaries suspected that
these ostensible Christians were carrying out Jewish rituals in the privacy
of their own houses. (Is it purely a coincidence that—as in the court case

Sisson cites—both *The Jew of Malta* and *Merchant* take us inside the Jew's house, as though to show us what is "really" there?) The 1588 deposition to the Inquisition that I have already cited claims that both their status as "racial" Jews and their Jewish practice are "public and notorious in London," and Barton also insists on the scandalous publicness of this "secret" community in his complaint. Wolf concludes that the "true character" of the converso community "could not have remained altogether unknown to the general public, while to the Government . . . it must have been in every sense an open secret."[23] For some in on the secret, the evidence of the community's continued practice of Jewish rites despite its outward conformity would doubtless have counted as another instance of Jewish perfidy. The clerk of the Privy Council's report to the Privy Council on the Lopez case, for instance, makes the capacity to swear oaths against one's own belief a particularly Jewish characteristic: "Lopez, like a Jew, did utterly with great oaths and execrations deny all the points, articles, and particularities of the accusation" during his first examination.[24] (But had he not denied the charges—had he, for example, gloried in them like Marlowe's Barabas—he would presumably also have proved himself a Jew.) The Judas-Jew homology was always ready at hand to confirm the treachery of any particular Jew: Barton uses it in 1594 in a letter to Burghley ("I have byne most iudasly and iewisly dealt with all by Aluaro Mendax Jewe"); and one summary of the evidence in the Lopez case calls him "a perjured murdering traitor, and Jewish doctor, worse than Judas himself."[25] Since Judas was the type of the false convert as well as the traitor, the reference to Judas here may serve to indicate not only the magnitude of Lopez's presumed treachery but also his status as a converso under suspicion.[26] (Even Lopez's name—echoed in Antonio's comparison of Shylock to a wolf in *Merchant*, 4.1.72—may have associated him with the unconverted Jew: the wolf was traditionally the emblem of Saul before he was converted into the lamb Paul.)[27] According to a later report, Lopez cried out on the scaffold that he "loved the Queen as well as he loved Jesus Christ," a declaration that the London crowd reputedly greeted with derision; the near-legendary status of these (perhaps legendary) last words suggests the extent to which the conviction that he was a crypto-Jew went hand in hand with the conviction that he was a treacherous would-be killer of Christians, in this case of a figure who represented simultaneously the body of the realm and the head of the church.[28]

But the outcome of the 1596 court case reported on by Sisson suggests that not everyone in the know was troubled by the secret practices of the conversos: the court eventually found in favor of the English widow Mrs. May and against the converso merchant Alvares, but "beinge moved with

the losses and trobles which the poore Straungers indured perswaded Mrs.
May being present to deale charitably with Alvares in regarde thereof" and
hence to forgo part of her claim against him, even after he had been revealed
as a practicing Jew—a remarkable display of sympathy, particularly in the
aftermath of the Lopez trial.[29] Moreover, in a climate in which the term
"stranger" was volatile enough to be subject to censorship, the court's use of
it for the converso merchants is far from neutral: the court's plea to Mrs. May
is of a piece with official responses to the anti-stranger riots that had plagued
London, most recently in 1593 and 1595, and with the powerful depiction
of Sir Thomas More quelling a similar riot in *Sir Thomas More*, in a scene
generally thought to be in Shakespeare's hand.[30] More's plea for sympathy for
"strangers"—"Imagine that you see the wretched strangers, / Their babies
at their backs, with their poor luggage / Plodding to th' ports and coasts for
transportation" (2.3.80–82)—is directed primarily to the mainly Dutch and
French Protestant population targeted by the riots in the 1590s.[31] But the
distinction between this population and London's Spanish and Portuguese
conversos was far from absolute: on the one hand, generalized anti-alien
sentiment could easily gain its force from anti-Jewish discourse during this
period;[32] on the other, anti-Spanish feeling could sometimes create sympathy
for Jews as well as Protestants displaced by the Inquisition. Reginaldus Gonsalvius Montanus's popular indictment of the Spanish Inquisition was translated into English in part so that the English might read their own potential
fate in its Protestant victims, among them strangers very like More's; the
translator's preface in fact calls "the pitifull wandring in exile and pouertie of
personages sometime rich and welthy, the wiues hanging on their husbands
shoulders, and the pore banished infants on the mothers brests" "a matter
fit for any Poet to make a Tragedie of hereafter."[33] And although "Jew" is a
term of opprobrium throughout the text and the translator familiarly calls
the Inquisition itself "the popish Sinagoge" (A2r), Montanus overcomes his
general aversion to Jews for long enough to use the Inquisition's treatment
of them as an additional way of excoriating its practices: the author's preface
refers indiscriminately to the "so many thousandes of people either Turkes
or Iewes, or true christians or heretikes (as they terme them) and reuolters
from the Romishe faith, as haue come within the Inquisitours iurisdiction
from the very first beginning of the Inquisition, till this daye," all of whom
have been burned, tainted with infamy, or "depriued of al their substance
[and] haue suffred at their hands for very trifles" (B2v).[34] At least in the context of Inquisition-bashing, Montanus is even willing to entertain the possibility that the unconstrained practice of their religion counts as "good"
for the Jews themselves: though he considers the conversion of the Jews "a

godly purpose surely," he notes that despite their "misery and thraldome" in Spain, the Jews were initially "notwithstanding in good case for one thing, in that they were not compelled by any to alter their religion till the time of *Ferdinando*" (B3r).[35]

Montanus's work suggests that compassion for the enforced conversion of the Jews and their mistreatment at the hands of the Inquisition could serve the needs of Protestant propaganda and that the court may not have been alone in sympathizing with the "poor Straungers" who were conversos in London. In fact, the scene of More quelling the anti-stranger riot seems to go out of its way to enable the inclusion of the conversos among its pitiable strangers. More wins over the members of the rebellious crowd by invoking a kind of handy-dandy changing of places.[36] He first reminds them that they might well find themselves in the position of London's strangers, should the king be lenient and exile (rather than executing) them for their rebellion, and he then asks them to imagine their reception in the countries to which they would be forced to flee:

> whither would you go?
> What country, by the nature of your error,
> Should give you harbour? Go you to France or Flanders,
> To any German province, Spain or Portugal,
> Nay, anywhere that not adheres to England,
> Why you must needs be strangers. (2.3.136–41)

Protestant strangers from France and Flanders were the contemporary rioters' primary targets; since More is asking the rioters to imagine themselves in the place of their victims, it makes sense for him to put France and Flanders at the head of his list of the countries to which the exiled English might be forced to go. But why Spain and Portugal? Though there were Spanish and Portuguese Protestants in England, they were not the particular targets of the stranger riots; the handy-dandy structure in itself does not require the English to imagine themselves as strangers in those countries. More's allusion to Spain and Portugal in effect asks the English to imagine themselves not only in the place of those they are rioting against but also in the place of those other victims of the Inquisition in their midst. And the conversos in London were prominent among those victims; in fact, the association of the conversos with Portugal was so strong that, at least in some quarters, any Portuguese doctor was subject to the suspicion that he was Jewish.[37] If the scene of More quelling the anti-stranger riot is indeed by Shakespeare, it implies not only his generalized sympathy for "strangers" but also his willingness to extend that sympathy to the strangers from Spain and Portugal, among them perhaps London's Jewish strangers.

But such sympathy is a double-edged sword. In *The Merchant of Venice* Shakespeare reserves two of his three uses of the volatile term "stranger" specifically for his Jews, despite the numerous others who might have been called strangers in the play: the would-be convert Jessica is ambivalently welcomed into Belmont as a "stranger" (3.2.236), and Shylock complains that Antonio has "foot[ed]" him "as you spurn a stranger cur" (1.3.114). The language of Shylock's complaint in fact closely duplicates the language in which More asks the English to imagine themselves forced to flee England for foreign countries in which they themselves would be the mistreated strangers:

> Would you be pleased
> To find a nation of such barbarous temper
> That breaking out in hideous violence
> Would not afford you an abode on earth,
> Whet their detested knives against your throats
> Spurn you like dogs, and like as if that God
> Owed not nor made not you, nor that the elements
> Were not all appropriate to your comforts,
> But chartered unto them? What would you think
> To be thus used? This is the strangers' case. (2.3.141–50)

But if *Sir Thomas More* asks the English to imagine themselves in the position Shylock occupies, spurned like stranger curs, it also invites them to imagine themselves in effect as his victims: if they were forced to migrate to a foreign country, its residents might "whet their detested knives" against their English throats, in a gesture that duplicates the stranger Shylock's whetting of his knife against the citizen Antonio (4.1.120).[38] In fact, the third occurrence of "stranger" in *Merchant* anticipates this turnabout: Antonio attributes the hold that Shylock has over him to "the commodity that strangers have / With us in Venice" (3.3.27–28). The passage in *Sir Thomas More* thus manages simultaneously to appeal for sympathy toward strangers and to reinforce the crowd's xenophobia, and the Shylock who inhabits the position both of victim and of victimizer perfectly replicates this doubleness: if he wields *Sir Thomas More*'s language of sympathetic appeal, he also wields its knife.

In *The Merchant of Venice*, I suggest, the contradictory elements of More's speech coalesce into the figure of Shylock, simultaneously a spurned

dog and a knife-wielder like More's strangers—and like the mixture of poor
stranger and Judas-Jew that contemporary English saw in their own local
conversos. Shakespeare's Jew has in fact become a converso of sorts by the
end of 4.1, when his conversion is mandated by the state; and like his analogues in *Sir Thomas More* and in London, this resident alien has the potential to trouble precisely the boundaries between homebred and foreign, self
and other. Shylock is already a Venetian alien; after his conversion, what
would he be—a Christian Jewish Venetian alien? Perhaps he never appears
again after his conversion in part because these combinations are both un-
tenable and close to home, for London's own resident Christian Jews—or
Jewish Christians—might have provoked similarly disquieting questions
about both religion and nationhood. Whether or not they practiced their
Jewish rites, they—like Shylock and Jessica—apparently carried the bodily
residue of their Jewishness with them. Indelibly alien within Christianity,
they were a kind of living contradiction within it, marking the place where
theological and racial differences intersect: in what sense could these Jews
be fully Christian? And their presence might similarly trouble developing
notions of nationhood. Hooker famously claimed that "there is not any man
of the Church of England, but the same man is also a member of the commonwealth; nor any man a member of the commonwealth, which is not
also of the Church of England"; insofar as church and commonwealth were
at least theoretically coterminous, would the conversos' conformity to the
Church of England make them "English"? As members by lineage of what
Shylock persistently calls the "nation" of the Jews, could they ever become
full members of the newly consolidating English nation?[39]

Alien by both religion and nation, the conversos—like Shylock—might
doubly serve as figures for the stranger within. More's appeal to the English
in fact plays exactly on this sense of uncanny "within-ness." His speech
works by asking the English to imagine themselves simultaneously as
spurned-dogs and as knife-wielding strangers; if we catch a preliminary
glimpse of Shylock-as-Jew here, it is Shylock as a figure for the English as
strangers, the English when they are most alien to themselves. And like
Shylock, the conversos not only trouble boundaries and definitions but also
gesture toward a certain strangeness both within Englishness and within
Christianity itself. The conversos were Jews who had become Catholics who
had become Protestants who were—maybe—still Jews after all; their own
history of conversion disquietingly echoed the vexed and imperfect recent
history of conversion in England. And it echoed the Protestant understanding of a broader pattern of conversion as well: the passing of the promise not
only from Jew to Christian but from Catholic to Protestant. But what if the

residue of the Jew remained within Christianity, as the residue of the Jew remained within England? Both Catholics and Protestants of various stripes were fond of accusing one another of Judaizing;[40] but what if the Jew was there, in the Christian, not through some inadmissible excess or residue but constitutively, at the heart of his Christianity? The converso is a haunting figure in part, I think, because the Jew-as-stranger has the potential to recall Christianity to its own internal alien; converted or not, he can become a figure for the disowned other within the self.

⌒∾

These questions—provoked in part by a kind of thought experiment about the presence of London's conversos—are at the heart of my reading of *Merchant*, which turns both of its primary Jewish strangers into problematic converts. But Venice is a long way from London, and it may seem merely capricious to link Venice's Jews with London's. Then again, perhaps Venice did not seem so far away to Londoners themselves. In its commercial success and its openness to strangers, Venice had become a model for those in England who argued that the trade of foreign merchants was good for the country;[41] when Antonio attributes the legal hold that Shylock has upon him to "the commodity that strangers have / With us in Venice . . . Since that the trade and profit of the city / Consisteth of all nations" (3.3.27–31), he simultaneously echoes their argument and illustrates in his own body the dangers that might come from this openness to strangers. One of Shakespeare's probable sources for *Merchant*—Robert Wilson's *The Three Ladies of London*[42]—in fact warns against the Venice-ification of England in terms that anticipate exactly what Shylock would do to Antonio. In Wilson's play, the danger is located right at home in London, and its source is a figure with a strong family resemblance both to Shylock and to London's conversos: he is a usurious Venetian Jew currently resident in London.

The Three Ladies of London is a fiercely xenophobic play, written very much in a climate that *Sir Thomas More*'s dissatisfied citizens would recognize: French and Flemish foreigners who don't mind dwelling "ten houses in one" drive up rents beyond what the presumably more fastidious English can pay (ll. 879–80); foreign artificers make intricately shoddy goods that outsell solid English workmanship, forcing honest English craftsmen to join with them in Dissimulation; and foreign merchants trade essential English goods to foreigners in exchange for foreign baubles, all for the sake of Lucre.[43] The play opens with the image of London as a kind of spoiled Belmont, flooded with foreigners seeking to woo a Lady Lucre whose drawing power resembles that of Portia: two of the London ladies—Love and Conscience—lament that the third now "rules the rout," for "euerie man doth sewe, / And comes from cuntreyes straunge and farre, of her to haue a vewe" (ll. 7, 11–12); even "the Pagan himselfe, / Indaungers his bodie to gape for her pelfe" (ll. 18–19), anticipating *Merchant*'s Morocco. As Love and Conscience predict, the play allegorizes the eventual triumph of Lady Lucre over England with the help of her servants Dissimulation, Simony, Fraud, and especially Usury; and in this xenophobic climate, it is not surprising that Lucre is the only one of these three London ladies who turns out to have foreign roots. She and Usury in fact reveal their common origin in their first conversation:

> LUCAR: But Usery didst thou neuer knowe my Graundmother the olde
>   Lady Lucar of Uenice.
> VSURY: Yes Madam I was seruaunt vnto her and liued there in blisse.
> LUCAR: But why camest thou into England, seeing Uenis is a Cittie
>   Where Usery by Lucar may liue in great glory?
> VSERY: I haue often heard your good graundmother tell,
>   That she had in England a daughter, which her farre did excell:
>   And that England was suche a place for Lucar to bide,
>   As was not in Europe and the whole world beside. (ll. 278–86)

England has become in effect the new Venice, with Lucre and Usury as the carriers of its values.[44]

The Three Ladies of London does not explicitly identify this transplanted Venetian Usury as a Jew, but the play's audience would have no trouble making the connection. Usury was understood as a particularly "Jewish" crime even when it was practiced by Christians: Thomas Wilson, writing on usury in 1572, called English usurers "worse then Iewes" and wished that they could be banished like the Jews ("for thys cause, they [the Jews] were hated in England, and so banyshed worthely, wyth whome I woulde wyshe all these Englishmen were sent, that lend their money or other goods what-soeuer for gayne, for I take them to be no better then Iewes. Nay, shall I saye? they are worse then Iewes");[45] and Francis Bacon thought that all usurers should wear the distinctive clothing that Jews were forced to wear "because they do Judaize."[46] Perhaps Wilson's Usury is not identified explicitly as a Jew in *Three Ladies* in order to encourage English Christians to recognize themselves in him, but it would come as no surprise to the audience to learn in the play's successor that his "parentes were both Iewes" (*The Three Lords and Three Ladies of London*, ll. 1441–42). But it might have come as a surprise to discover that—despite his apparent origins in Venice—he was "borne in <u>London</u>" after all (*Three Lords*, l. 1442): by 1588, Wilson's Venetian usurer has become a native-born Jew, a kind of shadow-cousin to the conversos residing there. And although his comrades Dissimulation, Fraud, and Simony all plan to leave a newly purified England at the end of that play, he plans to stay right where he is, in London, despite all those who would like to have him banished: "here can I liue for all their threatning. . . . here will I stay sure, to keepe what I haue" (*Three Lords*, ll. 1446, 1450).[47]

Sisson is doubtless right that Shakespeare is not likely to have met a Shylock among London's conversos,[48] but *Three Ladies* in effect locates him there. For Usury functions as a kind of Shylock-in-London; his murder of Hospitality in fact anticipates Shylock's attempt to kill the liberal Antonio, underscoring the extent to which that attempt reiterates an issue of intense topical concern in England.[49] Throughout *Three Ladies*, Usury is portrayed as Hospitality's opposite and natural enemy. Conscience tells us that Usury "hates Hospitalitie, and cannot him abide, / Because he for the poore and comfortlesse doth prouide" (ll. 811–12); and Usury sneeringly confirms this basis for his hatred once he has brought Hospitality to ruin: "O haue I caught your olde gray bearde, you be the man whome the people so praise: / You are a franke Gentleman, and full of liberalitie, / Why, who had al the praise in London or England, but M. Hospitalitie?" (ll. 1023–26). The plot of *Three Ladies* in fact turns on their enmity: it depicts the contamination of Love and Conscience by Lucre, and that contamination—and therefore the trajectory of the play—depends centrally on the death of Hospitality.[50] For only Hospitality can protect Love and Conscience from bondage to Usury and thus to Lady Lucre; once he is dead—once (as Usury boasts) "you shall haue Hospitalitie in London nor England no more" (ll. 1059–60)—both London ladies are forced to become Lady Lucre's servants, ensuring London's thorough contamination by Venetian values.

Merchant in effect returns to the source of that contamination in Venice, embedding the relationship of Usury and Hospitality in the characters of Shylock and Antonio. Shylock's pursuit of Antonio is given psychological plausibility by Antonio's treatment of him and by Christian complicity in Lorenzo's theft of his daughter, but he is nonetheless the avatar of Usury in a more realistic mode. The motive for his hatred that he repeats most often and most explicitly—a motive not in Shakespeare's major source[51]—is Antonio's interference with his business practices: "I hate him for he is a Christian; / But more, for that in low simplicity / He lends out money gratis, and brings down / The rate of usance here with us in Venice" (1.3.37–40); "I will have the heart of him if he forfeit, for were he out of Venice I can make what merchandise I will" (3.1.105–7); "Tell me not of mercy. / This is the

fool that lent out money gratis" (3.3.1–2). And if Shylock is the avatar of
Wilson's Usury, Shakespeare positions Antonio as the avatar of his Hospitality, in effect reclaiming the gentlemanly virtue of hospitality for a mercantile society through him. His largesse, Antonio tells us as he is taken to
prison, rescues those who—like Love and Conscience—would otherwise be
bound to Shylock: "He seeks my life. His reason well I know: / I oft delivered
from his forfeitures / Many that have at times made moan to me. / Therefore
he hates me" (3.3.21–24). His speech here not only borrows its rationale
for Shylock's enmity from Wilson's Usury but also echoes the key terms—
"seeks," "hates"—of Hospitality's panic-stricken entry immediately before
Usury kills him: "Usurie hath vndone me, and now he hates mee to the
death, / And seekes by all meanes possible for to bereaue me of breath"
(ll. 1016–18). Both Antonio and Hospitality are "undone" by their Jewish
usurers (Merchant, 3.1.103; Three Ladies, l. 1016), who have unalterably
"hard" hearts (Merchant, 4.1.78; Three Ladies, ll. 229, 1304), and both plays
take pains to demonstrate that those hearts cannot be softened: Conscience
(Portia-like) tries and fails to "mollifie" Usury's heart (l. 1051), and Antonio
himself observes that "You may as well do anything most hard / As seek to
soften that—than which what's harder?— / His Jewish heart" (Merchant,
4.1.77–79).[52] And Shylock threatens Antonio with Usury's own weapon, the
knife with which he cuts Hospitality's throat.

   Three Ladies (I am arguing) provides something like the allegorical scaffolding for Merchant, a scaffolding that links Shylock to anxiety about the
foreign, and specifically "Jewish," values that are contaminating England;
for those who remembered the earlier play, Shylock's attempted murder of
Antonio would seem eerily familiar despite its foreign location. But of course
Shakespeare's version ends differently, and to assess exactly how differently,
we need to turn to the second of Shakespeare's probable sources for Shylock
within Three Ladies. And that second source suggests that, despite its xenophobia, Three Ladies is in some respects more magnanimous than Merchant:
in addition to Usury, who is explicitly identified as Jewish only in the play's
1588 sequel, Three Ladies forces its audience to confront the spectacle of a
Jewish moneylender who is the antitype of both Usury and Shylock. Soon
after the death of Hospitality, Wilson takes us to Turkey and introduces
us to "Gerontus a Iewe," a moneylender who is trying to collect his very
Shylockian bad debt—three thousand ducats for three months—from Mercadorus, an Italian merchant. Gerontus's explicit marking as a Jew—"we
that be Iewes," he says a few lines after he enters, in case his audience was
in danger of not noticing (l. 1243)—promises initially to make the Turkish
scenes a satisfyingly explicit location for the enactment not only of general-

ized "foreign" evils but also of the "Jewishness" implicit in Usury, and the
first scene does little to destroy this expectation; though it seems geographi-
cally askew—all of the preceding scenes are firmly localized in England—it
is comfortably congruent with the play's xenophobic logic. Lady Lucre has
instructed Mercadorus to go among the "Moores, Turkes, and Pagans" (l.
891) to find suitably worthless foreign baubles to exchange for substantial
English goods; after a long intervening scene showing the devastation caused
by the "bloudsucker" Usury (l. 957), we arrive in Turkey, where Gerontus
offers to further Mercadorus's scheme by providing him with commodities
to "sucke away mony" from the English (l. 1280), thus tidily allying himself not only with a familiar anti-Jewish stereotype but also (and more specifically) with the foreign bloodsucker back in England. But when Gerontus
declines to act like a Jew in the next scenes, he undoes this alliance and,
with it, any secure distinction between homebred good and foreign evil—or
between Christian and Jew.

Mercadorus, it turns out, has come to Turkey not only to gather worthless merchandise but also to take advantage of the Turkish law that rewards
converts by dissolving their debts. Although Christians routinely suspected
Jews of insincere conversions, this would-be convert is a Christian; and here
at least the Jew is not only steadfast in himself but the cause of steadfastness
in others. He twice registers disbelief that Mercadorus will so lightly change
his religion: "I cannot thinke you will forsake your faith so lightly" (l. 1558);
"I trow he wil not forsake his faith" (l. 1711). Moreover, when Mercadorus
insists that he will convert "Not for any deuotion, but for Lucars sake of
my monie" (l. 1725), Gerontus explicitly attempts to secure this Christian's
faith, in the process demonstrating his own startling indifference to Lucre.
Just as the Judge instructs Mercadorus to say "I forsake my Christian faith"
in order to complete his conversion, Gerontus interrupts: "Stay there most
puissant Iudge. Senior Mercadorus, consider what you doo, / Pay me the
principall, as for the interest, I forgiue it you" (ll. 1729–32). When Mercadorus refuses, Gerontus asks for only "the one halfe" (l. 1737); and when
Mercadorus responds, "No point da halfe, no point denere, me will be a
Turke I say, / Me be wearie of my Christes religion" (ll. 1738–39), Gerontus
forgives him the entire debt, and in terms that make the Jew the locus of a
traditionally Christian liberality like Hospitality's: "Well seeing it is so, I
would be loth to heare the people say, it was long of me / Thou forsakest thy
faith, wherefore I forgiue thee franke and free" (ll. 1740–42).[53] And Wilson
makes sure that we don't miss the point: the Judge summarizes this scene's
exchange of roles by saying "Iewes seeke to excell in Christianitie, and the
Christians in Iewisnes" (l. 1754).

The Judge of course reassuringly keeps the categories of Jew and Christian intact while scrambling their occupants. But this is nonetheless by any measure an extraordinary moment: although the Jewish usurer in England is (again, reassuringly) the embodiment of foreign evil, the Jewish usurer out of England turns out to be the embodiment of the "Christian" values no longer current there. How might we understand the presence of this turnabout in this otherwise largely xenophobic play?[54] It is relatively easy to read the Gerontus scenes as a kind of metaphorical exclamation point given to the triumph of Lady Lucre in England: if subjection to the material world is the sign of the Jew, the English in *Three Ladies* have become so thoroughly Judaized by the end of the play that one must leave England to find the virtues formerly known as English; and the measure of their subjection is that even a Jew in Turkey outdoes the Christian who is devoted only to Lucre.[55] And in at least one respect, the scenes seem perfectly congruent with the play's xenophobia, despite their "Christian" Jew. Mercadorus, after all, is not English: the play continually marks him as a foreigner not only through his name but also through his comically "Italian" accent; even in the Turkish scenes, where everyone is presumably foreign, only he is given this marker of difference.[56] But in one crucial respect, Mercadorus is distinctly less foreign than we might expect. Given both that his nationality would tend to identify him as Catholic and that Protestant propagandists frequently accused Catholics of exactly the Judaizing subjection to Lucre that he demonstrates, it is striking that the play never marks him as specifically Catholic and thereby as religiously foreign to the normative Christian in England. Wilson is perfectly willing to engage in anti-Catholic polemic in the case of Simony, who is Roman in origin but has been kidnapped from Rome by English merchants and brought to England to increase their wealth and who nostalgically recalls a time when England was forced to pay tribute to the pope (ll. 293–309, 340–57). But Wilson does not engage in anti-Catholic polemic in his Turkish scenes. Unlike in Marlowe, who enjoys triangulating between Muslim, Catholic, and Jew in *The Jew of Malta*, religious difference in the Turkish scenes of *Three Ladies* tends to harden into the simple opposition between Jew and Christian;[57] and in this configuration, from Gerontus's initial opposition of Jew and Christian—"if we that be Iewes should deale so one with an other, / We should not be trusted againe of our owne brother: / But many of you Christians make no conscience to falsifie your fayth and breake your day" (ll. 1243–46)—to the Judge's final summary, in which Christian and Jew have changed places, Mercadorus is given the role not of the Catholic but of the unspecified Christian.

Insofar as the Turkish scenes function in part to underscore Lucre's tri-

umph in England, it matters, I think, that it is the Christian Mercadorus's
"Jewish" willingness to convert for worldly gain that marks the full extent of
his subjection to Lucre: for this willingness brings the problem of the Turkish
scenes back home to the problem of conversion in England—and not only to
the problem of the Jewish converts who were suspected of a similarly opportunistic conversion there. In fact, we have already met Mercadorus's homegrown counterpart well before we get to the Turkish scenes.[58] Shortly before
our apparent detour to Turkey, Sir Peter Pleaseman enters "like a Parson"
and asks Simony to prefer him to Lady Lucre; and when Simony asks him
about his religion, he proves to be at least as convertible as Mercadorus:

> SYMONY: . . . but of what religion are you can ye tell?
> PETER: Mary sir of all religions, I know not my selfe very well.
> SYMONY: You are a Protestant now, and I thinke to that you will graunt.
> PETER: Indeede I haue bene a Catholicke, mary nowe for the most part a
>   Protestant.
> But and if my seruice may please her, harke in your eare sir,
> I warrant you my Religion shall not offend her. (ll. 935–41)

We do not need to go to Turkey to find a man willing to forswear his religion
for the sake of Lucre. And although Lucre is a Lady rather than a Queen,
she rules (ll. 6, 22) and has a court (l. 457); her structural similarity to either
of the queens who presided over England's mass conversions would probably have been uncomfortably clear to the audience, and Sir Peter's repeated
interjections of "Mary" may have helped them to hear the name of one
of them, as well as recording Sir Peter's old allegiance to Catholicism. Sir
Peter's willingness to switch religions for material gain—in other words—
makes him nothing if not English.

Sir Peter's religious instability thus anticipates Mercadorus's. And not
only his religious instability: if Mercadorus had promised to forsake everything for love of Lucre at their first meeting—"Madona, me doe for loue
of you tinck no paine to mush, / And to doe any ting for you me will not
grush: / Me will a forsake a my Fader, Moder, King, Countrey & more den
dat" (ll. 396–98)—Sir Peter Pleaseman proves himself to be even more willing to please.

> SYMONY: Then your name is sir Peter Pleaseman.
> PETER: I forsooth.
> SYMONY: And please woman too now and then.
> PETER: You know that homo is indifferent. (ll. 925–28)

Mercadorus apparently thinks that he can change both his religion and his nationality as easily as his clothes,[59] but Sir Peter thinks that he can change even his gender: when Simony slyly sexualizes Sir Peter's name, making clear his pleasing "service" to both men and women, Sir Peter responds with a grammatical joke that implies his willingness not only to please but also to be both genders.[60] And in this conflation of the shifting object of desire with the shifting of a self that is as "indifferent" as the word that denominates it, England's own local version of Mercadorus becomes the ultimate slippery signifier, achieving a shape-shifting that goes well beyond even the "more den dat" that Mercadorus promises to forsake for Lucre. Sir Peter's habit of opportunistic conversion turns out to trouble the stability of identity per se: it is not only his religion but himself that he "know[s] not . . . very well" (l. 936).

Sir Peter provides a kind of compacted history of recent English conversions, and the instability of identity that affects him seems to affect all England as well, for his England is no more categorically secure than the "Turkey" Mercadorus would convert to. Although the play ends with Lucre and the London ladies she has contaminated condemned to jail, both her domestic and her foreign servants are still thriving in London. Homegrown Fraud is "in the streetes walking in a Citizens gowne" (l. 1853), but even Usury and Simony are equally at home there: Usury is last seen "at the Exchainge" and Simony "walking in Paules" (ll. 1855, 1857). How long before this Jew born in England and this Roman imported to England by English merchants (ll. 293–309) become "Englishmen"? It is not surprising that the judge who restores an ostensibly English order at the end is named Nemo: in the various migrations, transformations, and conversions that characterize the England of this play, there is no longer any reliable principle of authority, and little secure identity—national or religious—on which such a principle might be based.[61]

To put matters this way is to suggest that the steadfast Jew Gerontus stands opposed not only to the changeable Mercadorus but to Sir Peter and the English themselves—and stands opposed to the English not only in their generalized contamination by Lucre but specifically in their categorical instability. I have already suggested that London's own multiply converted Jews may partly have served as figures for this instability. Although there are no literal conversos in *Three Ladies*—Usury's status as an allegorical figure apparently exempts him from the requirement that he adopt the protective coloration of a Christian—the shadowy presence of the conversos nonetheless seems to me to be refracted through this text: if Usury occupies their position as Jews who might spoil "Englishness" from within, Mercadorus and

Sir Peter exhibit their habit of opportunistic conversion. *Three Ladies* tell-ingly marks Mercadorus as a Jew exactly when he would turn Turk for gain; and insofar as the Judge's summary makes conversion for Lucre the sign of the Jew regardless of what religion one was converting from or to, the same logic would make England's own Sir Peter "excell in Iewisnes." But Sir Peter's history is England's; in making opportunistic conversion "Jewish," *Three Ladies* makes the English themselves kin to the multiply converted Jews in their midst. No wonder, then, that the principle of stability is vested in their antitype: a Jew who stays reassuringly the same, reassuringly alien, and—in the Judge's terms—reassuringly "Jewish" even when he seeks "to excell in Christianitie," a Jew so determinedly unconverted that he is able to prevent the conversion of others.

Gerontus functions as a principle of stability, I suggest, exactly because the English have come to resemble the conversos in their midst. But the topsy-turvy through which *Three Ladies* locates fixed value in an alien Jew has the effect of severely compromising the xenophobia which is the play's initial premise. Or, perhaps more accurately, of drawing attention to the ex-tent to which that xenophobia has been compromised from the start. Usury and Simony may be foreigners, but two of Lady Lucre's servants (Fraud and Dissimulation) are thoroughly English; and although Conscience tells us early on that Lady Lucre's suitors are strangers, among those suitors—Sim-plicity, Sincerity, Artifex, Lawyer, Sir Peter Pleaseman—only Mercadorus turns out to be a foreigner. It is the work of the play's post-Armada sequel—*The Three Lords and Three Ladies of London* was written in 1588 and en-tered in the Stationer's Register and printed in 1590—to dispense with this categorical confusion and to return evil to reassuringly foreign sources. In this sequel, all three London ladies have been redeemed from corruption and deemed fit to marry three allegorical London lords (Policy, Pomp, and Pleasure); even money—Lucre herself—has been magically remade both as English and as benign, and any hint of her Venetian origins or of her respon-sibility for the corruption of the other London ladies has been expunged from the plot. Evil enters this newly purified realm unsurprisingly through the persons of the three symbolically laden Spanish lords—Pride, Ambi-tion, and Tyranny—who would be husbands to the three London ladies; but in this new England, their attempted Armada-style invasion is so feeble that it is foiled merely by the scutcheons of the English lords. And in an England where (as Fraud says) "men are growen so full of conscience and religion, that Fraud, Dissimulation and Simony are disciphered, and being disciphered are also dispised" (ll. 1427–29), the old servants of the rehabili-tated Lady Lucre find themselves out of work (ll. 900, 1427) and are eventually forced to emigrate, predictably to Spain. In this climate, it comes as no surprise that even the apparently homegrown servants of the Lucre of *Three Ladies* are revealed to be foreign, or rather to have been foreign all along. When Usury—of all people—warns the others against emigrating and becoming "traitors to your natiue countrie" (l. 1438), Simony answers, "Tis not our natiue countrie, thou knowest, I <u>Simony</u> am a Roman, <u>Dissimulation</u> a Mongrel, halfe an Italian, halfe a Dutchman: <u>Fraud</u> so too, halfe French and halfe Scottish: and thy parentes were both Iewes, though thou wert borne in <u>London</u>" (ll. 1439–42). This move reinstates an unproblematic xenophobia in part by grounding the idea of a repurified England in an incipiently biological concept of the "native," and here that concept is directed specifically against the Jew born in London. The others are not "native" because they belong to other nationalities and presumably were not born in England. But Usury *was* born in England and hence is literally "native" there; he must be sharply reminded that England is nonetheless not his "natiue countrie." Unlike the others, he may be determined to "stay . . . to keepe what I haue" (ll. 1449–50), but at least in this play, he will never be "English."

Three Lords is a much less interesting play than its predecessor, and there is no evidence that Shakespeare knew it. Nonetheless, and despite all the famously Shakespearean complexity of *Merchant*, in some respects *Merchant* seems to me to revise *Three Ladies* in the spirit of *Three Lords*. If *Merchant*'s Portia is, like Lady Lucre of *Three Ladies*, sought after by foreign suitors, she is entirely liberated from any taint of that play's Venetian Lucre: her money comes not from the problematic commercial world of Venice but, like "manna" (5.1.293), from mystified sources; and her Belmont, like the England of *Three Lords*, is impeccably xenophobic. And if Belmont gives us the image of a purified England, mysteriously untainted by Lucre, Portia manages to reinforce something like a Belmont-style xenophobia even in Venice itself, in effect undoing the categorical instability that plagues *Three Ladies*: her rescue of Antonio depends crucially not only on the niceties of Venetian law but on her reinstating of the distinctions—between Christian and Jew, citizen and alien—that Venetian law had initially seemed immune to. And in that gesture, she seems to me to epitomize much of the work of the play itself.

I have already suggested that the relation between Usury and Hospitality serves as a kind of allegorical template for that between Shylock and Antonio. But I think that we cannot fully understand how that template works in *Merchant* unless we consider it in relation to the scene that Shakespeare simultaneously borrows from and occludes: the scene of the generous Jew. Frightening as the death of Hospitality is, the relationship between Usury and Hospitality is in its own way reassuring, since it makes the difference between a presumably Jewish usury and a presumably Christian hospitality abundantly clear. But the Gerontus-Mercadorus scenes threaten crucially to disrupt those secure distinctions: here the Jewish moneylender embodies the values of a "Christian" hospitality, and the Christian merchant embodies "Jewish" calculation as well as a "Jewish" tendency to convert for worldly gain. And if Portia accomplishes the rescue of Antonio partly by introducing categorical stability, *Merchant* itself seems to me to work toward much the same end. The play flirts with the categorical confusions—between merchant and usurer, Christian and Jew—of the Gerontus scenes, but by the time 4.1 is finished, the categories confounded in the Gerontus scenes have been tidily restored: the merchant of *Merchant*'s ambiguous title has proven to be emphatically a Christian, and its usurer emphatically a Jew. And it is just here, I think, that we can see the effect of *Three Ladies'* two Jews. For *Merchant* accomplishes this restoration in effect by rewriting the Gerontus scenes through the template of Usury-Hospitality, transforming Mercadorus/Antonio and Gerontus/Shylock into their simpler allegorical antecedents: the Italian merchant of *Three Ladies* is re-idealized in Antonio as the figure for Christian Hospitality, and its problematically generous Jew is debased in Shylock as the figure of hard-hearted Usury. The debt—three thousand ducats for three months—that *Merchant* borrows from *Three Ladies* seems to me to record something like the memory trace of this transformation, the reminder of what Shakespeare had to rewrite in order to produce his Jew; and Portia's famous opening question in 4.1—"Which is the merchant here, and which the Jew?"--records the anxieties to which that rewriting responds. For her question is oddly out of place in *Merchant*, where everyone can tell the difference; but it is perfectly congruent with the Judge's summary of the Turkish scenes, in which Mercadorus the Christian and Gerontus the Jew have switched places. And even as her question gestures back toward the categorical instabilities of the Gerontus scenes, it reveals the process of revision: just where we might expect the opposition of Christian to Jew or of merchant to usurer, Portia opposes merchant to Jew—a pairing that has the effect of radically separating out the categories of merchant and Jew compounded in Mercadorus, thus underscoring the play's drive to re-Christianize its merchant and re-Judaize its usurer.

And what of conversion and the conversos? Here too *Merchant* works to stabilize what is most troubling in *Three Ladies*. Mercadorus goes to Turkey not only to buy the baubles that will weaken the English economy but also to avoid a debt by converting; he becomes functionally "Jewish" by becoming a kind of Christian converso, a suspect convert who points toward the porousness of religious boundaries and whose own religious slipperiness is measured against the steadfastness of the play's manifest Jew, Gerontus. Turkey plays a special role in this exchange, for it is not a neutral "foreign" space: it is specifically a place where a Jew might go to practice his religion openly (as Gerontus apparently does, and as many did after the expulsion from Spain and Portugal) and where a Christian might become a Muslim or, for that matter, a Jew. In that sense, Turkey in *Three Ladies* might be understood as a kind of anti-England, where the suspect convert is more likely to be a Christian than a Jew. But the case of Sir Peter insists on the fragility of this opposition, for he is no better than Mercadorus; in effect, he Turkifies England, suggesting that its conversos too are Christian. And if *Merchant* rids London of its resident Jew by returning him to his original home in Venice, it also undoes the problem of Christian conversion: at the same time as it stabilizes the categorical confusions of Christian/Jew and merchant/usurer in *Three Ladies* by rewriting the Gerontus scenes through the template of the Usury-Hospitality scenes, it emphatically rewrites conversion—willing or enforced, "sincere" or as opportunistic as Mercadorus's—as entirely the province of the Jew.

⟨✑⟩

I have thus far been speculating about some possible consequences of the shadowy presence of the conversos within two texts—*Sir Thomas More* and *Three Ladies of London*—that have a proximal relation to *The Merchant of Venice:* one a strong analogue probably written by Shakespeare, and the other a probable source. I use the figure of the converso here not only to fill in a historical absence (how can we speculate about the effects of their presence unless we first acknowledge that they were there?) but also to suggest some of the ways in which that figure may be woven complexly into Shakespeare's reworking of these texts in *Merchant. Merchant*'s Jewish converts are not conversos—they are not Spanish or Portuguese; they are not victims of the Inquisition—but they nonetheless seem to me to draw the urgency of the questions they provoke in part from the proximity of "real" Jews—and real Jewish converts—in London. It is the burden of this book to draw attention to the forms in which these questions emerge in *Merchant*, particularly in some of its out-of-the-way corners. But before turning to *Merchant*, let me consider one additional pre-text for the play, one that illuminates with particular clarity just how problematic the figure of the Jewish convert within Christianity might be.

On April 1, 1577, at Alhallowes Church, the great Protestant propagan-

dist John Foxe preached a sermon at the christening of Yehuda Menda, re-
named Nathanael. The written form of the sermon was subsequently translated from Latin into English and published, along with the translation of
the new convert's "Confession," in 1578 in a cheap edition for popular con-
sumption.[62] The day of the christening must have been a glorious occasion
for Foxe—what better testimony to the truth of Christianity than the confession of a Jew that he and his forefathers have been misled, and to the truth of
a specifically Protestant Christianity than his laying the blame for the Jews'
stubborn disbelief on Catholic idolatry? And what better testimony to the
special suitability of Foxe's England to be the standard-bearer of a reformed
and united Christianity than the fact that this particular Jew attributes his
conversion to his coming to the "blessed" land of England?[63] But if the presence of the conversos in London may have raised vexed questions about
opportunistic conversion and the persistence of "Jewishness" both within
the English nation and within the ostensible Christian, the document that
records this triumph suggests that even the celebration of an apparently
successful conversion was not trouble-free. The sermon is in fact filled with
signs of anxiety about the foundational relation of Christian to Jew apparently provoked by Yehuda's conversion: anxiety that (I will argue) is reflected
in the much more ambiguous triumphalism of *Merchant.*

This anxiety is inherent in the trope of the olive tree that governs Foxe's
sermon from its beginning. The sermon is usually referred to by its short
title, "A Sermon Preached at the Christening of a Certain Jew"; but the full
title that introduces it in the text—"A Sermon of the true and gladsome
Oliue tree, mentioned in the Epistle of Sainct Paul to the Romanes, chap.
xi. preached at London by a faithfull Minister of God, Iohn Foxe, at the
christening of a certaine Iewe" (A1r)—foregrounds the olive tree as much
as the occasion.[64] Foxe immediately tells his audience that he "could not
determine vpon any one text of the whole scripture to be opened vnto you,
more profitable for your learning, more effectuall for exhortation, more applyable to our age, and more agreeable for this present occasion" than Paul's
olive tree (A2r–v). Why the olive tree? Because through it Paul holds out the
promise that some remnant of the Jews will be regrafted onto the holy root
from which they have been broken off:

> I speake vnto you Gentiles in as much as I am the Apostle of the Gen-
> tiles, I wil magnifie mine office, if by any meanes I may prouoke them
> which be my fleshe, and may saue some of them, for if the casting away
> of them be the receyuing of the worlde, what shal the receyuing of them
> be, but life from the dead? For if the first fruits be holy, the whole masse

is holy also: And if the Roote be holy, the braunches will be holye also:
And if some of the braunches be broken of, and thou beyng a wilde Oliue
tree, wast graffed in amongest them, and made partaker of the Roote and
fatnesse of the true and naturall Oliue tree, boaste not thy selfe agaynst
the braunches, for if thou do boaste, thou bearest not the roote, but the
roote beareth thee. Thou wilt say then, The braunches are broken of, that
I may be engraffed in. Thou sayest well: for vnbeliefe sake they were broken of: and thou stoodest stedfast in faith. Be not high minded therefore,
but feare, for if God spared not the natural braunches: Take heed lest it
come to passe, that he spare not thee. . . . Or els thou shalt be hewen of,
& they, if they continue not still in vnbeliefe, shalbe engraffed in agayne.
For God is of power to graffe them in againe. For if thou were cut out of
a naturall wilde Oliue tree, and contrary to nature were engraffed into
the true Oliue tree, how much rather shall the braunches be graffed in
agayne into their owne Oliue tree?[65]

"More applyable to our age, and more agreeable for this present occasion,"
then, because Yehuda's conversion is one such regrafting, and perhaps because of the millenarian hopes such regrafting might create.[66] And "agreeable" also because the olive tree is one of Paul's central tropes for the mystery of God's casting away of the Jews and election of the gentiles in their
place; through it, Foxe can bring the whole weight of God's originary choice
of gentile over Jew to bear on poor Yehuda-turned-Nathanael and, through
him, on his audience, as though the conversion of any single Jew reiterates
this defining moment of election for the whole Christian community. But
despite the title of Foxe's sermon, the "gladsome Oliue tree" is not entirely
"gladsome": if Paul promises that the Jews can be regrafted, he also warns
the Christians that they can be broken off, and he frames the regrafting of
branches as a zero-sum game ("thou shalt be hewen of, & they . . . shalbe engraffed in agayne"). Moreover, even if the Christians do not become as reprobate in their turn as the Jews, the displacement of Jew by gentile registered in
this trope turns out to carry with it its own burdens of anxiety and guilt.

   First of all, there is the matter of ancestry. Paul's olive tree poses the
issue of election and the supersession of Jew by Christian in the language
of the rupture of a family tree, in which the natural branches were broken
off—"contrary to nature"—so that wild branches can be grafted in. In a culture in which ancestry conveyed legitimacy, this cannot have been a neutral
trope. And Foxe raises the ante by stressing both the violence of the rupture
and the abjection of gentile ancestry, delegitimizing gentile claims to the
legacy of the "root" of Abraham[67] and separating contemporary Christians

from the lineage of Christ even more starkly than Paul does; in his gloss on
Paul's trope, the "proper and olde growen branches" are sawed off so that
"very abiect, & rascall Gentiles, barbarous & uncircumcised heathen" can be
grafted in through the "incomprehensible mercie of God" (A5v, L2r–v). This
exaggeration serves the argument for election well, since it underscores the
extent to which divine mercy rather than human merit leads to salvation: if
election is merited, Foxe reminds us, its "grace can not be said to be grace
at all . . . for that which is giuen according to the proportion of deseruings,
and not according to grace, seemeth in Augustines iudgement, a reward
rather of dutie, then a free gift of promise" (B6v).[68] In fact, Foxe later takes
pains to tell his contemporary auditors—now conflated with the gentiles
at their original moment of election through the same collapse of time that
elsewhere allows him to excoriate contemporary Jews for their torture of
Christ[69]—that they are inferior to the Jews not only in ancestry but also in
righteousness and "excellencie of zeale" (M2v): "Do ye thinke that any of
you were endued with any such excellencie, as ye myght thereby challenge
any preeminence aboue the Iewishe nation? . . . What vertue was in thee,
that myght procure thee to be engraffed in their place. And wherfore should
they, beyng natural branches, be hewen off?" (M1v–M2r). Foxe thus succeeds
in making both originary and contemporary Christians the perfect poster
children for the doctrine of election—but only at the cost of acknowledging their continued inferiority to that most abjected of categories, the Jew.
And—at least if Foxe's sermon is any indication—this acknowledgment is
perforce unstable: if the doctrine of election mandates that the gentiles must
be "sauage slippes" rather than rightful heirs, illegitimate interlopers who
replace the "proper and olde growen branches" (A5v), Foxe's text continually
strains against that position even while the logic of election requires it.

   Luther in his philo-Semitic days may have said that "we are but Gentiles, while the Jews are of the lineage of Christ. We are aliens and in-laws;
they are blood relatives, cousins, and brothers of our Lord,"[70] and the superior blood lineage of the Jews may serve the argument for election well, but
Foxe clearly finds the continued Jewish claim to this lineage galling. If on
the one hand he needs to insist repeatedly that the Jews "by so long continuance of inheritably discending race, did lawfully enioye the interest of
the true Oliue tree, as the true naturall ofsprings thereof" (B8r), on the other
he subtly rewrites that lineage, downgrading it to deprive it even of the
merit that he wants to claim counts for nothing. The Jews begin as "proper
and olde growen branches" replaced by "sauage slippes" (A5v), but they do
not remain so for long: they are immediately redescribed as "vnfruitefull
sproutes," "wyndshaken bowes and starued branches" that should be cut

off in order "that new plantes may prosper the better" (A5v, A6r). Foxe here sounds briefly like *King Lear*'s Edmund, discrediting his older brother's legitimacy by tracing it back to the "dull, stale, tired" bed in which he was conceived (1.2.13); and Edmund's use of horticultural imagery—"Edmund the base / Shall top the legitimate. I grow, I prosper" (1.2.20–21)—suggests how readily the language of superior vegetable vigor comes to the supplanting younger brother as he justifies replacing the old-grown branches on the family tree.[71] But the Jews refuse to recognize their weakened state, and Foxe is continually nettled by their claims to superior legitimacy. Theologically, he knows—and frequently reminds his auditors—that fleshly lineage no longer counts and that Christians are now "the true offspring of Abraham" (C7r); Abraham himself, he imagines, would cast off his merely fleshly sons if only he were alive to do so: "woulde he euer haue accompted you for his sonnes: or euer haue acknowledged such impes to haue proceeded out of his loynes?" (E3v). Hence the utility of Yehuda/Nathanael's testimony that his fathers have "estranged them selues and their posteritie from the common wealth in deede of Israel" ("Confession," B8r) and of the new name chosen for—or perhaps by—him: Calvin's commentary on that name points precisely toward the displacement of Abraham's fleshly lineage and the redefinition of who can lay claim to the name of Israel.[72] But Foxe no sooner counters Jewish pride in lineage theologically than he reinstates it rhetorically so that he can counter it again: as though his own answers—or perhaps his own ancestors—do not entirely satisfy him.

The Jews (he complains) "being otherwise a people most abhored of God, & men . . . would neuerthelesse most arrogantly vaunt them selues to bee more esteemed, and more precious in the sight of God, then all other nations, people and tongues: and that they were his only darlings" (C1v). Unconverted Jews were hardly likely to have been present in the parish church of Alhallowes in London on April 1, 1577, but Foxe makes them rhetorically present,[73] invoking their words in order to ventriloquize their claim to Abraham and their disdain for all other nations: "Very well now. And whereupon doth the blinde arrogancie of the Iewish Nation magnifie their race? do we not deriue our petigree (say they) lyneally from our most holy father Abraham?" (C2v); "Will ye flee backe againe to your rotten wormeaten poesies? we are the seede of Abraham, and were neuer subiect to anie other: well we may wander, but we can neuer perish. The holy Patriarches are our progenitours: we are the yssue of an holy roote" (E2v). In fact, for much of the sermon (as in this last instance), he speaks as though the Jews were literally present, addressing Yehuda/Nathanael's reprobate brothers as though they were sitting in front of him, making their outrageous claims:

This one thing perhaps doth raise vp your crestes, and puffe you vp with pryde, because you doe conueye vnto your selues so long a discent of your genealogies and kinred from so famous Auncestoures: because ye fetche your petigree and families from Abraham, and the holy Patriarches, and in that respect you do reprochefully disdayne all other nations, as though God had created them to no purpose at all. (C6r–v)

And vnder colour of this prerogatiue, beeyng pufte vp with pride, you swell with immeasurable vayne glorious persuasion of fleshly courage, and sette all other nations at naught, as though you alone were the onely inheritaunce of the Lorde, and as though you helde him fast tyed to your generation. (K2v)

Foxe—in other words—insistently dramatizes a contest over the value of blood lineage that his theology should allow him to regard as long since won. His key terms in these passages—"pedigree," "prerogative," "inheritance," "generation"—allow us to see exactly what is at stake in this contest between "the Iewish Nation" and "all other nations." And the fiction through which Foxe invokes the presence of the Jews has the effect of bringing the contest into the present moment in England, thus allowing Foxe to represent himself as heroic in the face of a contemporary danger, boldly defending the claim of "the nations"—his underdog "Gentiles"[74]—who are threatened by what amounts to an imaginary invasion of Jews claiming unproblematic lineal descent from Abraham. Moreover, despite what Foxe knows theologically, his rhetoric sometimes points toward a residue of uncertainty about the contest's outcome. Both the hint of a whiny petulance in his various "as though" clauses—"as though God had created [all other nations] to no purpose at all," "as though you alone were the onely inheritaunce of the Lorde"—and the notably phallic prowess he attributes to his Jews, who are puffed up with pride and swollen with fleshly courage, and whose roosterly, as well as familial, crests are raised up, seem to me to register a covert anxiety that the superior fleshly lineage of the Jews may still have the power to trump the more remote claim of the younger "nations" to the inheritance of the Lord. And in fact, sometimes Foxe projects the outcome of this contest into the future, as though it had not yet been settled. Assuming the voice of a prophet writing before God has cast the Jews away, he taunts the imaginary Jews in his audience—once more conflated with their ancestors—by predicting their fate: "I haue declared vnto you, what shall become of your nation and people"; "Dost thou not perceyue . . . howe thou shalt be cast away, thou proude generation? And . . . you shal knowe that God wil neuerthelesse not be destitute of a people, that shall glorifie his name" (K2r). But this prophetic prediction has the effect of destabilizing the triumph of the gentiles by projecting it into the same futurity: "it shall come to passe, that you your selues being Iewes, & your whole race for the most parte beyng cast away, . . . the Lord wil transpose his louing countenaunce, not into one angle of the worlde among the Iewes onely, but wil be magnified, & haue the glory of his name called vpon, in euery place throughout all nations & tongues" (K3r–v). Foxe's imagined temporal location here allows him the pleasure of assuming a prophetic voice like that of Isaiah or Malachi, from whom he has just finished quoting, but it nonetheless fixes him in an uncertain rhetorical present in which he has only the prophet's provisional "you'll see" with which to console himself: the standard consolation of the underdog, whether weaker sibling or weaker nation.

Perhaps Foxe writes the triumph of the gentiles into the future rather than the past in part because he is not entirely satisfied with how that triumph is going. Though Foxe generally looks toward a unified Christianity in the sermon, his curious use of the singular—"God wil neuerthelesse not be destitute of *a* people, that shall glorifie his name"—may gesture toward England's special role as the new Israel;[75] but if so, this was a role that England had only imperfectly assumed.[76] The turn to futurity in this passage would allow for whatever historical disappointments Foxe might have felt about England's church, and it would also—at least in fantasy—narrow the potentially awkward temporal gap between God's abandonment of "Israel" and England's eventual assumption of its status: if the Jews were only now about to vacate the premises of "Israel," that would leave those premises available for immediate English occupancy. Another of Foxe's curious phrases seems in fact to gesture toward this wished-for transfer of "Israel" from the Jews to the English even in the course of arguing for God's universal presence. When Foxe insists that God will transpose his countenance "not into one angle of the worlde among the Iewes onely, but . . . in euery place throughout all nations" (K3v), he conflates the "one angle" of the Jews with a traditional term for England itself, as though the countenance of God must be made manifest in the angle that is England before it can be universalized; in an earlier sermon he had in fact already claimed that "onely a little angle of the weast partes yet remaineth in some profession of [God's] name."[77] But the Jews refuse to give up their claim to their special "angle," and Foxe is clearly troubled by the persistence of their claim; his insistence on importing imaginary Jews into England and into his audience to make that claim gives it an urgency and force that seem altogether out of proportion with the danger represented by any actual Jews in England or elsewhere. Speaking to his imaginary Jews, Foxe boldly proclaims the firmness of his audience's "vnshaken faith" even in the face of Jewish provocation: "now neither the raging railing of your blasphemous mouth . . . nor the cruel curse & continuall accusations of the Lawe . . . can in any respect appall & terrifie our setled consciences" (G4v–G5r). But this denial rests, as all such denials do, on first imagining that your enemies in fact possess this terrifying power. No wonder that Foxe has to rewrite those "proper and olde growen branches" as "starued" weaklings, despite the utility of their legitimacy for the doctrine of election.

"And now (ye men of Israel)," Foxe asks triumphantly, rhetorically undoing the uncertainty of his own projection into futurity, "where is that your arrogant vaineglorious vaunt of the ofspring of your kindred? If to be issued of the race of Abraham be prised so highly in the sight of God, what meaneth then this casting away of the Israelites?" (L1v–L2r). But Foxe can reassure himself and his auditors about the worthlessness of Jewish ancestry only by undermining his own argument about election: if he earlier revises the "excellencie" of the proper old branches, here he discounts the merit of ancestry itself—the very ancestry that had initially served as the basis for his demonstration that God's election does not depend on merit. And like his progressive rewriting of the language of illegitimate usurpation as a language of desert, in which the proper old natural branches are cut off because they merit cutting off, this contradiction registers not only Foxe's unease at Jewish claims to ancestry but also a broader double bind at the heart of a Christian culture dependent on its sense of difference from—and superiority to—the Jews. On the one hand, Foxe needs to maintain the inferiority of Christian to Jew that makes God's casting off of the Jews and grafting in of the gentiles the supreme instance of election; on the other, despite his warning against "disdayneful triumphing vpon forlorn abiects" (A4v), he is not willing to give up the pleasures of excoriating the Jews. As a consequence, he wrestles not only with the familiar issue of the abstract justice of God's election but also with the awkward double conviction that though the Christians cannot have merited being chosen, the Jews must have merited being unchosen—or, more precisely, that though the distinction between Christian election and Jewish reprobation cannot strictly speaking be attributed to Jewish desert, the Jews must nonetheless be uniquely at fault.[78]

Jewish reprobation is—Foxe begins by telling us—ordained by the "vnchaungeable decree of [God's] incomprehensible wisedome" (A8v); and yet (however incomprehensible God's wisdom) that reprobation is surely merited: if the Jews are "ouercharged with the seuere rigor of Gods Iustice . . . so much the more haynous must the canker be, that prouoked [a punishment] so sharpe and bitter" (B1r). Despite their own apparent superiority, the Jews are thus reassuringly responsible for their own reprobation after all: the Jewish canker is "vnbeliefe," and "it is out of all question [that their punishment] proceeded from their owne default, and through vnbeliefe" (B1r, B5r–v). But the reassurance signaled by Foxe's emphatic "it is out of all question" proves to be very unstable, and Paul's own metaphor of the olive tree points toward this instability. Just before Foxe proclaims the Jews responsible for their own reprobation, he questions the apostle's use of "cut off" to describe their fate: "Wherefore chose he to say that they were cut of, rather then that they did fall away?" (B5r). And immediately after, he asks again, "What moued the Apostle then to vse this figuratiue phrase of speach of cutting of rather, saying that they were cut of, and fell not away of their owne accord? . . . The things that are cut of can not choose but fall away. . . . What is ment therfore by this word cutting of?" (B5v). Foxe repeats the question as though it were an irritation, a bone in his throat that he cannot quite be rid of, for his question returns him to the conundrum of merit that he has apparently just resolved: he perforce concludes that the apostle chose this figure for "nothing els, but to make vs conceiue, that the heauenly and vnsearchable hande of almightie God dyd ouerthrowe this buylding. . . . no endeuours of man can auayle, much lesse can mens merites or deseruings be of anie force . . . but the only election of almightie God" (B5v–B6r). But if neither merits nor—in this case—demerits are of any force, then the Jews are once again relieved of responsibility for their own reprobation. This is not a tolerable conclusion, and so Foxe reopens the question again, as though for the first time: "a question may bee moued here perhappes . . . whether the Iewes were not supplanted from the true Oliue for their vnbeliefe?" (B6v). And then he answers it as though he had not just settled firmly on the opposite position: "what els doeth it explane vnto vs, then a manifest demonstration as wel of the meritorious desert, as wel of faith, as of vnbeliefe?" (B6v).

Fault/no fault/fault: the need simultaneously to make the Jews guilty of their own reprobation and to attribute reprobation and election to the unsearchable hand of almighty God rather than to human merit leads Foxe in an apparently endless circle. And it leads as well to what comes to seem even to Foxe like a potentially infinite regress of questions. For positing unbelief as the Jewish fault that may—or may not—have led to their reprobation merely moves the conundrum of election one step backward, to the prior question of why God chooses some to believe and others to disbelieve. In the "iudgement of some," gentile/Christian faith and Jewish infidelity may be "deemed the very originall causes of the free acceptation of the Gentiles, and likewise of the repulse of the Iewes" (B6v), Foxe says, but the matter cannot rest there: "But for all this we heare not yet, what were the causes of the faith of the one, and of the vnbeliefe of the other" (B6v). And his answer leads him immediately back to the familiar problem: "when as if the cause of their dismembring from their true naturall Oliue tree be enquired: I answere, For their vnbeliefe vndoubtedly: And yet this answere doth not satisfie the purpose of Pauls disputation. For sithence faith is an especiall gift of God, issuing from out the only mercie and grace of God, and not from mans free choise, the question reboundeth backe againe from whence it began" (B7r). Belief and unbelief may be signs of "meritorious desert" (B6v), but neither proceeds from man's free choice, and so Foxe is forced to ask the question yet again: "Wherefore then were the Iewes forsaken, and the Gentiles receiued?" (B7v). The rebounding questions admit of no satisfactory solution, and their repetition suggests the extent to which Foxe can neither answer them nor let them go. For Jewish reprobation must be simultaneously merited and unmerited: even in the concluding paragraph of his argument about Jewish unbelief, the Jews' "wilful blyndnes" merits reprobation in one sentence, but in the next, "God was the worker of their blindnes" (B7v).[79]

In response to this conundrum, Foxe briefly attempts to preserve a secure relationship between cause (Jewish unbelief) and effect (Jewish reprobation) by reversing their order. Perhaps, he speculates (citing Paul), the unbelief of the Jews was the result—not the cause—of their reprobation; perhaps God arranged for Jewish unbelief in effect to justify himself after the fact: "did they therefore offend, because they shoulde bee cast away?" (B7v). But this "were as much to say, as though God should be delited in their destruction";[80] and as though in recoil from this conclusion, Foxe answers himself with an emphatic "God forbid," once again citing Paul: "Nay rather, that by their fal saluation should happen to the Gentiles: & that by their vnbeliefe the Gentiles might obteine mercie" (B7v–B8r). Foxe has already explained that "the safetie of the Iewes might haue byn an estoppell to the receauing of the Gentiles, & so haue procured their vncouerable destruction, through false opinion of the doctrine of righteousnes. . . . there was none other meane or way for the Gentiles, to haue due accesse to true righteousnes" (B4v). "There was none other meane": as Paul says, the Jews must be cast away "that so the decaye of the Iewes might be the riches of the Gentiles" (B4v). Foxe's "God forbid" in effect rescues God—or Foxe—from the impiety of Foxe's own thought by gesturing toward this necessity. But this conclusion not only produces the image of a singularly impotent or unimaginative God; it also makes the mercy extended to the gentiles uncomfortably contingent on the suffering of the Jews, who by definition were in themselves no more deserving of unbelief and reprobation than the gentiles were of belief and election. Foxe immediately registers this discomfort by questioning the necessity of Jewish reprobation for Christian election, in effect returning again to his original question: if the gentiles may obtain mercy only by the fall of the Jews, then "question wilbe moued here againe, whether it were not as easy for almighty god to haue giuen mercy to them both, if it had pleased him" (B8r). And many pages later, he is still asking the same question: "The Gentiles [who were chosen] were sometymes as voyde of fayth, as they [the Jews] are nowe" (M1v); "why was not this benefite of fayth and beliefe in Christ impartened to the Iewes, as well as to the Gentiles indifferently?" (M3v).[81] And if God could have done otherwise—if the Jews cannot be reliably made responsible for their unbelief or their reprobation—then perhaps they are not satisfying villains but rather innocent victims subject to a capricious God after all: "by this example it may happely bee thought, that God did execute too much crueltie and rigour agaynst those seely wretches the Iewes. Admitte in deede, that it was so. This was therefore a good lesson to forewarne vs" (M4r). But if the Jews are merely "seely wretches,"[82] and if their fate is fully applicable to *us*, then there is no essential difference between them and the Christians who have superseded them.

The spectacle of the converted Jew that begins in celebration returns Foxe and his auditors to God's originary election of gentile over Jew and therefore ends by producing the set of anxieties to which Foxe continually returns: anxieties about the merit of Jewish claims to superior ancestry, about God's justice, about the foundational distinctions between Christian and Jew, and about the "seeliness" of the Jews, who suffer only for the benefit of the gentiles. And as though in response, Foxe offers two local antidotes to these anxieties, both of which function to mark the Jew indelibly with his crime and thus to justify God's choice—and both of which have powerful analogues (I shall argue) in *The Merchant of Venice*. The first serves to racialize the Jewish unbelief that seems to be problematically undistinguishable from the unbelief of the gentiles who were chosen; the second produces the spectacle of the monstrous Jew who could not possibly be mistaken for a Christian—and who therefore deserves whatever punishment is meted out to him.

Although Foxe acknowledges that the gentiles may have been "sometymes as voyde of fayth, as they [the Jews] are nowe" (M1v), he interrupts his circular discussion of the causes of Jewish reprobation to establish that Jewish unbelief is nonetheless somehow—reassuringly—*Jewish*. After describing several lesser varieties of unbelief familiar to Christians, he comes to "this kind of infidelitie of al others . . . most horrible & execrable, when as

men do rushe headlong into such obstinate resistance, that they wil not only
not acquaint themselues with the trueth, being layd open before their eyes,
but will wittingly shut vp their senses from the beholding thereof, because
they will not see it . . . . And this is that vnbeliefe, which being more noy-
some then any pestilent botch, may rightly & properly be called the Iewish
Infidelitie" (B3r).[83] But the willful blindness of Jewish unbelief is not enough
to attach it securely to Jewish (and only Jewish) bodies; for this, Foxe needs
a discourse of bodies. He has already implicitly established that discourse
through a series of metaphors of unbelief as disease that anticipate the "pestilent botch" of this passage: Jewish unbelief is the "cankred contagion that
wrought their perdition" (B1r), the "infection" of their "fretting fistula"
(B1r). But insofar as this metaphoric disease is a pestilence, a contagion, an
infection, it points toward the undifferentiating dangers of contamination
rather than the specificity that Foxe needs. He therefore crucially shifts from
the model of contagion to the model of inherited disease; and in this shift,
Jewish unbelief becomes a kind of spiritual Tay-Sachs, a disease that marks
all Jews, and only Jews: "Iewish Infidelitie . . . seemeth after a certaine maner
their inheritable disease, who are after a certaine sort, from their mothers
wombe, naturally caried through peruerse frowardnes, into all malitious
hatred, & contempt of Christ, & his Christians" (B3r). Jewish unbelief thus
becomes the property of any Jew who had a mother—and so God "must
needes auenge him vpon the whole nation, and roote out the remnant of
the whole race altogether" (B3v). In the face of radical no-difference, that is,
Foxe attempts to instate the absolute difference of an inheritable biology—
the difference that undergirds all discourses of racism, and specifically the
Inquisition's blood laws, to which I will turn in chapter 3.[84] And his turn
toward race not only reassuringly reestablishes difference; it also solves the
vexing problems of God's justice and of Christian guilt at Jewish displacement. For whether or not the Jews have done something wrong to merit reprobation, they *are* something wrong; and who would not justly punish a race
thus biologically stained? Who would not guiltlessly take their place?

This is a brilliantly economical move: it not only affixes Jewish unbelief to Jewish bodies and assuages Christian guilt; it also creates an alternative genealogy for the Jews in which their race and nation—in Foxe's use
here, the terms are synonymous—are defined by contaminating mothers
rather than by holy fathers. And with that readjustment, Foxe can imagine
that God will do away with the whole Jewish problem: after all, he "must
needes . . . roote out the remnant of the whole race altogether." (Foxe's word
"roote" seems to me a good indicator of the stakes of his shift from fathers

to mothers, and hence from honorable ancestry to inheritable stain. If Foxe's imaginary Jews claim that they can never perish because "the holy Patriarches are our progenitours: we are the yssue of an holy roote" [E2v], here their derivation from mothers enables Foxe to transform that "roote" into the verb that registers their annihilation by God.) But the extent to which this local antidote—Foxe's fantasy of an inherited contamination and an attendant racial cleansing—runs counter to the avowed purpose of the sermon seems to me a good indicator of the strength of the anxieties the antidote is designed to assuage. For of course Foxe knows full well that God has no plans to root out the entire remnant of the Jewish race. In fact, he elsewhere takes pains to warn his auditors against believing "that the whole race was drawen all together into the same gulfe of perdition" [B5r], explicitly reminding them that "this one caution ought diligently to be marked: That no such thought enter into any our minds, as though the Iewes are so altogether forsaken of god . . . as that no sparkle of mercie is reserued in store for them to hope vpon: Neither that the whole stocke of that Nation is so altogether supplanted that no remnant of all the roote therof, hath any droppe of moysture layed vp for them in the fountaine of Gods free election" [A8r]. After all, his entire sermon rests on this possibility: it both begins and ends with a prayer for the conversion of the Jews [A1v, N2r]. But how can any Jew—even his new convert Nathanael—be converted if Jewish unbelief is indelibly attached to Jewish bodies and the whole race is to be destroyed?

Foxe's prayers for the conversion of the Jews are underwritten by Paul's testimony that they will eventually be returned to their holy root in the olive tree, but his desire for their conversion is nonetheless marked everywhere by ambivalence. Even when he "hope[s] well of [their] amendement" [L7r], he cannot imagine that amendment without first exaggerating their villainy by once again conflating contemporary Jews with their bloodthirsty ancestors: "Be not dismayed with despaire to attayne euerlasting life, because you crucified the sonne of God. . . . To racke the sauiour of the world vpon the crosse, is of all other [crimes] most execrable. Yet hath the Lorde promised to forget all these iniuries, if ye wil but repent you of them" [L7v]. God may forget, but Foxe won't: Foxe apparently needs the spectacle of the permanently bloodthirsty Jew as much as he needs the Jew whose unbelief is indelibly fixed in his body. As though he cannot quite count on the Jew to be reliably "Jewish" enough, he invokes just this spectacle in what is probably the most peculiar moment in the sermon, this time not only conflating contemporary Jews with their ancestors but also urging them to keep on reiterating their original crime:

Being swallowed vp of extreame madnes, & ouerwhelmed with blinde
rancour, & canckred malice, you did most cruelly despoyle him of life,
and spilt his guiltlesse blood, without all cause of offence. For why may I
not iustly accuse you, as partetakers of the same crime, sithence yee doe
with whole bent affection of hatefull despite, pursue the embrued steppes
of your bloodie sires, and gladly allow of that execrable murther?

And therefore (thou cursed Iewe) thou are duly charged with the guilt
of innocent blood: englut therfore thy greedie guts with goare. (L3r)

"Englut therfore thy greedie guts with goare": only the spectacle of the Jew
permanently engaged in the killing of Christ and the ritual murders[85] that
imitate that original crime can assuage the anxieties provoked by Nathanael's conversion—and so Foxe asks the Jews to keep on repeating their crime
in contradiction of everything he ostensibly hopes for, insisting that the Jew
remain a "cursed Iewe" forever, forever enacting the bloody site of his difference.

⸙

I take conversion and the trope of the Jewish stranger within Christianity
as the starting point for my reading of the relationship between Christian
and Jew in *The Merchant of Venice* because that relationship seems to me
to turn everywhere on anxieties about the difference between Christian and
Jew that they provoke: anxieties both about the permeability of religious, national, and personal borders and about the justice of God's purposes and the
Christian's unpaid debt to the Jew. These anxieties circulate in *Merchant*,
I argue, around three broad topics: the Jewish paternity of Christianity and
therefore the legitimacy of Christianity's claim to father Abraham and the
promise; the universalizing mandate of conversion, with its necessity for
incorporating the abjected body of the Jew into Christianity; and the Pauline promise—after centuries of abasement of the Jews, now more a threat
than a promise—that the uncircumcised Christian could, like the converso,
be a Jew within. Each of these topics is localized at a site of conversion in
Merchant, as befits their origin in the anxieties conversion provokes: the
first in Lancelot's turn from Jew to Christian in 2.2 (chapter 2), the second
in Jessica's vexed attempt at conversion by marriage (chapter 3), and the
third in the conversion and counter-conversion of Antonio and Shylock in
4.1 (chapter 4). Moreover, whatever the theological differences between Foxe
and Shakespeare may have been,[86] and despite Shakespeare's famous "humanizing" of Shylock, *Merchant* seems to me to display the same strategies

to contain anxiety that Foxe employs in his sermon, where the spectacle of the Jewish convert to Christianity requires the desperate remedies of a proto-racism and a contradictory desire that the Jew continue at all costs to play the bloody role assigned to him by the Christian. For if (as I argue) Lancelot's conversion enacts the guilt-ridden conundrums of election and of Christianity's relationship to its paternity in Judaism, as though in response, Jessica's reinforces the indelible attachment of Jewishness to Jewish bodies, and Shylock enacts the blood-englutted Jew who can secure Jewish difference—and Jewish guilt—even as the state mandates his conversion. Shakespeare in fact has the advantage over Foxe here: whereas Foxe can call up the figure of the monstrous Jew only as a rhetorical device in the midst of his sermon on conversion, Shakespeare can actually make him present to his audience in all his terrifying bloody-mindedness. And as the scene in which he whets his knife implies, the relation between Christian and Jew in *Merchant* turns crucially on blood: on the Jewish blood lineage of Christianity, on Jessica's inability to rid herself of her father's blood, and on the spectacle of the bloodthirsty Jew and Portia's final reification of Christian blood. Hence my shorthand for this entire complex of anxieties and defenses in *Merchant:* "blood relations."

CHAPTER TWO

Leaving the Jew's House:
Father, Son, and Elder Brother

It hath pleased our Lord God and heauenly father, to reueale his sonne vnto me, & to gather me againe into the stocke of my father Abraham (from whence I was cast out through vnbeliefe with my forefathers, the stifnecked and disobedient).
—"The confession of faith, which Nathanael a Iewe borne, made," C3r–v

O father Abram, what these Christians are.
—*Merchant of Venice*, 1.3.156

Conversion from Judaism to Christianity in *The Merchant of Venice*—at least before Shylock's enforced conversion in 4.1—is represented as a child's deception and then abandonment of a father. This representation is most explicit in Jessica, who leaves her father's house and his religion in the same gesture, taking his precious stones with her. But Jessica is not the only child who leaves Shylock's house and deceives a father in the process: just before we meet Jessica planning her escape in 2.3, we meet Lancelot attempting to escape from Shylock's house and deceiving his own father. Moreover, since Lancelot tells us that he is "a Jew" if he serves the Jew any longer (2.2.99–100), his leaving Shylock's service is itself a kind of mock conversion from Jew to Christian, as though he were parodying Jessica's conversion before the fact. But why? In this chapter I attempt to understand the connection between these two scenes and, more particularly, to answer a question that seems to me to underscore the implicit emotional exchange between them: why should Lancelot's decision to leave Shylock's house in 2.2 be so much more difficult, and so much more fraught with guilt, than Jessica's?

Shakespeare, I suggest, shapes Lancelot's throwaway scene of conversion in terms that encapsulate Christianity's anxieties about its vexed paternity in Judaism, simultaneously providing a kind of portal to the troubled relationship elsewhere occluded in the play's smoothly Christian triumph and warding off acknowledgment of that relationship by engaging it in the register of comedy. As I shall argue in the next chapter, Jessica's is not an entirely guilt-free, or problem-free, conversion; but by making his primary convert a daughter and eliding her conversion with her marriage, Shakespeare occludes the paternal betrayal inherent in that conversion, in effect "covering" it—and perhaps himself—in at least two ways: by assimilating her conversion story to a familiar comic pattern, in which daughters routinely leave blocking fathers in order to marry; and by nodding toward the legal and social "coverture" of wives by their husbands, as though Jessica's status were naturally contingent on Lorenzo's. But Lancelot's small scene in effect removes those covers, exposing the anxious familial relation between the would-be Christian and the figure Lorenzo calls "my father Jew" (2.6.25). As Lancelot manages the transition from Shylock's house to Bassanio's, and hence secures his status as Christian rather than Jew, his passage obliquely reiterates one of the central narratives through which Christian tradition understands that transition at its point of origin: a narrative that turns radically on a son's deception of his father in order to secure the blessing intended for his older brother. By alluding to this narrative as Lancelot enacts a comic version of the conversion from Jew to Christian, *Merchant* links the story of leaving the Jew's house with this problematic originary moment, reproducing the anxiety encoded in this narrative of the transition from Judaism to Christianity. And through this convergence, *Merchant* implies that all Christians can in effect be read as converts from an originary Judaism they must disavow, figured as a father they must deceive in order to secure a blessing they do not deserve. Hence I think the weird and apparently unmerited guilt in the scene of Lancelot's conversion, a guilt far out of proportion to its ostensible occasion, and hence also perhaps the need to make the father Jew despicable enough that there need be no shame in deceiving and abandoning him.

Leaving Shylock's house should be easy for Lancelot. After all, Shylock himself shows no signs of minding his departure—he has already "preferred" him to Bassanio (2.2.131) and is apparently glad to be rid of him (2.5.44–49). And initially, leaving Shylock's service seems unproblematic to Lancelot: he enters 2.2 proclaiming, "Certainly my conscience will serve me to run from this Jew my master" (2.2.1–2). But his conscience will not in fact serve him to run. Lancelot immediately shifts the imperative to leave Shylock from the domain of conscience—which now says, "do not run, scorn running with thy heels" (2.2.7)—to the domain of the devil, who "tempts [him], saying . . . 'use your legs, take the start, run away'" (2.2.2–5): he may think that the Jew is "the very devil incarnation" (2.2.21–22), but the voice that tempts him to leave the Jew also turns out to be demonic. This shift is, I think, worth emphasizing: when Lancelot reports that his conscience now tells him that he "should stay with the Jew [his] master" (2.2.18), he phrases his leaving Shylock's house as something like a betrayal or a breach of contract.

   Technically, of course, this is a problem that Lancelot should never have had to worry about: a whole series of regulations (at least from the Fourth Lateran Council on) prohibited Jews from hiring Christian servants.[1] Lance-lot himself gives an explanation of sorts for the prohibition: given that he has just complained that he is famished in Shylock's service (2.2.94), his claim that he is a Jew if he serves the Jew any longer comically exaggerates the effects of Shylock's stinginess on him, but it nonetheless suggests the fears of contamination that are at stake in this prohibition. But the prohibition—and hence the mandate to leave the Jew's service—also had a strong theological basis, one that moreover aligns Lancelot's escape from service in Shylock's house with the originary conversion of Jew to Christian. In Galatians, Paul's account of the passage of the promise from Jew to Christian turns crucially on the metaphor of service: "Then I say, that the heire as long as he is a childe, differeth nothing from a seruant. . . . Euen so, we when we were children, were in bondage. . . . [But now] thou art no more a seruant, but a sonne" (4.1, 3, 7); "Stand fast therefore in the libertie wherewith Christ hathe made vs fre, and be not intangled againe with the yoke of bondage" (5.1).[2] The Jew is bound and the Christian free, and it stands to reason that the theologically free should not serve the bound;[3] in fact, as though he had precisely these analogies in mind, Lancelot promotes himself from servant to Master Lancelot (2.2.40, 42) as soon as he decides to leave Shylock's service. For if his change of masters in effect marks Lancelot's conversion from Jew to Christian, then it also marks his conversion typologically from bound to unbound: hence, in Lancelot's literalizing imagination, Master Lancelot.[4] Given this theological warrant, nothing should be easier than leaving Shylock. But though Jessica apparently has few qualms about leaving her father, Lancelot can hardly bring himself to leave the old Jew; and his queasy conscience about leaving Shylock is immediately played out in his relationship to his own father.

   Paul tells the new Christian that he is "no more a seruant, but a sonne"—

and sure enough, as soon as Lancelot has decided to leave Shylock's service, his own father appears, carrying a basket of doves no less; and the scene between them ends in the recognition that Lancelot is indeed his son, as though in a literalization of his newfound Christian status. But why introduce Lancelot's literal father at this Pauline moment of transition? It's worth noting, I think, that this is Gobbo's only appearance in the play, and also that Lancelot seems to predict his appearance by conjuring him up immediately before he appears. In fact, his father intrudes somewhat awkwardly into Lancelot's conversation with his conscience at the beginning of the scene: "my conscience . . . says very wisely to me, 'My honest friend Lancelot'—being an honest man's son, or rather an honest woman's son, for indeed my father did something smack, something grow to; he had a kind of taste—well, my conscience says, 'Lancelot, budge not'" (2.2.10–15). His father enters Lancelot's mind—and therefore ours—as an interruption, as though called up by Lancelot's anxiety about leaving Shylock; and he materializes onstage as soon as Lancelot has made his decision: "I will run. *Enter old Gobbo*" (2.2.25). And although Gobbo first appears to serve as a kind of auxiliary to Lancelot's conscience—insofar as Lancelot is an honest man's son, he will obey his conscience and budge not—in the end, he acts to promote his son's service to his new Christian master, to whom he presents those symbolically laden doves.[5] But why? Lancelot does not need his father's help to move from Shylock to Bassanio; Bassanio specifies not only that Shylock has already preferred him but also that Lancelot himself has obtained his suit (2.2.128–29). Gobbo's appearance here thus seems to be entirely gratuitous, unmotivated by the plot. But perhaps its very gratuitousness from the point of view of the plot calls attention to an underlying logic that we might agree to call theo-psychological. For Gobbo's unmotivated appearance underscores the conjoining of theological and psychological anxieties about fathers in this scene, and more broadly in the transition from Jew to Christian: as though the guilt inherent in leaving one father—"my father Jew"—can be assuaged only by the presence of another who can mediate it.

The appearance of Lancelot's own father (I am arguing) helps to ward off Lancelot's anxiety about leaving Shylock: Lancelot apparently needs his father's blessing before he can make the transition from Jew to Christian and become a Pauline "son." But before he can claim that blessing, he apparently must "try confusions" with his own father (2.2.30), as though the scene with his father must simultaneously counter and replay his decision to leave Shylock. In fact, Lancelot no sooner imagines leaving Shylock than he plays at leaving his own father, in effect casting his status as father's son in doubt. When he initially describes himself as "an honest man's son, or

rather an honest woman's son, for indeed my father did something smack,
something grow to; he had a kind of taste," perhaps he means—or means to
mean—only that he has inherited his honesty from his mother rather than
his father. But his self-interruption ("or rather an honest woman's son")
nonetheless marks an interruption in his identity as father's son: though
logically he could be dislodged from that position only if his mother—not
his father—were dishonest, the sentence nonetheless performs this dislodg-
ing, shifting him from father's son to mother's son; in effect, he disinherits
himself in mid-thought.[6] We might take this as no more than the Shakespearean tic that often proclaims the son of the mother no more than the
shadow of the father (2 *Henry IV*, 3.2.121); and in fact Lancelot counters
this fantasy by proclaiming his father "true-begotten" (2.2.28) as soon as he
appears onstage, apparently securing his own lineage in him through the bizarre logic that his father's true-begetting would demonstrate his own. But
then Lancelot goes on to act out the uncertainty of his relation to his father,
disavowing him after all. First, he conceals his identity from his father; then
he claims an advancement in rank ("young Master Lancelot") that would
give him a different father ("No master, sir, but a poor man's son," his father
protests); and finally he tells the poor old man that his son is dead (2.2.40–43,
55). Even after he has reclaimed his father by revealing himself to him, he
continues to half-deny him, as though he were not altogether certain about
which father he belonged to: Gobbo presents him to Bassanio as "my son,
sir, a poor boy," and Lancelot interrupts him to say, "Not a poor boy, sir, but
the rich Jew's man" (2.2.108–10).

    This exchange between Lancelot and Gobbo reads social advancement as
a kind of betrayal of a father who is denied and left behind. But it also obliquely
reiterates Lancelot's attempt to leave Shylock, thereby reading Lancelot's religious "advancement"—his turn from Jew to Christian—in the same terms.
The two fathers have been linked associatively from the opening moments
of the scene, when Gobbo intrudes unexpectedly into Lancelot's meditation
on leaving Shylock; the deception Lancelot practices on his father seems to
me a kind of residue from the guilt expressed in that meditation, as though
Lancelot could receive his father's blessing and turn Christian only by first
playing out the scene of paternal betrayal implicit in leaving Shylock. And
though this scene of trying confusions seems far from central in *Merchant*,
it is nonetheless central to Shakespeare's imagination—central enough that
he will replay it in Poor Tom/Edgar's deception of Gloucester.[7] But what
exactly is it doing here? I have already suggested that the scene of deception
provoked by Lancelot's decision to leave Shylock plays out in comic mode
both guilt about leaving the father behind and anxiety about the uncertainty

of paternal lineage, in effect warding off both by making a game of them. But why should the decision to leave Shylock be so fraught with this anxiety and guilt? I think because it reiterates in miniature the originary scene of conversion from Judaism to Christianity—and because guilt toward the father and anxiety about his lineage crucially frame that larger scene of conversion. Lorenzo's apparently throwaway characterization of Shylock as "my father Jew" is resonant in part because Judaism is commonly figured as the father to Christianity: Foxe reminds his auditors in his sermon on conversion that "the very first yssues of our Christian faith sprang out of [Jewish] stocke" (*Sermon*, B5r), and Paul calls Abraham "the father of vs all" (Romans 4.16). But the turn to Christianity from Judaism depended radically on abandoning this Jewish lineage while nonetheless claiming it as one's own, simultaneously leaving the father behind and posing oneself as his true son. Lancelot's decision to leave Shylock reiterates this turn both insofar as it anticipates Jessica's own abandonment of her father and insofar as Lancelot himself imagines leaving Shylock as a conversion of sorts; it thus inherits the guilt and anxiety attendant on this larger moment of conversion. No wonder, then, that Lancelot has difficulty leaving Shylock and can do so only by playing out the deception of his father and his own disinheritance before he can secure his father's blessing and become a Pauline "son": here Shakespeare's habitual joke about the son's legitimacy maps onto larger theological concerns about the legitimacy of Christianity's claim to the Jewish lineage it has abandoned and thus to the inheritance of father Abraham.

∽

If Foxe's *Sermon preached at the Christening of a Certaine Iew* and the "Confession of faith" appended to it are any indication, something like bad conscience toward the fathers and anxiety about reclaiming their patrimony may have been a familiar accompaniment to Jewish conversion. Foxe's Jew Nathanael concludes his confession of faith with the words that serve as the first epigraph for this chapter: words that trace his torturous route back to the "stocke of [his] father Abraham" after he has disowned his fleshly forefathers. Throughout, he defines his conversion as much by his troubled relation to these fathers as by his newfound belief in Christ. He thus begins his confession by reminding his audience of God's promise "in the dayes of our forefathers," "the othe which he had sworne vnto our fathers Abraham, Isaac, & Iacob" ("Confession," B1r). These are his fleshly forefathers, and he clearly alludes to them with some pride. But his conversion turns on—and enacts—the displacement of these fathers, the "stocke of Abraham after the

fleshe" ("Confession," B2r); by the end of his confession, Nathanael's claim
to father Abraham depends on his disavowal of them. Nathanael thus enacts
for the benefit of his audience a move familiar from Paul, Christianity's most
spectacular Jewish convert, who similarly displaced his own fleshly fathers
in order to become a child of the promise: "all they are not Israel, which are
of Israel: Neither are thei all children, because thei are the sede of Abraham
. . . they which are the children of the flesh, are not the children of God: but
the children of the promes are counted for the sede" (Romans 9.6–8).[8] Like
a latter-day Paul, Nathanael can be counted for the seed of father Abraham
only if he casts off the "stocke of Abraham after the fleshe": a formulation
that must have been deeply satisfying for Foxe and his auditors, since it
rebuts the special Jewish claim to Abraham from as it were the horse's
mouth and poses Christians as what Lancelot might call the "truly begotten" sons of Abraham after all.

But the problem registered in this converted Jew's words is that Abraham must stand simultaneously for the fleshly fathers that he must disavow
and the spiritualized father that he desires access to: the heavenly father
he would worship remains, ambiguously, "the God of Abraham, Isaac, and
Iacob" ("Confession," B7v).[9] And this is, I think, not only Nathanael's problem. I have already argued in the last chapter that the spectacle of Yehuda's
conversion to Nathanael seems to have functioned for Foxe as much to stir
up anxiety about the Christian claim to be counted for the seed as to allay
that anxiety. Abraham may be, as Paul says, "the father of vs all" (Romans
4.16), but the route back to him for this new Christian is peculiarly cir-
cuitous, and that circuitousness suggests the peculiarity of Christianity's
relationship to its paternity in Judaism. For Christianity depends radically
both on its claim to a fleshly Jewish lineage and on its success in destabilizing that lineage, its claim that only the spiritual children are the true heirs.
Christ must be lineally—and in the flesh—descended from Abraham, Isaac,
and Jacob: as Paul says, the Israelites are those "of whome are the fathers,
and of whome concerning the flesh, Christ came" (Romans 9.5); and the first
words of the New Testament painstakingly trace Christ's fleshly lineage
back to David and, through him, back to Jacob, Isaac, and eventually Abraham (Matthew 1.1–17).[10] But Christians can claim to be the seed of Abraham
only by disclaiming this fleshly lineage; insofar as "the very first yssues of
our Christian faith sprang out of that stocke" (Sermon, B5r), every Christian has in effect enacted a version of Nathanael's—or Paul's—dispossession
of his original fathers in claiming Abraham for his own. The route back to
father Abraham thus requires exactly the kind of doublethink audible in
Nathanael's words or in Paul's when he asserts that "all they are not Israel,

which are of Israel" (Romans 9.6): like Abraham, "Israel" has to do double duty, in effect standing in both for the disowned fleshly and for the promised spiritual lineage—a confusion that the Geneva Bible's gloss to the first of those "Israels" attempts, not very successfully, to rectify by explaining, "that is, of Iacob whose name was also Israel."

Jacob is a telling figure here, and one whose status will be explicitly contested in *Merchant:* does he stand for the fleshly or the spiritual inheritance in this Geneva gloss? If Isaac and Jacob are lineally and in the flesh the guarantors of Christ's status as Messiah, they are also, from Paul on, the symbolic bearers of the promise that disinherits that fleshly lineage; typologically, they are called on to represent the proto-Christian children of the spirit, while their elder siblings Ishmael and Esau inherit the discredited position of the Jews, the children of the flesh. The argument with which the Geneva Bible introduces the book of Romans phrases this displacement thus, echoing Paul's double "Israel" but replacing it with Abraham: "the examples of Ismael and Esau declare, that all are not Abrahams posteritie, which come of Abraham according to the flesh: but also the verie strangers and Gentiles grafted in by faith, are made heires of the promes." In other words: the fleshly descendants of Abraham are to be displaced by sons of faith—and these sons of faith come to be typologically represented by none other than Isaac and Jacob, the fleshly ancestors of Christ. Isaac and Jacob are thus called upon simultaneously to represent both the Jews from whom Christ descends in the flesh and the triumph of Christian spiritual lineage over Jewish fleshly lineage. But they cannot comfortably stand for both at once; and the simultaneous embracing and displacing of this fleshly lineage enabled by the switch between typological and literal modes of interpretation registers the ambivalence of Christianity toward its ancestry in Judaism.

Augustine's attempt to keep the literal and typological separate in his discussion of Jacob and Esau illustrates the problem. He begins confidently enough: "*Esau* and *Iacob, Isaacs* two sonnes, prefigured the two peoples of Iewes and Christians," with Esau serving as the type of merely fleshly descent as opposed to Jacob's spiritual descent. But then Augustine is forced to interrupt himself to account for the literal, rather than typological, descendants of each son: "although that in the flesh the Idumeans, and not the Iewes came of *Esau*, nor the Christians of *Iacob*, but rather the Iewes." Here the typological is compromised by the literal, into which it threatens to collapse. And because Christ's lineage must be literal—in the flesh—the two modes of interpretation cannot be kept separate after all; fleshly and spiritual are hopelessly entangled in the figure of Jacob as literal and typological

threaten to change places. Thus, according to Augustine, Isaac's blessing of
Jacob is a prophecy of Christ because (like Jacob) Christ "is Lord ouer his
brother, for his people [i.e., Jacob's typological people, the Christians] rule
ouer the Iewes [i.e., Esau's typological people]." So far so good. But Augustine continues, "The sonnes of his father that is *Abrahams* sonnes in the
faith [i.e., Jacob's typological people, the Christians] doe honour him. For
hee is *Abrahams* sonne in the flesh [i.e., literally a descendant of Jacob]."[11]
Augustine's "for" serves as the switch-point between the Jews' typological
descent from Esau and their literal descent from Jacob, and it indicates the
point at which Augustine must abandon the typological for the literal, lest
Christ be misunderstood as the fleshly son of Esau rather than of Jacob. And
as such, that "for" carries the weight of Christianity's vexed relation to the
literal fathers of Christ: Christ can be adored by Jacob's typological sons of
the promise only if he is in the line of Jacob's literal sons, but those literal
sons must nonetheless be displaced—rewritten as the typological sons of
Esau—before Jacob's typological sons can claim their place as Abraham's
true posterity.

No such ambivalence or indirection attends Shylock's access to the line
of Jacob or his possession of the figure he calls "father Abram" (1.3.156).
Christians may nominate themselves the heirs of Isaac and Jacob and con-
sign Jews to their typological ancestors Ishmael or Esau, but for Shylock it
is the Christians who are in the line of Ishmael, son of the bondswoman
Hagar. When he calls his Christian servant Lancelot "that fool of Hagar's
offspring" (2.5.42), it is unclear whether "Hagar's offspring" refers to Lancelot himself or to Bassanio, whose "fool" Lancelot has just become.[12] But in
either case, it emphatically designates Ishmael as the ancestor of the Christians, not of the Jews. And if the Christians become the outcast spawn of
Ishmael in this formulation, Shylock elsewhere claims the lineage of Isaac
for himself; metaphorically at least, he leans easily on the staff of Isaac's
son Jacob, by which he swears shortly before this challenge to Christian
hermeneutics (2.5.35).[13] And in his early conversation with Antonio about
Laban's sheep—a conversation framed as a contest over who has the right
to interpret the Bible—Shylock traces his own possession of the figure he
calls "our" Abraham through his near identification with his ancestor Jacob: "This Jacob from our holy Abram was, / As his wise mother wrought
in his behalf, / The third possessor; ay, he was the third" (1.3.68–70).[14] In
fact, Shylock is so confident a member of Abraham's family that he can appeal to him to secure the distinction between that family and the outsider-
Christians who would lay claim to him: "O father Abram, what these Christians are, / Whose own hard dealings teaches them suspect / The thoughts of

others!" (1.3.156–58). Shylock's use of father Abraham to critique Christian suspicion of Jews here is brilliant if bogus: we already know that he intends to sacrifice Antonio to his "ancient grudge" if he can (1.3.42), an intention that (as I shall later argue) identifies him with a vengeful "Jewish" version of the patriarch rather than a salvific Christian one. And perhaps he appeals to Abraham as a form of rhetorical currency to guarantee his good intentions largely because he expects Christians to expect Jews to appeal to Abraham; Marlowe's Barabas appeals to Abraham well before his first scene is finished (*The Jew of Malta*, 1.1.104). But the figure of Abraham nonetheless does him double duty, enabling him simultaneously to conceal his anticipated (and, in the play's terms, "Jewish") revenge under a veil of filial piety and to reclaim the special relationship of the Jews to the figure that Paul would claim as "the father of vs all."

Shylock in fact refutes this Pauline claim every time he names the patriarch: in Shylock's mouth he is consistently "Abram" rather than "Abraham." For an alert Renaissance listener who was well schooled in the Bible, "Abram" would signify not simply as a convenient contraction of "Abraham" but as the undoing of the crucial moment when Abram became Abraham, when the father of the Israelites became, precisely, "the father of vs all": "Beholde, I make my couenant with thee, & thou shalt be a father of manie nacions, Nether shal thy name anie more be called Abram, but thy name shalbe Abraham: for a father of manie nacions haue I made thee" (Genesis 17.4–5). The change from Abram to Abraham is understood within Christian tradition as the decisive seal of the patriarch's new status as spiritual father to the gentiles as well as the Jews and is pointedly recorded as such in the biblical commentaries. The Geneva Bible's brief introductory summary of Genesis 17, for instance, specifies that "Abrams name is changed to confirme him in the promes"; its marginal glosses to Genesis 17.4 and 5 spell out that he is now father "not only according to the fleshe, but of a farre greater multitude by faith" and that "the changing of his name is a seale to confirme Gods promes vnto him," conveniently referring the reader to Romans 4.17—"as it is written, I haue made thee a father of many nacions"—lest the point be missed. The glosses to Genesis 17.4–5 in the Bishops' Bible similarly refer to Romans 4, reassure the reader that Abraham is now father "not of them only that were of his children: but also of the beleuyng gentiles," and interpret the changing of Abram's name as "a seale of gods promise."[15] Calvin's commentary on Genesis 17 specifically refutes the claim that "many nations" might refer only to the various peoples deriving from Abraham lineally according to the flesh: "the carnal stock of Abram could not be diuided into diuers nations. . . . Abram was not therefore called the father of many nations, bycause his seede was to be diuided into diuerse peoples, but rather that the varietie of nations should be gathered vnto him." The prophecy thus "extendeth the name of father, to the whole world, that the Gentiles from all partes might growe into one familie of Abram, whiche otherwise were forreigners, and a farre off"; and it is sealed by Abram's name change: "Also the chaunging of his name, is added in steede of a pledge & seale. For he beginneth now to be called Abraham, that the name it selfe might beginne to teache, that he should not be the father of one kindred: but that a progenie should arise vnto him out of an exceeding multitude, contrarie to the common manner of nature."[16]

In Christian tradition, that is, the name change from Abram to Abraham, which barely registers for most contemporary interpreters of *Merchant*,[17] encodes the contested genealogy that expresses Christianity's vexed relation to Judaism: it records the moment of Jewish displacement, the moment after which—in Christian hermeneutics—the claim to be a son of Abraham will be made as poor Nathanael is taught to make it, circuitously through the spirit rather than lineally through the flesh. And the significance of this displacement of the Jewish claim to unique lineal descent is—in the Christian reading—literally registered in the name itself: as Calvin says, Abram's name was changed so "that the name it selfe might beginne to teache, that he should not be the father of one kindred." Augustine elaborately spells out the way in which the name itself teaches:

> Thus this great and euident promise beeing made vnto *Abraham* in these words: *A father of many nations haue I made thee . . .* (which promise wee see most euidently fulfilled in Christ) from that time the man and wife are called no more *Abram* and *Sarai,* but as we called them before, and all the world calleth them: *Abraham,* and *Sarah.* But why was *Abrahams* name changed? the reason followeth immediately, vpon the change, *for, a father of many nations haue I made thee.* This is signified by *Abraham:* now *Abram* (his former name) is interpreted, an high father.[18]

The etymological understanding of the name shift shared by Augustine and Calvin was in fact widely available to a Renaissance audience: a similar explanation makes it both into a work as comparatively arcane as Ainsworth's *Annotations Upon the first book of Moses, called Genesis. Wherein the Hebrew words and sentences, are compared with, & explayned by the ancient Greek and Chaldee versions* and into Clapham's handbook for beginners, *A Briefe of the Bible.*[19]

Given Augustine's emphasis on the bond that links the patriarch's new theological status with his new name, it's not surprising that he half-apologizes for having referred to the patriarch as Abraham rather than Abram before his change of name; he excuses himself on the grounds that "all the world" calls him by that name. And within Shakespeare's world, he seems to be right: except for Shylock, Shakespeare's other characters follow the normative practice and call the patriarch Abraham—as of course do Foxe and his convert Nathanael.[20] But Shylock consistently uses the name the patriarch had before he became Abraham, "father of manie nations"—and hence before he was rewritten as spiritual progenitor of the Christians. His use of "Abram" insistently localizes the father-figure of all, making him particularly Jewish property, patriarch specifically to the Israelites; as Shylock says, he is "*our* holy Abram" (1.3.68). And Shakespeare guarantees that we will hear the specificity of this "our": a moment earlier, Shylock has anticipated it by referring to "our sacred nation" (1.3.43), the nation based precisely on the fleshly possession of Abraham. In chapter 3 I will argue that Shylock's blood claim to sacred nationhood might in itself be a cause of anxiety to the English during a period when new definitions of nationhood were developing and when there were new national contenders for the position of "sacred nation." But for now, I want to call attention to the surprising extent to which Shakespeare allows Shylock's claim to the patrilineage of Abraham to challenge Christian hermeneutic practices, or at least to signal that they are a matter of interpretation. Immediately after Shylock claims Abraham—and therefore Jacob—as his own, he and Antonio wrangle about the interpretation of the episode of Laban's sheep, a controversy Antonio attempts to settle first by argumentation (the increase in Jacob's flock was "A thing not in his power to bring to pass, / But swayed and fashioned by the hand of heaven"; 1.3.88–89) and then by retreat into platitudinous generalization ("The devil can cite Scripture for his purpose. / An evil soul producing holy witness / Is like a villain with a smiling cheek, / A goodly apple rotten at the heart. / O, what a goodly outside falsehood hath!" 1.3.94–98). These platitudes about the relation of outer to inner are congruent with the lesson of the casket scene and may be intended to reflect the supposed rottenness of literalistic Jewish hermeneutic practices (good literal outside; bad spiritual inside),[21] but Antonio's retreat into rhetorical excess nonetheless suggests a certain uneasiness about winning the interpretative contest on other grounds.[22] Like 2.2, the scene in which Lancelot can become one of Abraham's spiritual children only by playing out his uncertain relation to that paternal inheritance via his relation to his own father, Antonio's words suggest an undercurrent of doubt about his possession of the story—and therefore about his possession of the figure Shylock insists on calling father Abram.

⋙

When Lancelot leaves Shylock's house in act 2, scene 2, he plays out a particularly anxious version of that inheritance. I have already suggested the ways in which Lancelot alludes to Paul's trope of the transformation from servant to son as he enacts the uncertainty of paternal lineage in this scene. But that trope is from the first embedded exactly in the interpretative contest that Shylock reiterates when he calls Lancelot "that fool of Hagar's offspring" and claims Jacob for his own. Both Ishmael and Esau are positioned as servants to their younger brothers, and in Christian hermeneutics the passage of the paternal inheritance from them to their younger brothers signifies the passage of the promise from an "older" Judaism to a "younger" Christianity. But this is a potentially troublesome set of analogies. In the instance of the first pair of brothers—Isaac and Ishmael—the distinction between older and younger maps tidily onto Paul's distinction between bound and free, and thence onto the distinction between flesh and spirit: "For it is written, that Abraham had two sonnes, one by a seruant [Ishmael], & one by a fre woman [Isaac]. But he which was of the seruant, was borne after the flesh: and he which was of the fre woman, was borne by promes. By the which things another thing is ment: for these mothers are the two Testaments" (Galatians 4.22–24). And because the younger son, Isaac, was the free child of the promise, "In Isaac shal thy sede be called: That is, they which are the children of the flesh [the Geneva gloss to "children of the flesh" is "as, Ismael"], are not the children of God: but the children of the promes are counted for the sede" (Romans 9.7–8). In this reading, maternal status in effect trumps primogeniture: because the older is born bound and the younger born free, younger can fittingly supersede older; Hagar's status as bondwoman in effect puts the ordinary laws of primogeniture into abeyance. When Paul turns to the second set of siblings a few verses later, they seem initially to provide a simple parallel to the first: "also Rebecca when she had conceiued . . . It was said vnto her, The elder shal serue the yonger. As it is written, I haue loued Iacob, & haue hated Esau" (Romans 9.10–13). But in this case there is no conveniently different mother to blame, no "natural" difference to account for the triumph of younger over older; we are left merely with the bare fact of younger superseding older and the abrogation of ordinary conventions of inheritance.

For Foxe, this reversal of the conventions of inheritance becomes an opportunity to discredit "this ordinarie discent according to the lawe of the flesh" and thus the claims to fleshly descent both of Jews and of apostolic Catholicism: "when as God in stead of Cain, Esau, Ismael, Saul, to whom of right apperteineth the ordinary succession & discent of the Priesthode, of the birthright, & inheritance of the kingdome, he made especial choyce of Abel, Isaac, Iacob, & Dauid, who had no interest at all in the right of succession. In like maner forsaking the Iewes, he accepted the Gentiles contrary to all order" (Sermon, C3r–v). But in an age that valued fleshly ancestry so highly, a solution that makes the ascendancy of the gentiles "contrary to all order" may have been anxiety-provoking. Second sons who threatened to displace their brothers were notoriously troublesome: in Shakespeare's plays they tend to be called Duke Frederick, or Claudius, or Edmund, or Antonio, and Shakespeare's sympathy is almost invariably with the displaced older brother.[23] And not only is there no "natural" difference to account for the ascendancy of Jacob over Esau (as there is in the instance of Isaac and Ishmael): Jacob's triumph over his older brother is accompanied by the same sorts of disguises and manipulations that an Edmund might use. In the standard Christian reading of this episode, the blessing that Isaac gives to Jacob in place of Esau predicts "the preaching of Christ vnto all the nations" (Citie of God, 16.37 [611]); it prefigures the moment when the Abrahamic inheritance is transferred from fleshly older to spiritual younger child, and thus the turning of God's promise from Jew to Christian that underwrites all subsequent conversions from Judaism to Christianity. But Jacob's route to this blessing is both indirect and suspect. As Shylock reminds the audience (1.3.69), he secures it only by following his wise mother's advice: he disguises himself as his hairier brother Esau, lies about his identity to his blind father Isaac, and steals the blessing his father meant to give to his older brother. And this is the loaded version of Christian inheritance played out in 2.2 just as Lancelot is about to perform his own vexed turn from Jew to Christian:

LANCELOT: Do you not know me, father?
GOBBO: Alack, sir, I am sand-blind. I know you not.
LANCELOT: Nay, indeed, if you had your eyes you might fail of the knowing me. It is a wise father that knows his own child. . . . Give me your blessing. (ll. 63–68)

"It is a wise father that knows his own child": Lancelot's revision of the familiar proverb—"A wise child knows his own father"[24]—underscores this scene's resemblance to this famous biblical scene of misrecognition. And a moment later, Gobbo completes the reference by commenting on the hairiness of his son: "What a beard hast thou got! Thou hast got more hair on thy chin than Dobbin my fill-horse has on his tail" (ll. 82–84).[25]

Act 2, scene 2, thus replays a version of the story that Shylock has just confidently alluded to when he claims holy Abram as his own in the previous Venetian scene (1.3.68–70), in effect reclaiming that story for Christian hermeneutics: insofar as Lancelot becomes a figure for Jacob as he converts, then Christians rather than Jews inherit the Abrahamic line through Isaac and Jacob, and Jews rather than Christians are left in the position of Hagar's offspring Ishmael. But if 2.2 reclaims the story of Jacob for the Christians, it does so only by underscoring what is most problematic in that story; in its Shakespearean version, it is hardly a figure for an uncomplicated Christian triumphalism. First of all, it is never absolutely clear that Lancelot in fact secures his father's blessing: though he asks for that blessing twice (2.2.68, 74), there is no firm textual indication that he ever receives it. And if he does manage to secure the blessing, he does so not only by a deception akin to Jacob's but by invoking the obscure guilt that haunts this story: guilt that ultimately turns on exactly the displacement of Jews by Christians and therefore is an appropriate accompaniment to Lancelot's own turn from Jew to Christian.

The moral queasiness that dogs Lancelot as he prepares to leave Shylock is in fact a familiar component of commentary on this foundational episode, and so is its potential for the kind of uneasy comedy that Lancelot plays out in 2.2.[26] Calvin acknowledges that Jacob's deception of his father "seemeth . . . to be childish mockerie," and his commentary on Genesis 27.26 begins by gesturing toward exactly this potential: "Prophane men will say, that this is a meere iest, that the olde man hauing nowe a dull wit, and well stuft with meate and drinke, vttereth his minde vnto a counterfet person."[27] He exhorts the reader nonetheless to "reuerently beholde the secrete purpose of God,"[28] but the potential both for comedy and for moral queasiness remains. For insofar as "*Esau* and *Iacob, Isaacs* two sonnes, prefigured the two peoples of Iewes and Christians,"[29] they did so only by presenting severe interpretative difficulties, and not only about birth order. The Geneva Bible's gloss to Rebecca's plan to deceive Isaac in Genesis 27.9, for example, is "This subtiltie is blameworthie because she shulde haue taried til God had performed his promes"; the gloss to Jacob's representing himself as Esau in 27.19 is "Althogh Iaakob was assured of this blessing by faith: yet he did euil to seke it by lies." Or, in the pithier formulation of the gloss to 27.14 in the Bishops' Bible: "Iacob was not with out fault, who myght haue taried vntyl god had chaunged his fathers mynde." Augustine himself can argue against reading Jacob's trick as "fraudulent deceipt" only by uneasily asking, "What can the guile of a guiltlesse, true hearted soule be in this case, but a deepe mistery of the truth?"; he thus removes the problem from the realm of human morality altogether, in effect excusing Jacob's behavior by locating it in the realm of a mystery not to be understood by ordinary human means.[30]

Augustine's move is prototypical: the interpretative skills designed to de-problematize the moral problems in Jacob's theft of his older brother's inheritance in order to make the story comfortably available for typological use in fact end up calling attention to the very problems they would deny. In Gervase Babington's commentary on Jacob's earlier seizure of Esau's birthright in the mess of pottage incident (Genesis 25.29–34), for example, the capacity to read through Jacob's behavior becomes the mark of the reader's—not Jacob's—moral stature as "good": "But was this a brothers parte, to praye as it were vpon his brother, and to lye in waite for a vantage. . . . Howe then may Iacob be excused heere? The answer of good men is, that in an extraordinarie thing, we may not vse an ordinarie measure. . . . The Lords purpose was to deriue the birth-right to Iacob." He concludes his discussion of this episode with a specific warning to his readers not to judge Jacob and not to use his behavior as a model for their own: "Let vs leaue all to God, and make no doctrine eyther of rebuke to others, or imitation to ourselues by extraordinarie facts."[31] That he needs to warn his readers against trying this at home suggests the subversive political potential of Jacob's act; it's no wonder that Jacob's behavior has to be read through the lens of mystery. And the theological stakes of this interpretative strategy are high, as Henry Ainsworth's commentary on Genesis 27.19 points out: "This though it were not so properly [sic], (& cannot in that respect be excused,) yet was it true in mysterie, & spiritually, as Iohn Baptist was *Elias, Mat.*11.14, and we gentiles, are the *Circumcision, Phil.*3.3. *Rom.*2.28. & the children of promise, are counted for the seed *Rom.*9.8. *Gal.*4.28."[32] If Jacob's apparently immoral behavior could not be read through the lens of mystery, then neither could the claim that the Christians had superseded their theological ancestors and were now to be counted for the seed of Abraham.

These acts of reading against the grain of ordinary morality thus become acts of faith: to read through Jacob's deception to the mystery of God's choice is in effect to proclaim one's own status as the new inheritor of the promise. And precisely because it was so problematical, the Jacob and Esau story became a prototypical key text for the doctrine most explicitly concerned not only with the mystery of individual salvation but with the mystery of God's originary election of gentile/Christian over Jew.[33] For Paul, God's choice of Jacob over Esau provides an explanatory framework for the mystery of God's choice, and specifically for the role of "works" in that choice: "yer the children were borne, & when they had nether done good, nor euil (that the purpose of God might remaine according to election not by workes, but by him that calleth) It was said vnto [Rebecca], The elder shal serue the yonger" (Romans 9.11–12). Paul founds the doctrine of election not on the easily distinguishable (flesh/spirit, bound/free) brothers Ishmael and Isaac but on the indistinguishable Jacob and Esau—and founds it on them precisely because they are morally indistinguishable. And in fact, most of Paul's followers go further than Paul does here, locating evidence for election in God's choice of Jacob not simply in his moral neutrality but specifically in his moral weakness—hence, for example, the gloss to Jacob's deception in Genesis 27.26 in the Bishops' Bible: "We must not so muche beholde the outwarde doinges here, as the prouidence of God, who woulde by suche weaknesse, haue his election declared."

Jacob's weakness declares God's election: exactly the fact that Jacob does not deserve the inheritance makes him its ideal recipient. According to Calvin, God even goes out of his way to emphasize that Jacob did not deserve to be chosen:

> For in deede he might haue wel placed Iacob the formoste, when the Infants should coome forth from their mothers wombe. . . . And why then did not hee permit & ordaine that Iacob should haue the priuiledge of birthright? . . . And why doth God then pull him back, & make him inferiour to his brother, as touching the law of nature, and afterwards setteth him aboue him? In this we see that God would shut out all glory of man, that he would that al height should be thrown down, and that men should bring nothing of their owne.[34]

Calvin in fact puts Jacob at the center of one of his primary works on election—the *Thirteene Sermons . . . Entreating of the Free Election of God in Iacob, and of reprobation in Esau*, published in English in 1579—exactly because he did not merit election either by "law of nature" or by moral superiority. And an English interlude from 1568 (*A newe mery and wittie Comedie or Enterlude, newely imprinted, treating vpon the Historie of Iacob and Esau*) similarly insists on Jacob's exemplary status for the doctrine of election.[35] For Calvin and his followers, the more morally dubious Jacob's actions are, the more strikingly God's choice of him repudiates the idea of salvation by works—and hence repudiates the claims of the Jews or the Catholics, the people of the external vocation. Both in his sermons on election and in his lengthy commentary on Genesis 27, Calvin consequently takes pains to establish not only Jacob's moral weakness but also Esau's distinct superiority. Here is Calvin's commentary on Genesis 27.30:

> For if thou compare both their works together, Esau obeyeth his father, bringeth the fruite of his hunting, of the prey gotten by his labour, he dresseth meat for his father, he affirmeth nothing but the truth: to be short, thou shalt finde nothing in him, whiche deserueth not praise. Iacob going not from home, appointeth a kid, in sted of venison, insinuateth himselfe with many lies, bringeth nothing whiche may rightly commende him, and in many things he deserueth reprehension.

His conclusion is by now predictable: "Therefore, we must needes confesse, that the cause of the euent dependeth not vppon workes but lyeth hid in the euerlasting purpose of God"—to which the marginal gloss adds, in case we were in danger of missing the point, "Election dependeth not vpon workes."[36]

Calvin's desire to associate Esau with Catholics and Jews—both of whom need to be distinctly blameworthy—occasionally taints the purity of his claim that Esau did nothing to merit deselection. In his thirteenth sermon on election, for example, Calvin rewrites Esau's virtue as merely an "outward shewe" in order to mark it as the type of Jewish or Catholic outward observance; specifically—and in a notably circular argument—Calvin decides that Esau's apparently repentant tears before his father must signify false, rather than true, repentance since he is one of the reprobate.[37] And despite the language about meritless election with which *Iacob and Esau* begins ("before Iacob and Esau yet borne were, / Or had eyther done good, or yil perpetrate: / . . . Iacob was chosen, and Esau reprobate"; Prologue, ll. 8–11), the interlude finds Esau deserving of reprobation from the start: he is in every way a lout, compared with his obedient younger brother. Whatever the claims of the doctrine of election, the idea of a purely meritless selection or deselection was clearly hard to sustain.[38] Nonetheless, that doctrine—and, with it, the secure sense that Jacob and the Christians have been selected over Esau and the Jews in a moment of mysterious ur-election—depend exactly on this difficulty and therefore on the conviction that ordinary moral norms have not been followed in God's choice. If the "right" child had been chosen, there would be no necessary recourse to the doctrine of election and no appeal to mysteries beyond human understanding: "works" would stand triumphant.

As in Foxe's *Sermon preached at the Christening of a Certaine Iew*,[39] election thus understood must always begin from a suspicion that God may have been unjust: the doctrine could not discount both the power of works and the capacity of human beings to make judgments about God without first provoking the anxiety that God had made the wrong choice. Indeed, if such anxieties were not aroused, the doctrine would not be doing its work. Paul himself models this passage through anxiety specifically in relation to the Jacob and Esau story in Romans 9, where he moves directly from God's apparently unmotivated election of Jacob in the womb to a striking invocation of God's injustice in order ultimately to arrive at the insufficiency of man's understanding of God's choices:

> For yer the children were borne, & when they had nether done good, nor euil . . . It was said vnto her, The elder shal serue the yonger. As it is written, I haue loued Iacob, & haue hated Esau. What shal we say then? Is there vnrighteousnes with God? God forbid. For he saith to Moses, I wil haue mercie on him, to whome I wil shewe mercie. . . . Therefore he hathe mercie on whome he wil, & whome he wil, he hardeneth. . . . But, o man, who art thou which pleadest against God? shal the thing formed say to him that formed it, Why hast thou made me thus? (Romans 9.11–20)

Calvin's commentary on Paul's question—"What shal we say then? Is there vnrighteousnes with God?"—is "Fleshe cannot heare that wisedome of God, but straightwayes it is troubled with tumultuous questions, and in a sort striueth to bring God to a count."[40] And his thirteenth sermon on election uses Jacob's moral inferiority to his brother to trace the same passage through tumultuous questions about God's injustice before returning to rest in the mysteriousness of God's wisdom:

> Iacob was not preferred, but by the free goodnes of god of which thing there appeareth no reason vnto vs, for lo Esau which went to hunt, who lied not, who deceiued not his father, and did not thrust in him self craftily. . . . But what doth Iacob? he deceyueth, hee lieth, and dealeth dissemblingly, and presenteth him selfe as it were his brother Esau: . . . Wee might well saye then, that Iacob deserued too bee reiected and cut of: but neuerthelesse GOD would that he shuld haue the birthright. . . . Albeit then that we know not what moued & induced God to this, yet notwithstanding let vs hold for most certaine, that he doth nothing but most iustly, because his will is the rule of all rightuousnes: hee is subiect too no lawe, and much lesse to our fantasie . . . all that which shall enter into our braine, must of necessitie bee ouerthrowen: as it is sayde, that hee shall always bee iustified, yea albeit men condempne him.[41]

"Wee might well saye": for Calvin, questioning God's righteousness, or even condemning God, is construed as a necessary first step toward recognizing the folly of human reason and the incomprehensibility of God's justice.

If Jacob and Esau serve as poster children for the doctrine of election and therefore for the question of God's justice, they do so not in the abstract but specifically in relation to God's transfer of the promise from the Jew to the Christian. Paul cites the brothers' story to epitomize this transfer; and the language in which he explicates God's apparently arbitrary choice of younger brother over older underscores the problem of divine justice already implicit in election:

> he saith to Moses, I wil haue mercie on him, to whome I wil shewe mercie: and wil haue compassion on him, on whome I wil haue compassion. So then it is not in him that willeth, nor in him that runneth, but in God that sheweth mercie. For the Scripture saith vnto Pharao, For this same purpose haue I stirred thee vp, that I might shewe my power in thee, and that my Name might be declared through out all the earth. Therefore he hathe mercie on whome he wil, & whome he wil, he hardeneth. (Romans 9.15–18)

In this passage, Paul draws on the trope of the hard heart, which would come to be associated—as it is in *Merchant*—with the Jewish refusal of Christian mercy and therefore of salvation ("You may as well do anything most hard / As seek to soften that—than which what's harder?— / His Jewish heart"; 4.1.77–79). But the hard heart here is itself the work of God; as Paul makes clear, it is associated with Pharaoh, whose heart God notoriously hardened. The Geneva gloss to "I wil haue mercie" is "As the onelie wil & purpose of God is the chief cause of election and reprobacion: so his fre mercie in Christ is an inferior cause of saluacion, & the hardening of the heart, an inferior cause of damnacion"; insofar as the hardened heart is another trope for reprobation, it returns emphatically to the problem of God's justice. Locating the Jews in the position of Pharaoh (as Paul does) may have the effect of leaving the position of "Israel" free for the gentile nations, who will now occupy it: hence "all they are not Israel, which are of Israel." But it does so only at the cost of underscoring the injustice of a God who first hardens the heart and then condemns the heart so hardened to damnation. And if the Jew's heart, like Pharaoh's, is hardened by God so that God's name "might be declared through out all the earth" to all nations (Romans 9.17), then Christian salvation depends precisely on Jewish hard-heartedness: a hard-heartedness for which the Jew himself can hardly be blamed.

Perhaps in response to this conundrum, Antonio attempts to natural-
ize the hardness of Shylock's "Jewish heart" as though it were a given of
nature—a flood, a wolf, or a gust of heaven (4.1.70–79)—rather than the
consequence of God's choice; and the play works to reaffirm the stereo-
typical view of the monstrously hard-hearted Jew in Shylock as though to
deflect any residual guilt that the Christian triumph at the expense of the
Jews might cause. But Antonio's phrase "gusts of heaven" (4.1.76) threatens
to give the game away, underscoring the heavenly hand in that hardened heart. And as I have already suggested, the allusion to the Jacob and
Esau story as Lancelot negotiates his anxious turn from Jew to Christian
serves in effect as a concealed portal that invites exactly that residual guilt
into the play. As in Foxe's Sermon, the spectacle of one particular Jewish
conversion—here, Jessica's as anticipated in Lancelot's—evokes the originary moment of election that undergirds all such conversions and, with it,
acute concern about God's justice in casting off the Jews only (as Foxe says,
citing Paul) "that so the decaye of the Iewes might be the riches of the Gentiles" (Sermon, B4v). And the conjunction of Lancelot's pseudo-conversion
with the Jacob and Esau story has the effect of framing the supersession of
Judaism by Christianity as a conversion of sorts and of articulating the guilt
of that supersession/conversion specifically in familial terms. Act 2, scene
3, poses Jessica's attempt to become Christian specifically as a betrayal of
her father Jew; by anticipating Jessica's conversion attempt in Lancelot's attempt to leave Shylock in 2.2 and then reenacting the anxiety-ridden story
that epitomizes God's originary choice of Christian over Jew, Shakespeare in
effect makes every Christian into a convert from Judaism and underscores
the complex familial relationship between Christianity and the Judaism it
superseded—a relationship that turns on displacement of the legitimate heir
and theft of the father's blessing. Hence, I think, the odd moral queasiness
of the scene, both in Lancelot's deception of his father and in his qualms of
conscience about leaving Shylock: for this reenactment poses the Jew as the
betrayed father not only in relation to his daughter Jessica but also in relation to all those who consider themselves inheritors of the promise under
the type of Jacob.

If act 2, scene 2, allows Christians to reclaim Jacob for themselves, it does
so only by assuming the burden of guilt he carries as he figures the transmission of the promise from Jew to Christian. In the scene that echoes this
transmission, Shylock occupies the position both of betrayed father and of

displaced elder brother: no wonder, then, that Lancelot's anxiety at leaving him is in excess of its ostensible occasion. And that anxiety surfaces
once more in 2.2, just as Lancelot's own transition from Jew to Christian
appears to be completed. Lancelot seals the deal with Bassanio with a line
that apparently encapsulates his understanding of the relation between his
old master and his new: "The old proverb is very well parted between my
master Shylock and you, sir: you have the grace of God, sir, and he hath
enough" (2.2.134–36). Editors routinely direct readers to "The grace of God
is gear enough" as the proverb in question;[42] they do not comment on the
witty sleight of hand by which Lancelot turns the proverb into its own opposite by separating "enough" from "the grace of God" and then attributing
the one to the Jew and the other to the Christian. But what exactly does it
mean to say that Shylock has "enough"? Bassanio has just contrasted his
own poverty-stricken state with that of the "rich Jew" (2.2.132–33); presumably Lancelot means that Shylock has the material goods and Bassanio the
spiritual ones, and in the commercial atmosphere of Venice—at least up
until the trial scene—that would indeed appear to be enough. But an alert
audience member might have heard in Lancelot's revised proverb an echo of
a particularly troubling moment in the history of Jacob and Esau—a moment
that moreover points beyond them toward another vexed pair of brothers
that haunt this play.

When Shylock's reference to Jacob's staff (2.5.35) stakes his claim to be
in the line of the third possessor from Abraham, it simultaneously directs us
to this moment. At first glance, however, his reference might be understood
as predicting his own people's displacement once again, despite his own hermeneutic intentions. The most prominent reference to Jacob's staff in the
New Testament serves to refer readers back to a moment of paternal blessing
that reinscribes the triumph of younger brother over older and thus of gentile
over Jew: "By faith Isaac blessed Iacob and Esau, concerning things to come.
By faith Iacob when he was a dying, blessed bothe the sonnes of Ioseph, and
leaning on the end of his staffe, worshiped God" (Hebrews 11.20–21). The
marginal gloss directs readers to the scene in which Jacob blesses Joseph's
younger son Ephraim rather than his older son Manasseh, despite Joseph's
best efforts: "And Ioseph said vnto his father, Not so my father, for this is
the eldest: put thy right hand vpon his head. But his father refused, and said,
I knowe wel, my sonne, I knowe wel: he shalbe also a people, & he shalbe
great likewise: but his yonger brother shalbe greater then he, and his sede
shalbe ful of nations" (Genesis 48.18–19).[43] The Geneva glosses to the scene
in Genesis make sure that we don't miss the point: Joseph "faileth in binding Gods grace to the ordre of nature"; his younger son Ephraim is the one

"in whome Gods graces shulde manifestly appeare." Moreover, if this scene reinscribes the triumph of younger over older, it does so in a singularly reassuring way: the insistence that (unlike Isaac) Jacob knows what he is doing here—"I knowe wel, my sonne, I knowe wel"—has the effect of simultaneously keeping the scene of Jacob's own stolen blessing in view and mitigating some of the guilt associated with it, as though undoing that earlier scene of paternal deception.[44] Shylock's reference to Jacob's staff thus might be seen as an inadvertent argument against his own claim to Jacob insofar as it takes his auditors to Hebrews 11 and thence to this guiltless scene of displaced inheritance. Or rather, it might be seen in this way except for one curious detail: despite the assertion of Hebrews 11 and its gloss, there is no staff in this scene of blessing in Genesis.[45]

But the staff does occur in a more vexed moment of Jacob's career—a moment moreover in close proximity to a startling "enough" that returns not to this compensatory scene of blessing but to a scene that reinforces Jacob's sense of guilt. Shortly after the episode of Laban's sheep, which we know that Shakespeare read closely, Jacob leaves Laban's house with all his possessions and receives word that his brother Esau is approaching with four hundred men; reasonably enough, given what he has done, he "was greatly afraid" (Genesis 32.7). In response, he prays for God's protection, in effect bargaining for God's continued favor by recalling all that God has already done for him: "I am not worthie of the least of all the mercies & all the trueth, which thou hast shewed vnto thy seruant: For with my staffe came I ouer this Iorden, and now haue I gotten two bandes. I pray thee, Deliuer me from the hand of my brother, from the hand of Esau: for I feare him" (32.10–11).[46] The staff stands out in this prayer as the marker of how much God has already given to Jacob: the Geneva gloss to "staffe" is "that is, poore, & without all prouision"; and Babington's commentary adds, "I cannot omit this godly remembrance that Iacob here maketh of his first estate when he came into the countrey, and of his estate now when he doth return. . . . A notable meditation morning and euening for rich merchantes, wealthie lawyers, and men and women of all degrees, whom God hath exalted from little too much."[47] But Jacob is provoked to this godly remembrance less by gratitude than by a sense of unworthiness—"I am not worthie"—and by fear, and he uses his wealth in an attempt to buy off the brother he has cheated: even before he prays, he arranges to offer him extravagant gifts. And despite the determination of commentators to make Esau into the merely material man as befits his status as the type of the Jew—in the Geneva gloss to Genesis 25.33, for example, he is the type of the wicked who "preferre their worldelie commodities to Gods spiritual graces"—the meeting of the brothers does nothing to assuage the anxious sense that Esau may be more worthy than his brother after all.

When Jacob last saw Esau, he was vowing to kill Jacob (27.41), in effect justifying God's deselection of him after the fact; but when Esau sees Jacob here, he "ran to mete him and embraced him, and fel on his necke and kissed him, and thei wept" (33.4). And this unexpected gesture of forgiveness is apparently not motivated by Jacob's offer of gifts: when Jacob repeats the offer, Esau replies, "I haue ynough, my brother: kepe that thou hast to thy selfe" (33.9). Jacob has just attributed his wealth to the grace of God (33.5), and Esau replies that he has "enough": this extraordinary encounter seems to me to stand behind Lancelot's revised proverb, both generating and complicating its terms. When Lancelot attributes the "grace of God" to the Christian and "enough" to the Jew, his words should function to register the transition his "conversion" enacts and hence the triumph of the spiritual over the merely material realm.[48] But his echo of this encounter muddies the waters of this easy typology: it poses the "Jewish" brother as far less anxious and far more generous than his "gentile" brother.

Commentators scurry to make this Esau consistent with their desire to have him serve his function as merely material man. Babington, for example, manages to transform Esau's response into the sign of the rich man's pride: "Esau his speech that hee had inough, sheweth the pride of rich mens hearts, bragging stil of their plentie."[49] And Calvin continues to consider him the type of the "cruell" man who can still serve as the anti-type to his brother: though his hard heart has been temporarily mollified here, that is merely a sign of God's grace toward Jacob.[50] What is problematical in the story is characteristically allegorized out of it: thus, when Jacob calls himself Esau's servant and his family bows to Esau (Genesis 33.5–7), apparently reversing Isaac's promise that Jacob would be lord over his brethren (Genesis 27.29), Calvin hastens to reassure his readers that in this episode "we may beholde the forme of the Church, as it appeareth in the worlde" and take comfort "if at this day also the glorie of the Church, being couered with a base shewe, be a scorne to the wicked."[51] The Geneva gloss to the same passage goes even further to reassure its readers about Esau's moral inferiority, despite the evidence of the narrative: "Iaakob and his familie are the image of the Church vnder the yoke of tyrants, which for feare are broght to subiection"—a formulation which tidily does away with any hint of Esau's generosity or of the wrong that Jacob has done to him.

But the questions raised by Esau's generous insistence that he has "enough" seem to me not so easily contained; and although no one would suspect Shylock of the spiritual generosity that Esau demonstrates here,

Lancelot's citation of this episode as he moves from Jewish to Christian master invites these questions into the play. What, for example, would count as
"enough" for the Jew? Specifically, what is "enough" for Shylock? He tells
his Christian auditors, "You take my life / When you do take the means
whereby I live" (4.1.371–72); does the "half" he will be given if he turns
Christian still constitute "enough"? And is "enough" only the domain of
the Jew? If the Jacob-Esau encounter muddies the distinction between Christian and Jew by making Esau more generous than his guilt-ridden brother,
Merchant famously muddies that distinction from the opposite direction,
by making its Christians too reliant on the merely material "enough" that
should be the province of the Jew. Lancelot's revised proverb implies a clear
opposition between material enough-ness and the spiritual "grace of God,"
assigning the first to Shylock and the second to Bassanio. But as Bassanio accrues wealth at the expense of Antonio, and using Shylock's "enough" as col-
lateral, we can no longer securely differentiate between Shylock's "enough"
and the purportedly spiritual wealth Bassanio accrues.[52] By the end of the
play, Shylock's wealth has been magically "spiritualized" and transformed to
"manna" (5.1.293) that will pass to his Christianized children; but it is worth
remembering that manna spoils when it is used with the kind of greed that
Jessica and Lorenzo have already amply demonstrated, and also that Jesus
himself rejects manna in favor of the bread of heaven that he brings.[53] So
under what conditions is the "enough" of material wealth compatible with
"the grace of God"? Or (to return to the proverb Lancelot has scrambled)
should the grace of God be gear enough?[54]

   If one line of inquiry about this episode takes us to troubling questions
about wealth and grace that are familiar to critics of the play, another returns us specifically to questions about the justice of God's choices. For
Jacob ambiguously offers Esau his blessing—"I praie thee take my blessing"
(33.11)—along with his gifts, as though he could pass his father's blessing
on to his brother along with his wealth, or perhaps as though the guilt of
that blessing had become a burden to him. But apparently God wants only
one of these brothers to be blessed. When Esau discovers Jacob's deception
in Genesis 27, he cries out, "Blesse me, euen me also, my father. . . . Hast
thou not reserued a blessing for me?" (27.34–36); when Isaac answers that
he has no blessing left for him, Esau's response is even more poignant: "Hast
thou but one blessing my father? blesse me, euen me also, my father: and
Esau lifted vp his voyce, and wept" (27.38). Calvin insists on Esau's wickedness here, just where those attending to the story might be most tempted to
feel sympathy; his tears, for example, are "rather a signe of outragious and
proude displeasure, then of repentaunce. . . . Euen so the wicked, when they

are vrged with punishment, do bewaile the losse of their saluation: but yet for all that, they ceasse not to please them selues in their wickednesse." And he considers Esau's desire that there be more than one blessing evidence of his "blind incredulitie"—his lack of faith—"for whereas there rested but one blessing with the father, he requireth to haue another giuen vnto him, as though it were in his will to breath out blessings without the commandement of God."[55] But Calvin knows perfectly well that faith itself is the unmerited gift of God, and exactly Esau's pained question—"Hast thou but one blessing my father?"—continues to haunt Foxe, who repeatedly asks why God did not choose to give the blessing of faith to both gentile and Jew: "were [it] not as easy for almighty god to haue giuen mercy to them both, if it had pleased him?"; "why was not this benefite of fayth and beliefe in Christ impartened to the Iewes, as well as to the Gentiles indifferently?" (Sermon, B8r, M3v).[56] Why—in other words—must the decay of the Jews be the riches of the gentiles? And what, in this zero-sum game of blessing, would it mean for Esau—or Shylock—to have "enough"?

Another pair of brothers whose shadowy presence is invoked in 2.2 provides a provisional answer to those questions. The sheer profusion of the term "prodigal" in Merchant has made the presence of the parable of the prodigal son (Luke 15.11–31) nearly unmistakable in the play, and several critics have observed its traces not only in Antonio, Bassanio, and Jessica but also in the scene between Lancelot and his father: like the prodigal, Lancelot is starving, and his father welcomes him back as though from the dead; and like the prodigal, he receives new clothes.[57] Since the parable often served as a trope for conversion, its relevance to Lancelot's scene of transition from Jew to Christian is clear.[58] Shylock himself invokes the context of the parable both when he accuses Bassanio and Antonio of prodigality (2.5.15, 3.1.37) and when his self-righteous logic—"What judgement shall I dread, doing no wrong?" (4.1.88)—echoes that of the Pharisees against whom the parable is directed.[59] Insofar as Shylock makes himself into a Pharisee, he tidily illustrates the necessity of a Pauline supersession: the Jewish regime of self-righteousness and Law must be superseded precisely because it can only call down judgment; Shylock-as-Pharisee thus sets himself up not only for his defeat, but specifically for his defeat by the "no-blood" clause, that is, by the agency of a Law that can only conduce to death.[60] And he once more takes on the position of the older brother, traditionally understood as a stand-in for the pharisaical Jews.[61] For insofar as the parable reiterates the familiar division between the righteous older brother and the younger one who does not merit his father's grace but nonetheless receives it, it quadrates comfortably with the Christian interpretation of the Jacob and Esau story:

once again the excluded older brother stands in for the Law-bound Jews who are displaced and the younger brother for the wayward Christians who are received. But with this difference: this time there is more than one blessing.

When this older son complains ("Lo these manie yeres haue I done thee seruice, nether brake I at anie time thy commandement, & yet thou neuer gauest me a kid that I might make merie with my friends"), this father answers, "Sonne, thou art euer with me, and all that I haue, is thine" (Luke 15.29, 31). "Thou art ever with me, and all that I have is thine" is a far cry from the exiling of Esau from his father's blessing: this parable points not toward the displacement of the older son but toward the father's inclusive love.[62] The errant younger son is received as his father's son rather than as his servant despite his unworthiness ("Father, I haue sinned against heauen, and before thee, And am no more worthie to be called thy sonne: make me as one of thy hired seruants"; Luke 15.18–19, repeated in 15.21); but "all" that the father has continues to be his older son's. Read thus, the prodigal son parable severely qualifies the supersessionist narrative on which the Christian sense of "chosenness" depends. No wonder, then, that so many versions of the parable find a way to omit the older son from the story.[63] But in Lancelot's own supersessionist scene, Shakespeare's citation of Jacob and Esau undoes this omission. He might have written Lancelot's transition simply as a sanitized prodigal son story, in which Lancelot is welcomed home to Christianity. But by simultaneously allying Lancelot with the prodigal son and with Jacob at the moment that he deceives his father and displaces his older brother, he layers one story on top of the other, in effect doubling Esau in the prodigal son's older brother and therefore opening up the occluded question of the blessing reserved for him. And by reading the scene of the prodigal son's conversion through the narrative of Jacob and Esau, he returns us to the deceived father and the displaced older brother, thereby underscoring the familial guilt inherent in the zero-sum game of blessing—and in Christianity's supersession of the Jews.

⋅✵⋅

Lancelot plays out this guilt-ridden relation to Judaism when his own father appears onstage. And Gobbo himself stands in for the contradiction in the Christian figuration of Judaism. He can so easily substitute for Shylock, I suggest, because his blindness is typologically allied with the often-alleged blindness of Judaism;[64] and yet he is the bearer of those prototypically Christian doves. Like Isaac, whose role he takes on as he plays deceived father to his disguised son, he is simultaneously Jew and Christian: for the blind old Jew Isaac carries the promise of the Christian seed in his lineage and is typologically a figure for Christ.[65] Act 2, scene 2, thus encodes the sameness and difference that haunts Christianity's relation to its Jewish lineage: Lancelot's encounter with his father condenses not only anxieties about Christianity's originary deception of the father but also anxieties about its radical dependence on Jewish origins that must always be simultaneously embraced and denied, reminding us that the doubled figure of Isaac—archetypical Jew and type of Christ, betrayed father and bearer of the promise—will always shadow Christianity.

Through his encounter with Gobbo, Lancelot can simultaneously deny the father-Jew in Isaac and embrace Isaac as the bearer of Christianity, and he can complete his turn from Jew to Christian only by means of this complexly displaced negotiation. But an odd piece of byplay when he and his father first meet suggests that he can never entirely leave the Jew's house after all. "Which is the way to Master Jew's?" Gobbo asks, and Lancelot answers him, "Turn up on your right hand at the next turning, but at the next turning of all on your left, marry at the very next turning, turn of no hand but turn down indirectly to the Jew's house" (2.2.31–36). "Turn" (Latin *vertere*) is of course at the root of *conversion*; and the obsessive repetition here would seem to confirm that conversion is indeed on Shakespeare's mind as he encodes Lancelot's "conversion" in this encounter between father and son. Gobbo responds to his son's puzzling directions by saying, "By God's sonties, 'twill be a hard way to hit" (2.2.37); but Lancelot's language suggests rather that it will be hard to miss: the house that Lancelot would leave is apparently everywhere, up every road, the place you can never quite leave because all turnings take you there. In this play ostensibly concerned with the triumphant supersession of the Jews, 2.2 reminds us that Christianity itself represents a kind of originary turning away from Judaism, a turning that can never be wholly complete. Anxiety about this incompletion—displaced and denied elsewhere in the play, where Judaism is figured as the absolute other to Christianity—shapes almost every element in 2.2: if elsewhere Shylock is unequivocally the bad father who must be left behind, here, through his doubling in Gobbo, he turns out simultaneously to be the progenitor, the point of origin, the shadow-self.

CHAPTER THREE

Her Father's Blood:
Conversion, Race, and Nation

I most humbly beseeche Almightie God, that he will not onely vouch-
safe his gracious encrease to this glorious worke begunne with this Israelite stranger, but also to allure the whole remnant of the circumcised
Race, by this his example, to be desirous of the same communion: So
that at the length, all nations, as well Iewes, as Gentiles, embracing the
faith, and Sacramentes of Christ Iesu, acknowledging one Shephearde,
vnited together in one sheepefold, may with one voice, one soule, and
one generall agreement, glorifie the only begotten sonne our sauiour Iesus
Christ.
—Foxe, *Sermon*, A1v

LANCELOT: Truly I think you are damned. There is but one hope in it
    that can do you any good, and that is but a kind of bastard hope,
    neither.
JESSICA: And what hope is that, I pray thee?
LANCELOT: Marry, you may partly hope that your father got you not, that
    you are not the Jew's daughter.
JESSICA: That were a kind of bastard hope indeed. So the sins of my
    mother should be visited upon me.
—*Merchant of Venice*, 3.5.4–11

Iewish Infidelitie . . . seemeth after a certaine maner their inheritable
disease, who are after a certaine sort, from their mothers wombe, naturally caried through peruerse frowardnes, into all malitious hatred, &
contempt of Christ, & his Christians.
—Foxe, *Sermon*, B3r

After the many turnings of 2.2, we finally arrive at Shylock's house in 2.3, and we find therein another would-be convert. I suggested in the last chapter that Lancelot's escape from that house serves as a necessary prelude to Jessica's, a comic warding off of the anxiety that might otherwise be provoked by reading conversion as a betrayal of the father-Jew: for only Jessica can say "my father Jew" and mean it literally, and only she must literally leave the Jew's house in order to convert. In fact, the story that Lancelot enacts as he leaves that house turns up in a more attenuated form in Jessica's conversion, as though Shakespeare could not quite suppress the anxiety that story of stolen blessings expressed: when Jessica disguises herself, deceives her father, and steals her patrimony, she too enacts a shadowy version of Jacob's theft and therefore of the passing of the promise from Jew to Christian.[1] But she enacts Lancelot's story of conversion with a difference.

As with the convert Nathanael, Lancelot's conversion entails his disclaiming one "father" in order to claim the blessing of another. When Lancelot tells Jessica that she cannot be saved as long as Shylock is her father, he literalizes the terms of the conversion that he has enacted in 2.2: she too cannot become a Christian without changing fathers. But as Jessica points out, Lancelot is forgetting the place of the mother in his "hope" for her salvation, for Lancelot's solution can save her only by invoking the infidelity of her mother. The end of *Merchant* is full of cuckoldry jokes and thus of a barely concealed anxiety about the mother's place in the making of children; but it's nonetheless odd that this comic exchange about Jessica's conversion reiterates a concern about mothers that occurs in the midst of Lancelot's earlier scene of conversion. In that scene, Lancelot had briefly figured himself as mother's son rather than father's son; and although the emotional focus of the scene is securely upon fathers, he can claim his place as his father's son and receive his father's blessing only after he has successfully identified his mother, as though her identity provided the key to his own after all ("Her name is Margery indeed. I'll be sworn, if thou be Lancelot thou art mine own flesh and blood"; 2.2.80–81). Mothers are generally absent from this play: except for Lancelot and his pregnant Moor's unborn child, Jessica appears to be the only character who has—or had—one, and aside from the allusion to her in this conversation, where she (like the Moor) would make a bastard of her daughter, her presence is registered only when Jessica disowns her by selling off the ring that she gave to her husband Shylock. Particularly given this general absence, it's striking that both these mothers turn up in proximity to the play's comic meditations on conversion. Moreover, even if

most of *Merchant*'s characters do not appear to have had mothers, the prototype whom Lancelot imitates in his own scene of conversion definitely had
one, as Shylock reminds us just before 2.2: Jacob obtained his father's blessing and thus became the third possessor from Abram "as his wise mother
wrought in his behalf" (1.3.69). In the story that signals the transmission of
the promise from Jew to gentile, the figure of the mother notably intervenes,
as Lancelot's does, to secure the father's blessing. Commentators frequently
registered embarrassment about this wise mother's micromanagement of
her son's career;[2] and this embarrassment may reflect a larger anxiety about
the mother's role in the transmission of patriarchal benefits from father to
son—an anxiety bound to be exacerbated in the case of Jacob and therefore
in the case of Jacob's avatar Lancelot, who is in effect making a claim to
father Abraham on behalf of the play's Christians. Hence perhaps the odd
intrusion of Lancelot's mother into the scene of Lancelot's "conversion,"
where she threatens briefly to disrupt his identity as his father's son. But
why should Jessica's mother turn up in the conversation about the efficacy
of her conversion?

   Perhaps because Jessica herself has the problematic capacity to become a
mother, a possibility that the play gestures toward very soon after this conversation, when Lorenzo reminds Lancelot of his own pregnant Moor. And
Jessica's name itself may make the same gesture toward her problematic
maternity. Accounts of its derivation generally track it either to "Iscah" or to
Shakespeare's feminization of "Ishai," or "Jesse."[3] The Geneva Bible's gloss
to "Iscah" (Genesis 11.29) is "Some thinke that this Iscah was Sarai"; since
"Sarai" is Sarah's name before the prophecy of Isaac's birth and the name
change that, together with Abram's, signals the transmission of the promise
to the gentiles (Genesis 17.15), that derivation might register something like
the unregenerated "Jewish" remnant in Jessica—and in her offspring. But
derivation from "Jesse" is no less problematic. Jesse is familiarly the "root"
of Jesus's lineage, the crucial link that aligned Jesus with the house of David
and hence with the Old Testament prophecy that could establish him as the
Messiah. If Shakespeare feminized "Jesse"—or if some members of his audience heard that feminization in Jessica's name—then her name would point
toward something peculiar about that link back to the paternal root: given
who Jesus's father was said to be, the link to the root of Jesse could come
only through his mother. As Foxe says, "if ye require who was his father, he
came not in deed from man, but discended from God. But if you demaunde of
his mother: he is on the mothers side a Iewe borne, according to the flesh, the
sonne of Abraham" (*Sermon*, C7r). (Foxe's convert Nathanael is even more
emphatic in tracing Jesus's fleshly lineage through his mother's side, perhaps

because the rabbinic principle that Jewish identity was transmitted through the mother was less foreign to him: "the man Iesus Christ [was] borne of the virgin Marie . . . and so, by the flesh he toke of hir, descending of the seede & stocke of Dauid."]⁴ As with Lancelot, female flesh must intervene to secure Jesus's paternal lineage, his status as the son of Abraham, the stock of David: when Matthew 1.16 traces Jesus's lineage through Joseph rather than Mary ("And Iacob begate Ioseph, the housband of Marie, of whome was borne IESVS"), the Geneva gloss hastens to restore Jesus's fleshly link to Abraham by restoring Mary's claim to that lineage and then assimilating her lineage to her husband's ("Albeit the Iewes nomber their kinred by the male-kind: yet this linage of Marie is comprehended vnder the same, because she was maried to a man of her owne stocke & tribe"). So the father's line is transmitted through the mother's body, and the root of Jesse is thus in effect the root of Jessica, as Shakespeare's feminization of the name would suggest.

Even as she herself would convert to Christianity, then, Jessica's name carries the potential reminder that the fleshly lineage of Jesus comes from his Jewish mother. But if the Jewish womb is the bearer of the Jewish lineage that must authenticate Jesus's status as the Messiah, it is also the symbolic repository of the fleshly remains that should be left behind; and this double valence reiterates the double valence of Judaism within Christianity. The problematic maternal body—in other words—encodes ambivalence toward the fleshly lineage of Christianity itself. In Galatians 1.15–16—"it pleased God (which had separated me from my mothers wombe, and called me by his grace) To reueile his Sonne in me"--Paul makes his conversion simultaneous with his separation from his mother's womb, turning that womb into a metonymy for the ties of the flesh that he would eschew in favor of those of the spirit.⁵ Foxe reiterates and darkens this association of Judaism with the mother's part when he traces Jewish unbelief to the Jewish womb in one of my epigraphs for this chapter; and Graziano plays on it when he traces Shylock's "currish spirit" to the wolf that, "whilst thou lay'st in thy unhallowed dam, / Infused itself in thee" (4.1.132, 135–36). Lancelot may attribute Jessica's Jewishness to her father and believe that only her mother's sin of infidelity could free her from it, but the association of Jewishness with the Jewish womb seems to have been familiar enough for Shakespeare to have drawn on it here:⁶ in Graziano's depiction of Shylock's gestation as a kind of bestial incarnation, the wolf stands in for the Holy Spirit and Shylock's mother for an "unhallowed" Mary.⁷ To arrive at the source of Shylock's Jewishness, Graziano thus reaches back behind Jessica's father to the Jewish womb that bore him, in effect attributing his Jewishness to his mother's sin after all.

But if Jewishness is the consequence of the Jewish womb, then where does this leave Jessica? Poised on the threshold of her father's house, she would deny the status conferred on her as "daughter to his blood" (2.3.17) in order to claim entrance into what Foxe imagines as the union of all nations in the body of Christ. The reference to Jesse in her name may seem to endorse the possibility of her conversion insofar as it alludes to the fulfillment of the Davidic lineage in Christ, but its feminization also carries the reminder of her Jewish womb, and thus of the potentially unassimilated Jew within the Christian—and within the Christian community. Jessica's conversion story—in other words—is everywhere inflected by her gender, for her womb will be the carrier of her father's Jewish blood, in her and in the children that might be born of her. No wonder, then, that she is so anxious to be rid of her mother's ring.

In *Merchant*, as in Foxe's *Sermon*, the spectacle of conversion provokes the discourse of blood; but in *Merchant*, that discourse is rooted in the female body—and specifically, I think, in that body's capacity to reproduce itself. It is often said that Jessica's conversion is easier than Shylock's because she perforce lacks the defining bodily mark of Judaism[8] and thus is not quite a member of what Foxe tellingly calls "the circumcised Race" (*Sermon*, A1v). But in fact the play worries the issue of blood more strenuously in her case than in her father's, and it does so, I think, exactly because she lacks that defining mark and hence has the potential to infiltrate Christian society—in her own person and in her children—without being recognized. Much in *Merchant* would seem to endorse Jessica's conversion, but Lancelot's exchange with her at 3.5.4–11 is no mere aberration: it opens out into the vexed territory that lies between the universalizing claims of Christianity and the particularities of blood lineage and nation, for the contrary discourses of race, nation, and religion meet in her. Jessica may aspire to escape from her father's countrymen and his nation—both words that carry references to the womb within them[9]—to something like the merger of all nations in the oneness of Christ that Foxe imagines. But Belmont, the play's local stand-in for this imagined place of Christian harmony, ruthlessly excludes foreigners, and Jessica's escape is everywhere compromised by the limiting specifics of her father's blood.

Jessica herself seems to assume that her conversion will be an unproblematic consequence of her marriage.[10] Well before she assures Lancelot that her husband has made her a Christian in 3.5, she appears to imagine marriage and conversion as synonymous, as though her husband, rather than the church, had the power to make her a Christian and the laws governing the material conditions of women could unproblematically be applied to her spiritual state:

> Alack, what heinous sin is it in me
> To be ashamed to be my father's child!
> But though I am a daughter to his blood,
> I am not to his manners. O Lorenzo,
> If thou keep promise I shall end this strife,
> Become a Christian and thy loving wife. (2.3.15–20)

In fact, marriage appears to occur to her largely as a way to escape her father's blood or, more exactly, as a way to end the strife between his blood and her (presumably gentle/gentile) manners. Though her escape from her father's house to her lover fits conveniently into the conventions of a romance plot, her speech is not the love-longings of a typical romance heroine: Lorenzo is invoked not as the solution to the problem of Jessica's erotic desire but as the solution to the problem of being her father's daughter. Romance conventions would lead us to expect her to convert in order to marry, but the rhetorical weight of this speech moves in the opposite direction, suggesting that she would marry in order to convert.

Since Lancelot has just managed his own "conversion" from Shylock's house, it is perhaps fitting that he is the agent of her escape and would-be conversion: the shift in his status in fact allows him to carry the crucial letter to Lorenzo, who dines with his new master Bassanio. But his assumption that the only way out for Jessica is to have been begotten by some other father is so deeply embedded in him (and so endemic to the culture in which his author operates) that it occurs in a muted form even here, while he is ostensibly serving as the agent of her escape. Lancelot's response to Jessica's request to carry a letter to Lorenzo—"If a Christian do not play the knave and get thee, I am much deceived" (2.3.11–12)—half-anticipates his later stipulation that she needs a new father: his "get" hovers unstably between "get" in the sense of "possess" and "get" in the sense of "beget," despite the temporal illogic that "get" as "beget" would introduce (how can Jessica be begotten by a Christian in the present tense?).[11] The Second Folio reading— "if a Christian *did* not play the knave and get thee, I am much deceived"— suggests how readily Shakespeare's near contemporaries would have heard the "beget" in Lancelot's words: in effect, F2 stabilizes "get" as "beget" and then alters the tense to solve the problem of temporal illogic.[12] This revision underscores the way in which the latent pun in Lancelot's "get" satisfies the impossible condition that he sets for her conversion in 3.5.4–5: at least for an instant, it allows her to have been begotten by a Christian father after all. But by undoing the simultaneity of "get" and "beget" in Lancelot's response, F2 mutes the more complex fantasy that apparently drives Jessica's desire for marriage to Lorenzo. In Lancelot's condensation, the subject of "get" flickers ambiguously between Christian husband (who may get her in the present) and Christian father (who may have begotten her in the past). For a dizzying moment, through its elision of getting in the present with begetting in the past and its duck-rabbit flickering of father and husband as the subject of "get," Lancelot's response fuses Christian husband and Christian father—as though Jessica's Christian husband could do away with the embarrassment of her Jewish birth by becoming her Christian father, literally re-begetting her in the present with Christian, rather than Jewish, blood.

Lancelot's pun on "get" thus condenses the tension between Jessica's blood and her conversion and promotes its own impossible fantasy solution to that tension: a Christian marriage in the present that would convert Jessica by simultaneously solving the problem of her father's blood. And that fantasy briefly comes back into view in 3.5, when Jessica asks what hope there is that she will not be damned, and Lancelot answers, "Marry, you may partly hope that your father got you not," as if to say "marry—and you may partly hope for a new father," as though that father could be produced by her marriage.[13] But of course there can be no such marriage. Lancelot's puns—which initially seem to give Jessica what she wants—serve not to realize but to set the limiting condition to Jessica's fantasy of being saved by her husband. The pun on "get" in 2.3 suggests that Lorenzo can get (and hence convert) Jessica only if he can simultaneously re-beget her, effecting what amounts to a literalization of the trope of conversion as rebirth: "except a man be borne againe, he [or, in this case, she] can not se the kingdome of God."[14] And the pun on "marry" in 3.5 underscores the impossibility of this literalization, for neither marriage nor conversion will fulfill her hope that her father got her not. In the end, both puns return Jessica once again to the strictures of her father's blood.

Despite the play's apparent endorsement of Jessica's conversion, Lancelot is not alone in his insistence on those strictures: his version of conversion seems closer to the state of things in Venice—and especially in Belmont—than Jessica's assumption that her marriage will do the trick. Her would-be escape from her father's Jewishness seems to begin well enough; only a few moments after she has declared her desire to become a Christian through marriage, her husband-to-be imagines Shylock's "gentle daughter" as her father's ticket to heaven, as though she could convert not only herself but him (2.4.34). And as soon as she appears in the "lovely garnish of a boy" and gilded with her father's ducats (2.6.45, 49), Graziano seems to grant her wish for transformation: depending on one's text, he proclaims her "a gentle [or "a gentile"], and no Jew" (2.6.51).[15] (Does he respond thus enthusiastically to the "fair" skin Lorenzo has already lavishly praised at 2.4.12–14, to her "lovely garnish," or to her promise to gild herself with still more ducats? Perhaps the latter; in his spendthrift world, a person generous with money—even money not her own—by definition can't be a Jew.) But when the undisguised and ungilded Jessica arrives in Belmont with Lorenzo, it becomes clear that Jessica's status as no-Jew is as evanescent as her disguise as a gilded boy. There Graziano marks her apparently unanticipated appearance with "But who comes here? Lorenzo and his infidel!" (3.2.217); his use of the term with which he will later register the Christians' triumph over Shylock—"Now, infidel, I have you on the hip" (4.1.329)—underscores the extent to which she is still the child of her father's blood.

Graziano may later prove to be the play's most outspoken anti-Semite, but he is not alone in regarding Jessica as an alien creature whose marriage has done nothing to convert her; Shakespeare takes pains in 3.2 to indicate the extent to which she is an outsider in Portia's Belmont. At least Graziano notices that she exists; neither Bassanio nor Portia register her presence in this scene, and they barely register it elsewhere. (Bassanio manages never to notice her, and Portia speaks to Jessica only once, at 3.4.43–44, when the barest requirements of courtesy force the exchange upon her. Even when Portia tells Lorenzo and Jessica that she is leaving the two of them in charge of Belmont as its temporary master and mistress, she speaks at 3.4.38 as though only Lorenzo were present.) Bassanio's welcome to Belmont, reiterated by Portia, extends only to his "very friends and countrymen" Lorenzo and Salerio (3.2.222). And Graziano's somewhat belated instructions to Nerissa—"cheer yon stranger. Bid her welcome" (3.2.236)—insist on Jessica's physical isolation on the stage during the awkward moments in which she is pointedly not introduced: "yon" makes sense only if she is standing at some distance from the others who are welcomed into Belmont, and "cheer" suggests that she is in need of cheering. Moreover, if Graziano's earlier "infidel" underscored Jessica's status as alien by religion, his "stranger" here underscores her status as alien by nation: though the term could function to indicate simply that she is unknown to the present company, she is after all known at least to Graziano, who could introduce her by name; and other uses of the term in the period tend to register foreignness by blood or nation rather than simply lack of recognition.[16] "Stranger" would take on that resonance in

Graziano's instructions more particularly because Bassanio has just greeted Lorenzo and Salerio as his "countrymen." In this context, Graziano's term indicates how far Jessica is from inclusion both in the present company and in the category of Bassanio's countrymen, though she too comes from Venice. In fact, as a "stranger," Jessica remains allied to the father she would escape, who complains that he is spurned by Antonio like a "stranger cur" (1.3.114)—and perhaps also to the conversos of London, to whom the same term was frequently applied.[17]

No wonder, then, that Jessica tries to dissociate herself not only from her father's religion but also from his "countrymen" in her only speech in this scene:

> When I was with him I have heard him swear
> To Tubal and to Cush, his countrymen,
> That he would rather have Antonio's flesh
> Than twenty times the value of the sum. (3.2.283–86)

Jessica here attempts to ingratiate herself into the company from which she is excluded not only by confirming their sense of her father's bloodthirstiness but also by defining his "countrymen" as specifically his, not hers—as though her conversion (however questionable in itself) could have the effect of changing her country along with her religion and thus could enable her inclusion as one of Bassanio's countrymen after all. At her initial appearance, Jessica had distinguished between blood and religion, taking seriously the Christian universalist promise that she could free herself from her father's religion if not from his blood. But here, in the face of the continued designation of her as an infidel and stranger, she appears to absorb the lesson implicit in Lancelot's pun—and as though in response, she fantasizes a radical separation from her father's blood and "country" as the price of inclusion in the social club to which her husband belongs, and as the only way to cast off her status as a Jew.

Jessica's uncertain entrance into Belmont seems to me to reflect the play's distinct uneasiness about her marriage—an uneasiness that also leaves the marriage itself unspecified (*when* do she and Lorenzo get married? *do* they get married?). And perhaps because her conversion is contingent on her marriage, the play carefully does not distinguish a moment after which Jessica is definitively converted, an omission that allows for a chronic tension between Jessica and the others, in which she persistently regards her conversion to Christianity as complete, and they persistently regard her as a Jew. If the crucial distinction for her is religious, the crucial distinction for them is of blood lineage. But this much Graziano's initial riddling praise of her as "a gentle, and no Jew" might have told her, for his praise turns out to allow her escape from the category of Jew only insofar as she can change her blood or nation, becoming not a Jew but a gentile. As Graziano's word slides between "gentle" and "gentile," that is, it enters the territory of what we might agree to call a proto-racial distinction:[18] although "Jew" might function primarily as a religious category when it is opposed to "Christian," it becomes an incipiently racial category when it is opposed to "gentle/gentile." In that opposition, "gentile" invariably functions as a marker of those races or nations that are not Jewish[19]—as in Foxe's wish that "the whole remnant of the circumcised Race" might convert, so that "all nations, as well Iewes, as Gentiles" might be united in one sheepfold. Graziano's implied opposition between "gentle" and "Jew"—she is no Jew *because* she is a gentle—thus underscores the "gentile" in "gentle" and racializes both "gentle" and "Jew" by construing them as mutually exclusive: while "gentle" and "Jew" might conceivably be compatible terms (Jessica appears to imagine herself with gentle manners in her opening scene), by definition Jessica cannot be both a gentile and a Jew.[20] In Graziano's formulation, only status as "a gentile" can guarantee her status as "no Jew": Jessica hopes for a conversion from Jew to Christian; Graziano implies that the necessary conversion will have to be from Jew to gentile, shifting the grounds of conversion from religion to race even as he seems to grant her the conversion she wishes for.

Graziano thus establishes Jessica's status as gentile as the necessary— and impossible—condition for her escape from Jewishness: although Jews might become Christian, they are, axiomatically, not gentiles. His apparently liberatory comment thus returns her to the strictures of her father's blood as firmly as Lancelot's contention that the problem of her Jewishness could be solved only if a different father had gotten her. And this return to her father's blood is a move the play continually makes; even her beloved Lorenzo no sooner calls her "gentle" than he recalls her to her position as her father's issue:

> If e'er the Jew her father come to heaven
> It will be for his gentle daughter's sake;
> And never dare misfortune cross her foot
> Unless she do it under this excuse:
> That she is issue to a faithless Jew. (2.4.33–37)

The more Jessica appears to be "a gentle, and no Jew," the more vigorously her problematic lineage needs to be asserted. Lorenzo initially entertains the

possibility that Jessica will be able to convert not only herself but her father, reversing the trajectory—"the sins of the father are to be laid upon the
children" (3.5.1)—that Lancelot insists on. But blood wins out in the end.
As soon as Lorenzo distinguishes her gentleness/gentileness from Shylock's
Jewishness, he must undo the distinction: if misfortune visits her, it will
be because she is her father's issue and hence a Jew after all. By the end of
Lorenzo's speech, her lineage has trumped her "gentleness"; as soon as the
possibility of her "gentle/gentileness" is invoked, it inevitably calls up her
father's Jewishness and subjects her to its taint.

✦

In its attentiveness to Jessica's continued status as outsider and infidel, *Merchant* seems to me extraordinarily attuned to the plight of the outsider who
would assimilate and to the price of assimilation, registered not only in
3.2 but also in Jessica's melancholy in 3.5 ("how cheer'st thou, Jessica?"
Lorenzo asks after Lancelot has insisted that she is still a Jew) and perhaps especially in the absurdly self-denigrating paean to Portia that follows
his question. For Jessica's response—if "two gods" were to wager on "two
earthly women, / And Portia one, there must be something else / Pawned
with the other, for the poor rude world / Hath not her fellow" (3.5.69, 71–
73)—smacks of the sort of internalized self-loathing attendant on the infidel's recognition that she can never be such a heavenly paragon. Her "two
gods" is, moreover, hauntingly suggestive: does she imagine a Jewish and a
Christian god unequally matched in the contest Lorenzo provokes immediately after Lancelot tells her that she will be perennially a Jew?[21] Her final
exchanges with Lorenzo seem playful and affectionate, but their such-a-
night threnody on doomed relations (particularly exogamous relationships)
underscores the fragility of theirs and may remind us uneasily of Lorenzo's
tardiness in turning up for their elopement, which Graziano attributes to
sexual satiety (2.6.9–19).[22] And is Jessica herself having second thoughts?
When Lorenzo uses the loaded word "steal" to describe Jessica's flight to
him—she "did . . . steal from the wealthy Jew" (5.1.15) in such a night—he
risks a pun that equates her love for him with his love for the Jew's money;
and she responds with a reference to a much more serious kind of theft: "In
such a night / Did young Lorenzo swear he loved her well, / Stealing her soul
with many vows of faith, / And ne'er a true one" (5.1.17–20). The ordinarily
conventional language that equates love with soul theft has an extraordinary
resonance here: insofar as it echoes the language of conversion to a false
faith, it allows for the otherwise-unspoken possibility that Jessica is begin-

ning to regret the series of thefts that have converted her and her father's wealth to the Christian. Her final line in the scene and in the play—"I am never merry when I hear sweet music" (5.1.68)—functions both to register her alienation from the merry company at Belmont and to align her with her father's melancholy and musicless house; after Portia's return, she has nothing left to say.[23]

Nonetheless, despite these hints of sympathy with her plight, the play's treatment of her is at least partly in the service of the ideologies that prevent her escape from that house, convert or not. In that sense, her situation poses the conundrum of the conversos (including London's own conversos) and provokes the discourse of blood that their historical presence engendered. As I have suggested in chapter 1, despite claims that "Jew" was purely a theological category in Shakespeare's England and that racialized thinking about Jews is an inappropriate piece of anachronism—despite claims, that is, that Jessica's conversion would necessarily free her from the taint of her father's blood—proto-racialized thinking about conversos appears to have been both conceptually available and conceptually useful to Shakespeare's contemporaries. Jewish difference had long been expressed both through a language of genealogical descent—Foxe's "race and stock of Abraham"[24]—and through a language of (usually immutable) physical difference; and both languages map easily onto what would become the newer language of "race"; Jewish difference was in fact prototypically racialized in the early modern period, at least in Spain.[25] Waad, the clerk of the Privy Council, did not need to have available to him an entire scientific discourse of race in order to describe Pedro Rodriguez, a converso living in Lyons who planned to marry Lopez's daughter, as "a Jew by race" in 1597;[26] and when Gabriel Harvey accounts for Lopez's suspicious success as a physician—the trickiness of what he calls Lopez's "Jewish practis"—by noting that he was "descended of Jews," he implies that Jewish deception is a biological inheritance.[27] The theological and the proto-racial categories are, moreover, far from distinct, for despite the possibility of conversion, the religion of the Jews itself could be understood as simply a derivative from their race: hence Foxe's exasperated speculation that Jewish unbelief must be inherited from the womb; and hence the characterization of London's converso community as "by race . . . all Jews, and . . . in their own homes they live as such observing their Jewish rites,"[28] where "as such" does the work of making their rites contingent on their race.

No wonder that poor Jessica's conversion does not free her from the strictures of her father's blood: only a Christian father could do that. Perhaps the play toys with its own fulfillment of this fantasy-solution when

it forces conversion on Shylock in the scene after the one in which Lancelot tells Jessica that she needs a new father: his conversion in effect would
give her a Christian father in the same ex-post-facto way as Lancelot's pun
on "get." But the play never encourages the audience to take the possibility of Shylock's conversion seriously. The persistent association of his
hard-hearted Jewishness with natural phenomena—the wolf, the sea, the
stone—has the effect of naturalizing it in him, making it fixed and immutable. And the same "gentle/gentile" pun through which Graziano fixes the
limiting conditions of Jessica's conversion underscores the immutability of
Shylock's Jewishness in Antonio's initial joke about his conversion: "Hie
thee, gentle Jew. / The Hebrew will turn Christian; he grows kind" (1.3.173–
74). The sequence of terms here—gentle Jew, Hebrew, Christian, kind—in
fact beautifully illustrates the process of racialization as a response to the
prospect of Jewish conversion. As soon as he invokes the possibility of the
gentle Jew, Antonio shifts ground from "Jew"—a marker both of race and of
religion—to "Hebrew," more specifically a marker of genealogical lineage; in
effect he secures Shylock's indelible racial alterity, and therefore his status as
non-gentile, just at the moment when the fixity of his "Jewishness" comes
into question. The audience has of course already been assured by Shylock's
aside (1.3.36–47) that there is no danger that this Jew will become "gentle";
Antonio's lines give them what amounts to a biological basis for that as-
surance. For his sequence forces the racial strain not only in Jew but also
in Christian, through the implied chiasmus "gentile/Jew," "Hebrew/Chris-
tian"—a chiasmus that allies gentile with Christian as firmly as it allies Jew
with Hebrew. Antonio's formulation thus denies its initial premise: though
a Jew might conceivably turn Christian, a Hebrew by definition cannot turn
gentile. And this appeal to the realm of inalterable "natural" differences is
signaled by the tricky word "kind," which undercuts Shylock's apparent
turn to kindness by invoking exactly that inalterable realm. Like his nation
(gens), his nature (kind) is reassuringly fixed: this Hebrew will never become
gentle/gentile, will never lose his Jewish obduracy, the stony-heartedness
that allows Christians to recognize him; he will never change his nature
and "grow kind." And whether or not he is forced to convert, he can never
join the kind of the Christian: even at the end of the play, he remains "the
rich Jew" (5.1.291).[29]

Insofar as Shylock will remain the Jew, converted or not, he secures the
important distinction between Christian and Jew, the distinction that Jessica's conversion threatens to dissolve—and he secures it exactly through an
appeal to a proto-racial difference. The puns through which Antonio introduces the topic of conversion into the play suggest the set of anxieties about

sameness and difference, nature and nations, that the topic provokes—anxieties for which racialized thinking provided an easy remedy, whether or not racial categories were fully in place in the early modern period. By the time of *Merchant*, Christian societies had been worrying about the instability of Jewish difference for generations. Jews, for example, are generally depicted throughout the Middle Ages as physically unmistakable, with red or black curly hair, large noses, dark skin, and the infamous *foetor judaicus*, the bad smell that identified them as Jews. But apparently Jews could not be counted on to be reliably different: although allegedly physically unmistakable, Jews throughout Europe were nonetheless required to wear particular styles of clothing or badges that graphically enforced their physical unmistakability—as though they were not quite different *enough*.[30] Archbishop Stephen Langton's 1222 council in Oxford seems to have instituted clothing regulations in England explicitly for this reason, following both the Fourth Lateran Council regulations of 1215 and a particularly troubling local case in which a deacon married a Jew, was circumcised, and was burned for his apostasy. Maitland summarizes the reasoning behind the institution of the English regulations thus: "there being unfortunately no visible distinction between Jews and Christians, there have been mixed marriages or less permanent unions; for the better prevention whereof, it is ordained that every Jew shall wear on the front of his dress tablets or patches of cloth four inches long by two wide, of some colour other than that of the rest of his garment."[31] The regulations thus appear to have been an attempt to make a difference where none was reliably visible, presumably on the assumption that no one would knowingly marry a Jew.

Even apparently reliable physical signs of difference were tricky: some thought, for example, that the *foetor judaicus* might disappear at baptism,[32] effectively obliterating the difference between Christian and Jew. And not every Christian would greet this news with joy: despite the promises of a universalizing Christianity, the difference between Christian and Jew was too important a part of the mental map to be given up lightly. Already too different and too much the same, Jews were a contradiction that conversion—particularly state-enforced conversion—turned into a crisis. And insofar as *Merchant* worries the contradiction between Jessica's conversion and her blood, it responds in its own way to the pressures that were, elsewhere in the sixteenth century, forcing a proto-racialized definition of Jewish difference. Although one theological justification for hatred of Jews had always been their stiff-necked refusal to convert, it turned out that massive conversion brought on its own problems. In sixteenth-century Spain, the danger was not that Jews would remain an isolated community refusing Christian grace but that they would convert and infiltrate Spanish society at all levels, becoming indistinguishable from their Spanish hosts as they entered into the mainstream. For conversion threatened to do away with the most reliable signs of difference, provoking a crisis in a very mixed society obsessively concerned with purity of lineage. In response to this crisis and the category confusions it entailed, the Spanish Inquisition attempted to establish difference just where it was least visible, in the unstable arena of blood, through the imposition of a series of so-called pure-blood laws. Jerome Friedman's account of these laws identifies a pattern that precisely duplicates *Merchant*'s insistence on Jessica's Jewishness just when she is most liable to be mistaken for gentle/gentile or Christian: "The more ardently Jews sought acceptance as Christians, the more ardently Christians identified them as Jews"; "The more New Christians assimilated into their new surroundings, the more biological distinctions were needed to separate New Christian from Old Christian."[33]

In the face of massive Jewish conversion and acceptance into Spanish society, the pure-blood laws were a strenuous attempt to ground an increasingly invisible difference specifically in bodily inheritance; in Friedman's account, with the emergence of these laws, sixteenth-century Spain succeeded in transforming "medieval religious anti-Judaism into a racial antisemitism" precisely at the point that the difference between Christian and Jew threatened to disappear. According to the logic of the pure-blood laws:

> All descendants of converts were really still Jews because they came from Jewish ancestors. The sixteenth-century "purity of blood" laws stipulated that anyone with at least one Jewish ancestor was himself still a *converso* and therefore was not a real Christian. . . . [As late as 1628], one Grand Inquisitor noted that "by *converso* we commonly understand any person descended from Jews . . . be it in the most distant degree." . . . These new exclusionary legal conventions were called "pure blood laws" because it was maintained that degenerate Jewish blood was impervious to baptism and grace. If mixed with Christian blood, the Jewish blood would contaminate subsequent generations and would continue to do so indefinitely. . . . The result of this racialist thinking was that the courts of Inquisition were increasingly involved with determining if a given individual was genealogically 1/16, 1/32, or 1/64th part Jewish. The Toledo court of Inquisition for instance, *devoted four times more space in its records to this than to actual court procedures involving charges of judaization.*[34]

It is emblematic of the entire enterprise that the laws enforcing difference at the point of its disappearance employ a metaphorics of blood, since the blood of various individuals is not only notoriously miscible but also notoriously hard to distinguish. The king instructs the lineage-obsessed Bertram on this paradox with some precision in *All's Well That Ends Well:* "Strange is it that our bloods, / Of colour, weight, and heat, poured all together, / Would quite confound distinction, yet stands off / In differences so mighty" (2.3.114–17).[35]

England did not face the massive problem that Spain did, nor is it clear how many of the English knew about, or would have been sympathetic to, the pure-blood laws of their traditional enemy. But they surely would have recognized the impetus behind the pure-blood laws. Spanish obsession with purity of lineage was a familiar butt of English satire; Aragon himself enters Belmont insisting on his differentiation both from the "barbarous multitudes" and from those whose "estates, degrees, and offices" are "derived corruptly" (2.9.32, 40–41). Though he prides himself on employing "the stamp of merit" in his judgments (2.9.38, 42), his language immediately collapses the discourse of merit into the discourse of blood lineage, in which those "derived corruptly" must be distinguished from "the true seed of honour" (2.9.41, 46).[36] For an English audience, the joke of his boast—like the joke of the pure-blood laws and the ambition they encode—would be on the Spanish. For according to the anti-Spanish propaganda prevalent in England, Aragon would have good reason to be concerned about being ranked with the barbarous multitude: the Spanish are "this scumme of Barbarians," "this mongrell generation," "sprong from the race of the Iewes"; far from being "the true seed of honour," especially the aristocrats among them are contaminated by their debased historic internal others ("All the worlde beleeueth . . . that the greatest parte of the Spanyards, and specially those, that counte themselues Noblemen, are of the blood of the Moores and Iewes").[37] For audience members familiar with this propaganda, Aragon's emphasis on an uncorrupted lineage would be deliciously comic; for them, Jessica would not be the first Jew, nor Morocco the last Moor, to enter Belmont.

Through Aragon, *Merchant* allows its English audience to mock the Spanish simultaneously for their mongrel blood and for their obsessive concern with uncontaminated lineage. But if *Merchant* is any indication, members of Shakespeare's audience would have recognized the impetus behind the Inquisition's pure-blood laws not only because it sustained their mockery of the Spanish but also because they themselves shared some of the anxieties those laws were designed to address—for the play itself at least partly replicates the logic of the pure-blood laws and hence the racializing structure that underlies them. I have already cited evidence that the English regarded their own conversos as "racial" Jews; the play's repeated insistence that Jessica cannot escape her father's blood puts Jessica in the position of those conversos, who are Jewish whether or not they convert. The extent to which Jessica is trapped in this racializing structure even when she most seems to escape it can perhaps best be measured by the odd moment in which the play briefly posits a quasi-biological difference between her and her father. Just when Shylock himself is claiming his runaway daughter as his own "flesh and blood," Salerio responds, "There is more difference between thy flesh and hers than between jet and ivory; more between your bloods than there is between red wine and Rhenish" (3.1.33–35). Salerio seems willing to allow for the possibility of Jessica's escape into Christianity here, but he does so only by simultaneously reinstating the discourse of race. In his formulation, Jessica can be different from her father, and hence eligible to marry Lorenzo and become a Christian, only if her flesh and blood are literally and identifiably different from his—only if she is not his flesh and blood after all. In his refutation of Shylock's claim to kinship, Salerio appears momentarily to grant Jessica the impossible condition established by Lancelot, who insists that she could become Christian only if she were begotten by some other father. But that very refutation reinscribes the terms of a racialized discourse in her, even as Salerio appears to liberate her from them: flesh and blood are the only terms of difference he will allow.

Salerio's peculiar formulation simultaneously denies and affirms the ineradicable difference of race, and its exaggerations suggest what is at stake. In order to satisfy the contradictory mandates of a racializing discourse and a universalizing Christianity, Salerio must make a difference between Shylock and his daughter, one of whom will remain a "racial" Jew while the other escapes into Christianity;[38] but he can make this difference only through a fantasy that distinguishes between their flesh and blood, in effect rewriting the theological distinction between Christian and Jew as the flesh-and-blood distinction between Jessica and her father. And in that fantasy Salerio would go one better than those who would force Jews to wear badges in order to secure their otherwise-unreliable difference from Christians: he would stabilize the hypothetical and invisible blood difference between father and daughter in the visible distinction of skin color, making Jessica reliably different from Shylock by giving him skin of "jet" in comparison with her "ivory." But although any given director may decide to comply with Salerio's hyperbolical distinction by embodying it in his or her production, the text makes it dif-

ficult to sustain. If Shylock's skin were reliably jet—his difference both from
his daughter and from the Christians as permanently and visibly marked as
the proverbial Ethiope's—would Portia have to ask which is the merchant
and which the Jew? And the hyperbole surrounding Jessica's "ivory" suggests
that it may be equally suspect. Lorenzo's first words about her are apparently
determined to construe her as white, as though only his insistence on her
exceptional whiteness could justify and legitimate their union:

> I know the hand. In faith, 'tis a fair hand,
> And whiter than the paper it writ on
> Is the fair hand that writ. (2.4.12–14)

And his "gentle Jessica" (2.4.19) is "fair" again at 2.4.28 and 39, and again
in 2.6, when Graziano's proclamation that she is "a gentle, and no Jew" is
followed immediately by Lorenzo's insistence that she is "wise, fair, and
true" (2.6.56). But does the rhetorical overkill convince us that she is in fact
fair? Or does it suggest that she must be rhetorically constructed as fair by
Lorenzo and the other Venetians in order to enable her gentile-ification and
thus Lorenzo's theft of her—and the ducats she brings with her—from her
father?[39]

Salerio's formulation suggests that Shylock must be hyperbolically
blackened to make Jessica white, and hence to secure the uncertain difference between father and daughter that temporarily stands in for the uncertain difference between Jew and Christian. And insofar as Salerio can make
Jessica white only by making Shylock into the equivalent of a Moor,[40] in
effect grounding the difference between father and daughter in the visible
difference of the other great category of converts troublesome to the Spanish,
Merchant once again replicates an Inquisitorial logic and anticipates a racial
discourse increasingly obsessed with skin color. For skin color provides a
convenient analogy for fantasmatic distinctions of blood, particularly when
the idealized appeal to oneness that underwrites conversion threatens to dissolve them. Thus Fray Prudencio de Sandoval writes in 1604:

> I know that in the Divine presence there is no distinction between Gen-
> tile and Jew, because One alone is the Lord of all. Yet who can deny that
> in the descendants of the Jews there persists and endures the evil inclina-
> tion of their ancient ingratitude and lack of understanding, just as in the
> Negroes [there persists] the inseparable quality of their blackness . . . ?
> For if the latter should unite themselves a thousand times with white

women, the children are born with the dark color of the father. Similarly,
it is not enough for the Jew to be three parts aristocrat . . . or Old Christian, for one family-line . . . alone defiles and corrupts him.[41]

As with the Negro, one family-line—that is, one Jewish ancestor—corrupts
the would-be Christian: Fray Prudencio needs the fantasy of a permanent
and visible difference in skin color in order to underwrite his fantasy of the
Jew's equally permanent but invisible difference of blood—and he needs that
fantasy exactly because conversion has threatened to merge gentile and Jew
into a perplexing oneness. And Salerio's lines—"There is more difference
between thy flesh and hers than between jet and ivory; more between your
bloods than there is between red wine and Rhenish"—are I think driven by
the same imperative. Initially, his appeal to the enabling fiction that one can
read a blood difference between Jessica and Shylock through a difference in
skin color seems to undo the Inquisition's insistence that the taint of Jewishness is permanent, persisting through the generations; in his construction,
Jessica's "whiteness" is the sign of her differentiation from her father and
thus of her potential to become "one of us" in both religion and race. But he
can convert her whiteness into such a sign only by first making skin the sign
of blood and then by making Shylock hyperbolically black, in the process
stabilizing in him the invisible Jewish difference that threatens to disappear
in Jessica. In an impossible attempt to satisfy the contradictory mandates
provoked by conversion, he thus transmutes the difference between Jew
and Christian into a difference between Jew and Jew, distinguishing fantas-
matically between the "black" Jew-by-race, who will always be a Jew even if
the state forces his conversion, and the "white" Jew-by-religion, who could
perhaps become a Christian and one of us—if only she were not in fact her
father's flesh and blood.

⌘

The metaphors through which Salerio makes Shylock into a Moor in order
to secure Jessica's "whiteness" suggest that Jessica can be allowed her Christian marriage and conversion only if she leaves Shylock behind as a kind of
security deposit, guaranteeing that he at least will remain reliably Jewish,
as definitively different as a Moor. And this is not merely Salerio's construction: the play in fact secures Shylock's identification with the Moor when
it gives him Cush—or Chus—as one of his countrymen (3.2.284), for Cush
is famously one of Ham's sons and therefore the progenitor of the Moors.[42]
These elisions of Jew and Moor eerily anticipate the relation between Shake-

speare's two Venetian plays: in the face of the potential confusion caused
by the converso, Shakespeare (like Salerio or Fray Prudencio) moves from
the Christianized Jew of *Merchant* to the Christianized Moor of *Othello*,
stabilizing both the shifting categories of religion and the invisible differences of blood of the earlier play in the apparently immutable and visible
category of skin color in the later one. And when Cush's descendant and
Othello's countryman Morocco turns up on this stage, he appears to serve a
similar purpose. He enters Belmont in effect as a visual anticipation of what
Salerio would make of Shylock, and his first words call attention to his skin
color ("Mislike me not for my complexion"), invoking one of the familiar
explanatory tropes of blackness: like Cleopatra, he is black because of his
special proximity to the sun, whose "shadowed livery" he wears (2.1.1–2).
But if Salerio and Fray Prudencio would secure blood difference via skin
color, Morocco immediately counters this move, challenging Portia (and
the audience) to look inward, toward the red blood that he shares with "the
fairest creature":

> Bring me the fairest creature northward born,
> Where Phoebus' fire scarce thaws the icicles,
> And let us make incision for your love
> To prove whose blood is reddest, his or mine. (2.1.4–7)

Through his imagined incision, Morocco invokes blood sameness to undo
the difference his skin color makes: through the redness of his blood, he
would lay claim to his xenophobic hostess.[43]

Morocco's image of incision recalls Paul's great refutation of biological particularism in Acts 17.26: God "hathe made of one blood all mankinde, to dwell on all the face of the earth." And insofar as Morocco gestures powerfully toward the common blood lying just beneath the skin of
difference, his language would seem to underwrite his kinsman Shylock's
later—and weaker—claim to the universality of blood ("if you prick us do
we not bleed?" 3.1.54); both would refute Salerio's attempt to ground differences of blood in skin color, at the same time undermining the incipiently
racist view that would separate human beings by "kind" instead of by interior qualities. But perhaps Morocco is allowed to articulate the one-blood
claim precisely because his skin is so reliably different? Morocco's own religious affiliation is left hauntingly unspecific: he asks for the guidance of
"some god"—presumably not the Christian one—as he makes his casket
choice, but his choosing speech is rich in allusion to Catholic belief and practice (suitors come "to kiss this shrine, this mortal breathing saint"; 2.7.40);

and as Portia anticipates his entrance, she entertains the possibility that he might be a saint inside, or even a priest ("If he have the condition of a saint and the complexion of a devil, / I had rather he should shrive me than wive me"; 1.2.109–10). But as Shakespeare's next Venetian play about conversion suggests, a Christianized Moor is still a Moor and still bears the visible—and hence reassuring—signs of difference; one cannot imagine a messenger, say, walking into the Duke's chambers in Othello's Venice and having to ask, "Which is the Senator and which the Moor?" Fray Prudencio's—and Salerio's—move to ground Jewish difference in skin color depends precisely on the fact that Moriscos, or converted Moors like Othello, were far less threatening to category stability than their Jewish counterparts. Since Morocco's difference is secured by his complexion—since no one would mistake him for "one of us"—he can perhaps be allowed to make a compelling claim for the "one blood" that underlies Christian universalism in Paul's formulation; he can, after all, do so without compromising visible racial difference.

And at least in Belmont, there is never any doubt that skin-color difference will trump the appeal to blood likeness. Morocco may invite Portia to look within him, but she herself ignores the casket's lesson on the unreliability of what is "outside" (2.7.68): she concludes her "gentle riddance" of him by drawing attention to his skin color once more ("Let all of his complexion choose me so"; 2.7.78, 79).[44] By the time Portia has finished with him, Morocco can remain the sign of the secure racial difference that Salerio would attribute to Shylock—and that Belmont will reinstate in Jessica. For the figure of Morocco reiterates the conundrums of conversion and Jewish difference in his own person; the tension between Christian universalism and racial particularity always apparent in the play's treatment of its Jews is perfectly condensed in him. His claim for one blood in effect underscores the possibility of Jessica's conversion, but his skin color stabilizes the differences essential to the emergent racist discourses that keep a Moor a Moor—and a Jew a Jew. Even the apparently stable signifier of his skin color can work simultaneously to ground and to minimize Jewish racial difference; as Salerio's formulation suggests, it can serve both to blacken Shylock by analogy and to whiten Jessica by contrast. But though Morocco's skin color can thus stand as the guarantor of Jessica's difference from her father, and hence of her marriage and entry into the community of Christians, this guarantee always threatens to double back on itself; as Portia's "I had rather he should shrive me than wive me" reminds us, Christian universalism may be all well and good, but its limiting case is marriage. It's partly for this reason, I think, that Jessica's own marriage is framed by Morocco's unsuccessful wooing of Portia: his entrance into the virgin kingdom of Belmont (2.1) precedes

Jessica's first appearance in 2.3, where she articulates her desire to escape her father's blood through marriage; and her escape with Lorenzo in 2.6 is immediately followed by Portia's "gentle riddance"—gentile riddance?—of Morocco in 2.7. Compared to the threat Morocco poses to Belmont, Jessica's marriage may come to seem almost acceptable—but he also serves as a visible reminder that her marriage too represents a form of miscegenation.

This reminder will be sharply reiterated later in the play, when the threat of miscegenation represented by Morocco's wooing of Portia is replayed in a minor key, deflected from the body of Belmont's "Queen" (3.2.169) onto that of an anonymous servant—let in, as it were, by the back door. Lancelot has been reassuring himself and perhaps his audience that Jessica will be Jewish as long as her father is Jewish, in effect that her marriage to Lorenzo has not trumped her blood difference. When Jessica reports on this conversation to Lorenzo, adding Lancelot's charge that he is damaging the commonwealth by converting Jews to Christians and hence raising the price of pork, Lorenzo answers by accusing Lancelot of his own damage to the commonwealth: "I shall answer that better to the commonwealth than you can the getting up of the Negro's belly. The Moor is with child by you, Lancelot" (3.5.31–33).[45] How does this Moor get into Belmont? Because we have not heard of her before and because we never see her, she has only a rhetorical existence, as though she were born of Lorenzo's need for a convenient retort: accused of what amounts to miscegenation himself, he is able to silence Lancelot by producing a worse instance of miscegenation. But his retort has the effect of making his marriage to Jessica and Lancelot's impregnating the Moor equivalent, and therefore of making Jessica and the pregnant Moor interchangeable. Rhetorically if not literally, then, Jessica's own entrance into Belmont—the entrance Portia does her best to ignore—seems to have brought this Moor in with her.[46] As though the danger to the realm implicit in Jessica's conversion requires that she herself be collapsed into the category of the Moor in order to stabilize her vanishing difference after all, the subterranean logic of the play returns once again to the apparently solid ground of skin color, in its own way duplicating the move that Fray Prudencio makes when he attempts to secure an infinitely transmissible though invisible Jewishness by appealing to the allegedly infinitely visible transmission of skin color—a move similarly provoked by the category confusion attendant upon conversion. And this subterranean logic effectively undoes the difference between father and daughter that Salerio proposes. At her entrance into Belmont, Jessica denies her connection with her father's countryman Cush, in effect fantasizing her own variant of the difference Salerio had insisted on in the previous scene; the unexpected appearance of this Moor as a kind of stand-in for Jessica's racial difference answers to that denial, relocating her as Cush's countryman after all.

In the play's two Moors, the racial difference that Jessica would like to escape through marriage and conversion is expressed in pure form—as though the Moors were a necessary experiment to test out the hypothesis that racial differences could be absorbed into the Christian body politic. For that reason, it matters that both Moors appear in conjunction with the threat of miscegenation, and that they appear only in the virgin kingdom of Belmont, where xenophobia is rampant and marriage is the topic on everyone's mind. I have already noted that Jessica herself is never fully absorbed into Belmont; the surprise reference to Lancelot's pregnant Moor—apparently unmotivated by the plot—suggests why. Salerio's formulation had allowed for Jessica's escape into whiteness only insofar as two impossible fantasy-conditions were met: her father must be secured in the position of the Moor, and she must be imagined as wholly separate from his flesh and blood. The implied analogy with Lancelot's pregnant Moor compromises both of these conditions: it puts Jessica as well as her father in the position of the Moor, and it forces the question of her flesh-and-blood lineage. For the second of Salerio's conditions can be sustained in fantasy only insofar as Jessica remains childless: as soon as the possibility of her pregnancy is brought into play—as soon as she is imagined as producing flesh and blood of her own—her father's lineage in her becomes manifest and the separation between them collapses. A pseudo-Augustinian text had long before anticipated the threat implicit in Jessica's marriage ("In consequence of the curses upon their fathers, the criminal disposition is even now transmitted to the children by the taint in the blood"),[47] and the appearance of Lancelot's Moor underscores it, for her pregnancy locates the transmission of racial lineage—the taint in the blood—squarely in the mother's body.[48] Fray Prudencio avers that the children of Moors will always be Moors; the rhetorical presence of this Moor reminds us that Jessica's children will always be Jews, no less Shylock's flesh and blood than she is—just as Foxe had predicted when he traced Jewish unbelief to the Jewish mother's womb.

⌒◇⌒

No wonder Jessica's love song with Lorenzo alludes only to doomed and childless couples; as with the other exogamous couples they invoke, early death might be a more satisfying outcome for Shakespeare's audience than the mixed offspring of such a marriage would be. (In Shakespeare's next Venetian play, Desdemona will get herself in trouble as soon as she alludes to the possibility of "increase" in her marriage with Othello.)[49] Jessica's entrance has already threatened to trouble the boundaries of Portia's closed domain (hence perhaps Portia's determined ignoring of her); as though to underscore that threat, Lancelot's Moor breaches those boundaries—and reveals the fragility of the fantasy of self-same enclosure that Belmont encodes. But if Belmont is the place of Christian harmony to which Jessica aspires, it is also, I think, a stand-in for England itself, presided over by its own virgin queen. Jessica's entrance into Belmont thus troubles the serenity of that fantasy of England—and troubles it not only through her resemblance to the conversos in London but also because she carries with her a complex set of allusions to a narrative of nationhood that reopens the question of blood sameness and blood difference exactly where it is most likely to be perplexing to a contemporary Englishman: in the vexed arena of country and nation.

When Jessica names Cush and Tubal as her father's "countrymen" (3.2.284), she invokes a complex narrative of national origins. The names of Tubal and Cush/Chus both come from Genesis 10, the genealogical account of the formation of the separate nations after Noah's flood. Whereas Genesis 11 locates the origin of distinct nations in the linguistic divisions after the Tower of Babel, and thus in supernatural punishment for human arrogance, this chapter locates the dispersal of nations and hence national difference purely in the "natural" realm of kinship groupings deriving from Noah's three sons, Shem, Ham, and Japheth: the introductory summary for Genesis 10 is "The increase of mankinde by Noah and his sonnes. The beginning of cities, contreis and nations," and its concluding words are "These are the families of the sonnes of Noah, after their generacions among their people: and out of these were the nacions diuided in the earth after the flood" (Genesis 10.32). The progeny of Noah's three sons divide the known world; national history begins with them. Thus William Warner begins his history of England in 1612 with "the diuision of the World after the generall Flood," specifying that "To *Asia Sem*, to *Affrick Cham*, to *Europe Iapheth* bore / Their families. Thus triple wise the world deuided was."[50] Given this division, Chus, Tubal, and Shylock make a strange set of countrymen, and not only because the Jews famously had no "country":[51] Chus is Ham's son, and Tubal is Japheth's, while Shylock descends from Shem's grandson Eber, "of whome [the Geneva Bible's marginal gloss to Genesis 10.21 tells us] came the Ebrewes or Iewes." This is not an insignificant detail. At a time of increasingly self-conscious nationalist formation, biblical commentators and genealogically minded historians often expended a good deal of effort trying to pin down exactly which peoples derived from which grandsons;[52]

the habit was familiar enough that Shakespeare can count on his audience
to recognize Prince Hal's mocking reference to it when he tells Poins that
men will either claim to be kin to the king or "will fetch it [i.e., their lineage]
from Japhet" (2 Henry IV, 2.2.99–100). Any careful auditor of Genesis and of
Merchant would recognize the incongruity of the mixed lineages implied by
the names of Shylock's countrymen.[53] And when first a descendant of Chus
and then one of Tubal appear onstage in Belmont as suitors to Portia—for if
Morocco would have traced his ancestry to Chus, Aragon would have traced
his to Tubal[54]—we can be reasonably certain that Shakespeare is engaging in
a complex conversation with Genesis 10 and the dispersal of nations.

But what are the terms of this conversation? The extent to which Belmont is construed through the idea of something like national purity is
clear from the first Belmont scenes, in which Portia efficiently characterizes
and dismisses her foreign suitors—including those derived from Shylock's
countrymen—as though they were anathema to her body and her body politic. Given the frequency with which both Jews and Moors were depicted as
contaminants in the Spanish bloodstream, perhaps the names of Shylock's
countrymen register as nothing more than a xenophobic joke at the expense
of Spain, as though the integrity of Belmont/England could be maintained by
locating contaminating blood mixture—and, for that matter, contaminating
religious mixture—only in Spain. (One can imagine the beginning of such a
joke at the expense of Spain: a Jew, a Catholic, and a Muslim were in a . . .)
But Jessica's marriage, conversion, and entry into Belmont threaten to bring
the anti-Spanish joke home: for insofar as Tubal and Chus are her countrymen as well as her father's, their promiscuous mixture would be reproduced
in her potentially pregnant womb, as the incipient pun in "countrymen" reminds us. In her descendants in Belmont/England, crucial differences among
the descendants of Ham, Shem, and Japheth would be undone, as though
they had never dispersed—or as though their blood was one after all. For at
least one biblical commentator in 1592, that was in fact the point of Genesis
10's account of the dispersal of nations:

> Though we see heere diuisions of Countreys made amongst them, and
> some dwelling here, some there, as they liked, yet one bloud remained
> amongst them, as a knot euer to ioyne them, what distance of place
> soeuer seuered them. And is it not so still . . . ? We be all as we see of one
> bloud and parent.[55]

Insofar as Morocco and Aragon are satisfyingly distinct from each other and
from the Venetians, as easily categorized and dismissed as Portia's other for-

eign suitors, they testify vigorously to the reality of national differences; but insofar as both are in effect descendants of Shylock's countrymen—born to them through the same time warp that makes Shylock a stand-in for Shem in this Noachic division and thus something like his own grandpa[56]—they undo the dispersal of nations and testify equally vigorously to the artificiality of a nationhood that would make differences from a common blood.

One blood or the division into nations: the discourse invoked by Shylock's—and Jessica's—odd "countrymen" reproduces in a different register the tension between a universalizing Christianity in which conversion is open to all and a proto-racial particularism in which blood differences make all the difference; it insists both on our common ancestry in Noah's progeny and on the division into distinct nations from this common origin, just as Genesis 10.32 does ("out of these were the nacions diuided . . ."). And the more specific account of the Japhethic divisions in Genesis 10.5—"Of these were the yles of the Gentiles deuided in their landes, euerie man after his tongue, and after their families in their nacions"—underscores the same tension by anticipating the division into different languages that is attributed to man's pride in Genesis 11. For the two different accounts of the dispersal of nations offered in Genesis 10 (the generations of Noah) and Genesis 11 (the Tower of Babel) themselves enable competing claims for—and therefore competing valuations of—the origins of nations. If the fall into national differences is a consequence of man's sin and God's punishment in Genesis 11, the dispersal of nations is an occasion to marvel at God's grace in Genesis 10, where the postdiluvial derivation of nations from the generations of Noah serves to declare "the wonderfull power of God," "the maruelous increase in so smale a time."[57] One account promotes the image of an original unity, spoiled by sin and recoverable only through grace, when (in Foxe's words) "at the length, all nations . . . acknowledging one Shephearde, vnited together in one sheepefold, may with one voice, one soule, and one generall agreement, glorifie the only begotten sonne"; the other allows for the glorification of cohesive and distinct national identities and languages—for pride in precisely those differences between nations that Foxe would like to see subsumed into oneness.

But the Reformation for which Foxe was a major apologist had itself put an enormous strain on the idea of a universal Christianity. Foxe might await a time when all nations would be united together in one sheepefold to glorify Christ with one voice, but he would probably want that voice to pray in English. Despite his scrupulous denial that the spiritual kingdom belonged to any one terrestrial nation—a denial in any case designed in the *Sermon* more to counter Jewish claims to special status than to make the promise available to all nations—he (like many others) seems to have had little doubt that there was a special relationship between England and the new universally true form of Christianity.[58] And that relationship crucially depended on displacing not only the old "nation" of Shylock and his countrymen but also the old definition of nationhood on which the Jewish claim to the promise seemed to rest—a project to which the discourse of the dispersal of nations could be useful. Just as religions were becoming increasingly "nationalized," the idea of nationhood itself was in flux, in a kind of secular equivalent to the Pauline shift from literal to spiritual descent from Abraham. Initially firmly linked with blood and kinship, and specifically with birth through its Latin root, during this period "nation" was well on its way to becoming a political term in which the artificial "family" within a country's territorial boundaries was merely metaphoric, borrowing its force from exactly those presumptively natural family groupings of kinship—old-style "nations"—that were now to be superseded.[59] And the nation so conceived was ideally situated to inherit the promise originally given to the blood nation of the Jews.

But a nation composed of those residing within certain boundaries rather than those related by blood is a potentially messy affair. We can hear some of the stresses inherent in this new definition of nationhood in MacMorris's indignant response to Fluellen's reference to his "nation" ("Of my nation? What ish my nation? Ish a villain and a bastard and a knave and a rascal? What ish my nation? Who talks of my nation?" *Henry V*, 3.3.61–63); in their exchange, language, ancestry, and place of origin may all be suspected of pulling against the political, territorial, and spiritual unity of the nation—"our nation," in the words of the archbishop of Canterbury (1.2.219)—that Henry V would like to achieve against the French.[60] And if Foxe's often-repeated attacks on the Jewish nation's pride in ancestry are any indication, the Jewish claim to a sacred nationhood of blood derived from father Abraham remained a source of some anxiety, perhaps because its delineations are so clear. When Foxe imagines a Jew boasting "we are the seede of Abraham. . . . well we may wander, but we can neuer perish. The holy Patriarches are our progenitours: we are the yssue of an holy roote" (*Sermon*, E2v), he articulates exactly the basis for the indelible—and indelibly sacred—nationhood for which Shylock speaks in *Merchant*.[61] Of the four uses of the term "nation" in the play, three are his, and he always uses it in its older sense (1.3.43, 3.1.48, 3.1.73). For Shylock, "nationhood" rests securely on continuity of blood and kinship; it is an extension of the "tribe," a term that he uses interchangeably with "nation" (see 1.3.46, 52, 106). And though the term "tribe" is more subject to derogation than "nation"—even Shylock uses it with an odd mix of con-

tempt and irony when he conceals his plan for revenge under the claim that
"suff'rance is the badge of all our tribe" (1.3.106), with its allusion to the
badge Jews were forced to wear—the word in his mouth unmistakably serves
to register not only the blood kinship of the Jews but more particularly their
derivation from the tribes of Israel and hence their claim to a sacred nationhood based on that derivation:[62] his first reference to the collectivity of the
Jews is specifically to their *sacred* nation (1.3.43). Against the newer sense
of nationhood, that is, Shylock poses a claim to an older nationhood of blood
and ancestry: a claim that threatens to disrupt the developing definition of
nationhood—and particularly sacred nationhood—as coterminous with land
boundaries. For the Jews were landless, and yet they were indisputably a
"nation"; Foxe refers continually to the "nation" of the Jews in the *Sermon*,
even while he persistently mocks them for their "fantasicall hope of a terrene kingdome" (Civ).[63]

At a time when nationhood was increasingly identified with land boundaries rather than kinship bonds, the Jews' claim to sacred nationhood despite their landlessness had the potential to disrupt the developing concept of a nationhood—a sacred nationhood—based not in blood but in land.
(Hence perhaps Mistress Quickly's wonderful substitution of Arthur for
Abraham—"he's in Arthur's bosom, if ever man went to Arthur's bosom"
[*Henry V*, 2.3.9–10]—in her vision of Falstaff's final resting place: a substitution that gives the British their own home-grown progenitor in place of
the problematically particularistic Abraham.) But Jewish landlessness could
also be used to shore up the claims of the landed nations to sacred nationhood. Jewish "wandering" had long been read as God's punishment for the
Jews' stiff-necked refusal of Christ and thus as the sign that the promise had
passed from Jew to gentile, the sign that "the nations"—or "us Gentiles,"
as Foxe repeatedly calls them[64]—had replaced the sacred nation of the Jews
as God's chosen people. (Foxe reads it this way, and Foxe's converted Jew
Yehuda-turned-Nathanael signals his conversion by reading it the same way
in the opening of his confession.)[65] Moreover, as the term "Gentiles"—originally all the non-Jewish nations taken together—was becoming increasingly
firmly identified with the European land-nations,[66] the landless status of
the Jews could serve not only to indicate the passage of the promise to the
generalized group of the gentiles but also to reinforce the specific claims of
the new sacred nations based in land. For Genesis 10 designated only the descendants of Japheth—not the descendants of Ham—as "the Gentiles" (10.5
specifies that "Of these were the yles of the Gentiles deuided in their landes"); and as biblical commentaries and national histories became increasingly determined to trace the origin of the European nations to Japheth's

line, they effectively secured the transfer of the promise, and therefore of
the idea of sacred nationhood, to the European nations just when religious
differences were increasingly open to definition in national terms. For if
the "Gentiles" who are Japheth's descendants are localized in the European
nations, then Genesis 9's famous prophecy that Japheth will "dwel in the
tentes of Shem" (9.27)—a prophecy widely understood to refer to the transfer
of the promise from Shem's line to Japheth's—has the effect of grounding
this transfer in both blood lineage and territorial nationhood, thus in effect
trumping Shylock's claim to sacred nationhood on both counts.

Under the circumstances, Jessica's invocation of Tubal and Chus as
Shylock's "countrymen" is heavily charged. For her designation of them as
"countrymen" underscores not the "beginning of cities, contreis, and nations" for the Jews but Jewish countrylessness: of what conceivable country
could these three be countrymen? Their very names trace in their descendants the routes of the Jewish diaspora through Spain and northern Africa
and thus the loss of their "country" Israel. And as Christian identity is
increasingly grounded nationally rather than supranationally, that loss becomes increasingly available to serve as the great counterexample against
which the national and religious identity of the gentiles can be measured.
(No wonder that the tale of the Wandering Jew is reinvented or consolidated,
and becomes newly popular, during this period.)[67] For if the narrative of
the dispersal of nations that Jessica invokes has the potential to undermine
national differences in a common blood, it also has the potential to make
religious triumphalism one with nationalist triumphalism—especially perhaps in England, where the head of the state was also the head of the church.
While Foxe himself in the *Sermon* does not mistake earthly kingdoms for the
spiritual kingdom of God, his mockery of the Jews for their "fantasicall hope
of a terrene kingdome" inevitably functions partly to enable English hopes
for a kingdom at once "terrene" and sacred that might replace Shylock's
now-dispersed "sacred nation": hopes that Elizabeth gives voice to when she
represents herself as "the nursing mother of Israel."[68]

Elizabeth's phrase constitutes England as a sacred nation contained
within land boundaries—a "terrene kingdome"—that can replace the blood-
nation of the Jews, and it does so reassuringly via what amounts to a fantasy
of virgin birth: no intrusion of outsiders into this maternal body; no chance
for miscegenation. Like Belmont itself, this image suggests the anxieties
that it seems designed in part to ward off—anxieties specifically about the
potentially promiscuous openness of a nation once it is no longer defined as
a nation of blood. For if a nation is not a nation of blood, then what exactly
is it? What are its boundaries under the new dispensation in which nation-

hood, like Christianity, is potentially open to all? Venice is, of course, the ideal venue for addressing these questions, since it was a famously "open" city, a polyglot trade center which functioned like a nation-state but tolerated both religious and national diversity for economic reasons.[69] And in the only use of "nation" in *Merchant* that does not belong to Shylock, Antonio suggests the danger that attaches to this conception of the nation. Without Portia's help, his body would be open to Shylock's knife as a consequence of Venice's "openness" to strangers; the Duke cannot overrule Shylock, he tells Solanio,

> For the commodity that strangers have
> With us in Venice, if it be denied,
> Will much impeach the justice of the state,
> Since that the trade and profit of the city
> Consisteth of all nations. (3.3.27–31)[70]

Antonio's use of "nations" here hovers between the old and the new dispensation. Taken alone, it might carry the old meaning of kinship groups and hence refer to "strangers" defined as much by lineage as by country. But Antonio's sequence of terms—commodity, state, trade, profit, nations—implies a political economy in which states exist to ensure trade conditions among "nations" conceived as political and economic, rather than kinship, units; and nations so conceived are dangerously porous and dangerously subject to the strangers in their midst. Insofar as Venice has to protect the trade interests of other nations in order to protect its own trade interests, its own national body is threatened—a threat epitomized here by Antonio's body, which must be subject to Shylock's knife precisely so that the trade routes by which he and the state thrive will stay open. Like Venice itself, with all nations mingling in its markets, the thoroughfares of Antonio's body are subject to the invasion of others who cannot be kept at bay. This is the danger of the newly modern nation, its porous boundaries no longer defined by kinship and race, its blood no longer intact.

The virginal realm of Portia's Belmont would seem to be the antidote to such dangers: her little kingdom and her body will not be open to all nations. Her boundaries can apparently be perfectly protected because she is, in fantasy, coterminous with her realm: she tells us that she is "Queen o'er [her]self" (3.2.169), as in the Ditchley portrait in which Queen Elizabeth's body takes up virtually the entire space of her kingdom; and the name of her realm slyly figures her female anatomy, as though her kingdom and her body were one.[71] Though strangers from all nations come to her in a

barely idealized imitation of Venice's merchants—they are all Jasons seeking the fleece (1.1.172)—they are quickly dispatched without damage to this
enclosed body. If Portia's suitors read like a catalog drawn from Shylock's
kinsmen and the dispersal of nations, it is the work—and what passes for
the wit—of the first Belmont scenes in effect to ratify not their one blood
but the differences between them, to dispatch them for us cleanly in a group
while identifying each as reassuringly distinct from the others. And Portia is
helped in this work by the invisible will of her father operating behind the
scenes, maintaining fidelity to a kinship line and eventually enabling just
the right amount of exogamy in Bassanio. What a satisfying fantasy of England this is, with its virgin queen and its bloodlines protected by the opera-
tions of a father absent but still mysteriously efficacious—and how different
from the Venice in which Antonio is at risk from the mingling of the nations.
No wonder that only Portia seems capable of finding the law that protects
citizens from aliens (4.1.344–46), and no wonder that Portia is so unwilling
to recognize Jessica's entrance into her realm. For Jessica brings with her
exactly that muddying of bloodlines that is deflected by Portia's banter and
her father's will: brings it in her own person, in the strange set of "countrymen" to whom she is (willy-nilly) allied, and in the pregnant Moor, who is
apparently invoked by Jessica's own potential for miscegenation.

When Lorenzo invites the newly converted Jessica to look to the golden
floor of heaven (5.1.57–58), he seems to promise her the possibility of a
harmonious Christian oneness in golden Belmont, where blood difference
will disappear.[72] In the context of her conversion, we might even expect
the blood mixture that she brings to Belmont to be read as a providential
return to the one blood of Noah's children, a return that would literalize
the oneness of all nations in Christ. Spenser's Irenius, for example, reads
blood mixture in this way when he tells Eudoxus that there is "no nacion
now in Christendome nor muche farther but is mingled and Compounded
with others, for it was a singuler prouidence of god and a moste admirable
purpose of his wisdome to drawe those Northerne heathen nacions downe
into these Cristian partes wheare they mighte receaue Christianitye and to
mingle nacions so remote so miraculouslye to make as it weare one kindred
and bloud of all people and eache to haue knowledge of him."[73] But despite
the play's apparent endorsement of that conversion, I do not think that this
is how Portia's Belmont—or those who share in the fantasy of Belmont as an
idealized England—would read it. Gibbons, for example, reads such mixture
as punishment for human sin: he interrupts his commentary on the dispersal of nations to note that it is "follie to suppose those nations which now
remaine, to be purelie the ofspring of such parentage. For such hath bin the

wickednes of men, their vnthankefulnes to God, and their crueltie within themselues; and such the wrath of God for their offences; as that they haue bin by wars and seditions dashed one against another, and in their habitations mingled and confused."[74] And even Irenius glorifies this mingling of nations only by way of apology for having just said that the Spanish—from whom the Irish claimed to be descended—are "of all nacions vnder heauen . . . the moste mingled most vncertaine and moste bastardlie."[75]

Immediately after Lorenzo gestures toward the golden floor of heaven, he reminds us that access to its unheard harmony is not so simple here on earth: we can have only the merest intimations of it here, while souls are enclosed in their "muddy vesture of decay" (5.1.63). In the realm of the flesh, and perhaps especially in the realm of the dark flesh suggested by "muddy," the mingling of different bloods is not the route to one Christian kindred; it is, as Irenius says, a form of bastardy.[76] It is no accident, I think, that bastardy turns out to be the subtext of the scene in which Lancelot weighs the success of Jessica's entrance into Christianity and therefore by implication into Belmont, and no accident that Jessica's "bastard hope" (3.5.6, 10) generates Lancelot's bastard child: a child bastardized both by its legal status and in its mingled blood. For that child reminds us that the same bastard mingling would be reproduced in Jessica's womb were she and Lorenzo to have children: whether or not Jessica is married, whether or not she is converted, her own children can be nothing more than a kind of "bastard hope" in Belmont, troubling the fantasy of a pure-blood nation.[77]

∽

Conversion, danger to the commonwealth, race, and miscegenation come together in Jessica's body in the last Belmont scene before the scourging of Shylock because they represent the threats to the nation that scourging is designed to ward off: she threatens to carry to Belmont the boundary-danger of the new hybrid nation, no longer a nation of blood and perforce permeable by strangers—the boundary-danger epitomized by the subjection of Antonio's body to Shylock's knife. But that image of the nation vulnerable at its borders maps uncannily onto the central icon of Christianity in 4.1, where the vulnerability of Antonio's body to the Jew's knife makes him briefly a type of Christ. The flickering between the images—for Antonio's threatened body cannot represent both at once—may serve to underscore the tension between the dream of a new and exclusive "sacred nation" securely within its own boundaries and the dream of a universalizing Christianity in which "all nations . . . acknowledging one Shephearde, vnited together in

one sheepefold, may with one voice, one soule, and one generall agreement,
glorifie the only begotten sonne." And in the face of this tension, *Merchant*
rushes to forestall that boundary-danger and to reinstate the differences that
bind Jessica to her father's blood. By the end of 4.1, Shylock will have been
securely located in the position of the alien whether or not his state-ordered
conversion is complete; and Antonio's body will remain securely closed, no
longer the thoroughfare for the nations who pass through Venice. For when
Portia saves the day and the integrity of Antonio's body by citing not only
the absence of blood in Shylock's contract but also the law that protects citizens from aliens and the law against shedding specifically *Christian* blood
(4.1.344–46, 305), she simultaneously restores the integrity of the proto-
national state and ratifies the blood difference between Jew and Christian:
the blood difference that can always be cited to exclude Jessica and her father, like the conversos of London, both from Foxe's dream of unity and from
the new nationhood that would replace the sacred nation of the Jews.

CHAPTER FOUR

Incising Antonio:
The Jew Within

For he is not a Iewe, which is one outwarde: nether is that circumcision, which is outwarde in the flesh: But he is a Iewe which is one within, & the circumcision is of the heart, in the spirit, not in the letter.
—Romans 2.28–29

Repent but you that you shall lose your friend,
And he repents not that he pays your debt;
For if the Jew do cut but deep enough,
I'll pay it instantly, with all my heart.
—*Merchant of Venice*, 4.1.273–76

For why may I not iustly accuse you, as partetakers of the same crime, sithence yee doe with whole bent affection of hatefull despite, pursue the embrued steppes of your bloodie sires, and gladly allow of that execrable murther?

And therefore (thou cursed Iewe) thou are duly charged with the guilt of innocent blood: englut therfore thy greedie guts with goare.
—Foxe, *Sermon*, L3r

In the course of his opening prayer for the conversion of the Jews, Foxe uses a curious phrase—"the circumcised Race"—to refer to the Jews collectively (*Sermon*, A1v). The phrase catches exactly the ambiguity in Jewish difference that I have tried to describe in the last chapter, and at the same time it epitomizes the solution to that ambiguity that the newly developing discourse of race enabled: even as he imagines their conversion, Foxe's phrase hardens a distinction based on a religious ritual into a marker of racial—not theological—difference.[1] I will eventually argue that anxiety about the status of circumcision as a reliable marker of difference plays itself out in the incision that Shylock would make on Antonio's body, but for the moment, I want to begin by returning to Jessica: is she or isn't she a member of the circumcised race? Calvin's uncharacteristically murky gloss to Genesis 17.10—"Let euerie man childe among you be circumcised"—suggests that the topic occasioned some perplexity. He wants to include women under the sign of circumcision because it is the "signe [that] the promise is confirmed . . . and it is certeine, that women as well as men haue neede of confirmation"; therefore, "it followeth, that the signe was ordeined for bothe sexes sake." But how exactly women partake in this sign remains a mystery that Calvin simply dodges in his conclusion: "For the couenant of God was printed and grauen in the bodies of the males for this cause, that the women also mighte be partakers of the same signe."[2] Nashe does not share Foxe's theological scruples, but he runs up against the same problem: when he wants to designate the whole community of the Roman Jews in *The Unfortunate Traveller*, he calls them "all foreskin clippers—whether male or female" (263), a designation that makes sense only if he imagines that females have foreskins or that they clip the foreskins of their males. But what might provoke this question specifically in relation to Jessica? And why might it matter to *Merchant*?

It is, I think, a sign of the ways in which circumcision haunts this play's meditation on the relation between Jew and Christian that Jessica herself cannot make the transition from Jew to Christian without undergoing a symbolic circumcision of sorts: as though she must be marked as a member of the circumcised race before she can be allowed to leave her father's house. The play in fact takes pains to transform Jessica into a boy even as it insists that her transformation is quite gratuitous from the point of view of the plot: the masque which serves as the excuse for her disguise has been called off by the end of the scene in which she elopes (2.6.63), and Salerio's report that Lorenzo and a perfectly recognizable Jessica have been seen in a gondola shortly afterward makes it clear that she did not really need the disguise in the first place.[3] Why then give her what Lorenzo calls "the lovely garnish of a boy" (2.6.45)? Not only, I think, to enable Lorenzo's homoerotically tinged response to her. For her disguise and especially Lorenzo's appreciation of her "garnish"[4] function to give her what amounts to a potential site for circumcision; and in fact Lorenzo has no sooner called attention to the penis of this boy-actor turned girl turned boy than Jessica offers to "gild" herself with her father's ducats (2.6.49), punningly reproducing in herself not only the guilt of his money but also the gelding that her theft—"two stones, two rich and precious stones, / Stol'n by my daughter!" (2.8.20–21)—will produce in him.[5] But this gelding is itself only an extension of the bodily sign of his Jewishness. Through the mobile fantasy that equates circumcision with castration,[6] her offer to gild herself marks her inclusion in the race of the circumcised just as she seems on the point of leaving it.

Jessica appears to be made into a boy as she attempts to leave her father's house just so that she can be returned to his body, firmly (if only momentarily) under the sign of circumcision: at least for this moment, she is in effect both a male and a female foreskin clipper. But from one point of view, her "gelding" is perfectly superfluous. Insofar as she only pretends to be "accomplishèd / With that [she] lack[s]" (to borrow Portia's phrase about her own male disguise at 3.4.61–62), she is already gelded, through the equation that would make a woman equivalent to a gelded man: an equivalence neatly underscored by Graziano when he wishes a gelding that has in effect already taken place—"Would he were gelt that had it for my part" (5.1.143)—on the woman who pretends to be the man that has his wife's ring.[7] And here I think we can begin to assess the bizarre utility of Jessica's disguise for the larger concerns of *Merchant*. For Jessica by definition cannot be circumcised—unless in the set of fantasies that equates circumcision with castration, and castration with femaleness, in which case she cannot help but be circumcised. But the same set of fantasies is always available to turn any Jew into a kind of woman.[8] No wonder that Jessica seems to trade in her shame at being her father's child (2.3.16) for shame at her disguise (2.6.35, 41):[9] if, on the one hand, Jessica seems to escape from her father and "the circumcised Race" by virtue of her gender, on the other, as she assumes the masculine disguise that allows both for Lorenzo's pleasure and for her fantasy-circumcision, she embodies in her own person the stigmatized and feminized figure of the guilty/gilded/gelded Jew—a figure (I shall argue) that will eventually be realized not in her own body but in the eroticized and shame-filled body of Antonio, the play's ur-Christian.

⋅⊙⋅

Jessica provokes an image of this ambiguously gendered rent body even before she herself appears onstage in drag in 2.6. When Lorenzo is late for his own elopement, Salerio accounts for his delay with the Cressida-like statement that Venus's pigeons fly ten times faster "To seal love's bonds new made than they are wont / To keep obligèd faith unforfeited" (2.6.6–7); and Graziano expands upon this hint, in language that once again anticipates *Troilus and Cressida* ("Who riseth from a feast / With that keen appetite that he sits down?" 2.6.8–9).[10] Perhaps these meditations on the effects of sexual satiety serve to anticipate Lorenzo's later invocation of Troilus, but at least at this initial stage of their relationship, satiety would scarcely seem to be the problem: there is no evidence that Lorenzo has already "feasted" upon Jessica or that he is like Graziano's horse, bored with the measures that he has already paced (2.6.10–12). Graziano's next analogy in fact proposes a different source of unease:

> How like a younker or a prodigal
> The scarfèd barque puts from her native bay,
> Hugged and embracèd by the strumpet wind!
> How like the prodigal doth she return,
> With over-weathered ribs and raggèd sails,
> Lean, rent, and beggared by the strumpet wind! (2.6.14–19)

Everything in the organization of this passage—rhythm, syntax, repeated words and sounds—points toward the equivalence of "Hugged and embracèd" and "Lean, rent, and beggared": an equivalence that functions to attribute Lorenzo's delay not to male satiety but to the bodily danger inherent in lovemaking. And the ship that begins as decidedly male (a younker or a prodigal) becomes female as soon as it puts from her native bay and is hugged and embraced by the strumpet wind, as though through a kind of contagion. The contagion that threatens to transform the gender of the lover even as it transforms the gender of the ship is the familiar stuff of Shakespearean drama, but it has a peculiar relevance to Lorenzo's situation here. In the last chapter, I suggested the danger that intermarriage with Jessica represents to the commonwealth insofar as she might potentially reproduce her Jewishness in her children; this passage inscribes that danger more intimately on Lorenzo's body. And it does so, I think, because in addition to the ordinary dangers of effeminization, marriage to Jessica carries within it the reminder of two earlier intermarriages, each of which ends not with the spectacle of the Jew's conversion but with the circumcised male body.

When Jessica disobeys her father and "look[s] out at window" (2.5.39), she simultaneously enacts one possible meaning of her name[11] and recalls the action of one of her forerunners, Jacob's only daughter, Dinah.[12] Shylock familiarly draws on Jacob both to substantiate his claim to sacred nationhood and to give his actions weight: he refers at length to Jacob's management of Laban's sheep (Genesis 30.37–41) to secure his right to usury (1.3.67–86), and he swears by Jacob's staff (Genesis 32.10) immediately after he orders Jessica not to look out into the public street (2.5.31, 35). Dinah appears suddenly in Genesis 34.1 ("Then Dinah the daughter of Leah, which she bare vnto

Iaakob, went out to se the daughters of that countrey"), soon after the Jacob material that Shylock draws on here; it is very unlikely that Shakespeare was unfamiliar with her story.[13] And that story tellingly anticipates Jessica's: both daughters are poised on the threshold of their fathers' houses and drawn toward the world outside, and both are immediately taken by men in exogamous unions[14]—a resemblance later underscored when Shylock identifies Jessica's mother as Leah (3.1.101). Commentaries on the story routinely echo Shylock's instructions to Jessica in 2.5: Babington used the story of Dinah in 1592 to excoriate "Womens needles going abroad," and Ainsworth traces the restrictions that later kept women at home to the same story ("God noteth Dinahs going out, as an occasion of her evil; & after teacheth yong women to be *keepers at home*"); both of them follow the Geneva Bible's gloss to Genesis 34.1, which stresses the parent's responsibility to restrict the child ("This example teacheth that to muche libertie is not to be giuen to youthe"). Babington in fact sounds quite like the Shylock who warns Jessica not "to gaze on Christian fools with varnished faces" (2.5.32) when he tells us that Dinah "went a walking to gaze and see fashions, as women were euer desirous of nouelties, and giuen to needles curiositie."[15]

Shylock speaks to his daughter as though he has Babington's Dinah in mind; and given the extent to which he apparently likes to understand himself through the analogue of his great ancestor, it would not be surprising if he did; at least some members of his audience are likely to have found in Dinah the model for his fears about Jessica's curiosity. And if so, she would have been a disturbing model. Although Genesis 34 begins with Dinah's leaving her father's house and her rape, the focus shifts almost immediately to the consequences for her rapist. When Shechem falls in love with her, Dinah's brothers initially invite him and his kin to be circumcised so that they can become "one people" with the Israelites ("But in this wil we consent vnto you, if ye wil be as we are, that euerie man childe among you be circumcised: Then wil we giue our daughters to you, and we wil take your daughters to vs, and wil dwel with you, and be one people"; Genesis 34.15–16). Shechem accepts this bargain, but the promise of becoming "one people" is a ruse, and this conversion proves to be deadly: "on the third day (when thei were sore) two of the sonnes of Iaakob, Simeon and Leui, Dinahs brethren toke ether of them his sworde & went into the citie boldely, and slewe euerie male" (Genesis 34.25).

The story of Dinah is disturbing in part because it invokes and then catastrophically shatters the promise of becoming "one people": it is a kind of conversion story gone terribly wrong, with both parties to blame. Shechem may wish to convert for love, but the Shechemites want to become "one people" with the Israelites for notably self-serving reasons: if they become one people with Jacob's family, they reason, "Shal not their flockes and their substance and all their cattel be ours?" (Genesis 34.23). The *Glossa Ordinaria* accuses them of "false sanctity," and Calvin follows suit, blaming them for changing their religion so lightly and converting for reasons of profit;[16] Ainsworth similarly considers their circumcision, "being doon without the knowledge and faith of God . . . a profanation of this *seal of the righteousnes of faith, (Rom.* 4.11)," which "was not let goe unpunished of God."[17] But Calvin thinks that the Shechemites' sins are outweighed by those of the Israelites, who "care not for circumcision: but onely seeke howe to make the miserable men weake and vnapte to resist them in the slaughter" and who "drawe the signe amisse from his trueth [and] defile the spirituall signe of life, when without exception or regard, they make straungers partakers thereof"; he sardonically adds, "Let the Iewes goe nowe and boast of their noble originall."[18] This cynical tale of conversion for profit and misuse of God's covenant might thus apply both to many recent converts—Jewish strangers or English natives—whose reasons for converting were suspect, and to those who forced conversion upon them, misusing the signs of spiritual life.

In the context of *Merchant*, the story of Dinah is disturbing not only because of its potential critique of conversion misused but also—and more specifically—because sexual union with the Jewish woman ends in this image of circumcision and death. One could hardly ask for a more vivid illustration of the dangers of intermarriage. Circumcision itself is sometimes read as a warning against intermarriage. Donne, for example, reads it this way in his sermon on circumcision: the Jews "were a Nation prone to *Idolatry*, and most, upon this occasion, if they mingled themselves with Women of other Nations: And therefore . . . *God* imprinted a marke in that part, to keep them still in mind of that law, which forbade them *foraigne Marriages*, or any company of *strange Women.*"[19] If circumcision was instituted partly to prevent the exogamous marriages of the Jews, in Genesis 34 it serves that purpose with a vengeance. And the commentators of the Geneva Bible who modeled themselves upon the ancient Israelite community read the fate of Shechem and his kin as a warning for contemporary Christians who might be tempted to be similarly exogamous, but this time with the Christians in the position of the Israelites and the Jews in the position of the Shechemites: when Levi and Simeon insist that it would be a reproach to them "to giue our sister to an vncircumcised man" (34.14), the Geneva gloss is "As it is abomination for them that are baptized to ioine with infidels." If Shechem was the infidel for the ancient Jews, Jessica is now the "infidel," identified as such when she enters Belmont with Lorenzo (3.2.217)—and Lorenzo thus courts the punishment of Shechem.

That punishment is in fact anticipated in the second story of intermarriage and conversion for love that—like the story of Dinah—seems to me to haunt the edges of *Merchant*. But this time the story is closer to home. In England in 1222, in a case that had a certain amount of notoriety in the sixteenth century, a deacon circumcised himself in order to marry a Jewish woman and was burned for his apostasy.[20] If (as I argued in the last chapter) *Merchant* worries the problem of the visible difference between Jew and Christian and uses Jessica's entrance into Belmont to underscore the dangers of a mixed union and a mixed nation, this case epitomized those dangers; Archbishop Langton's Oxford Council in fact responded to it by mandating the wearing of the Jewish badge explicitly to prevent such unions,[21] in effect restoring the visible distinction that the deacon had compromised when he circumcised himself. But the failure of difference is not the only danger here, and the story of the deacon illustrates the threat latent in Lorenzo's marriage to Jessica in a different register. Jessica reassures the audience that she intends to convert to Christianity, and Lorenzo clearly has no intention of circumcising himself and turning Jew. But the historical precedent for intermarriage in England was that the Jewess will end up converting the Christian, reproducing not only her theological but also her bodily condition—circumcised/castrated—in him; and although *Merchant* never echoes this precedent overtly in the Jessica-Lorenzo plot, Graziano's metaphor of the rent ship suggests that it nonetheless lives on at the level of fantasy. For if the covert logic in the stories of Genesis 34 and the deacon condenses crime and punishment, as though lying with the Jewish woman was in itself tantamount to circumcision and death, Graziano's metaphor to account for Lorenzo's otherwise-unexplained delay reproduces just this condensation: it identifies Lorenzo with the ship and Jessica with the strumpet wind that would simultaneously embrace and rend the body of the younker who sets out so confidently.

Within the logic of the circumcision stories that haunt 2.6, Graziano's speech thus makes perfect sense, even though it is oddly dissociated from what little we know of Lorenzo as a character or what we see of his relationship with his tamed Jewess Jessica. But I think that just this dissociation signals what is most interesting about the speech. Ordinarily we might expect the speech to give some plausible explanation for Lorenzo's delay, but here the delay seems to exist to provide an occasion for the speech; and its very gratuitousness seems to me to register not only its weird emotional urgency but also its place as a kind of switch point or fulcrum between the intermarriage plot and the Shylock-Antonio plot. For surely what is oddest about this oddly placed speech is that it so perfectly anticipates the fate of Antonio's ships.[22] But why should one of Antonio's ships appear as it were under the eaves of the Jew's house?

Perhaps because in *Merchant* it is Antonio, not Lorenzo, who is threatened with the penalty of Shechem. I have been arguing that the combined stories of the deacon and Shechem haunt the edges of *Merchant*, and that this haunting adheres to the figure of Jessica and provokes Graziano's apparently gratuitous speech. But insofar as the penalty of Shechem has a place in the plot of *Merchant*, it is localized not in the Lorenzo-Jessica plot but in the Antonio-Shylock plot: specifically in the "forfeit" (as Shylock puts it) of "an equal pound / Of your fair flesh to be cut off and taken / In what part of your body pleaseth me" (1.3.144, 145–47). Many have heard the resonance of circumcision in this speech; and later, when Shylock (true to his designation as a foreskin clipper) whets his knife "to cut the forfeit from that bankrupt there" (4.1.121), the anticipation of "foreskin" in "forfeit" is nearly irresistible.[23] As the potential circumciser of Antonio, Shylock would be merely following in the footsteps of his allegedly bloody-minded ancestors, who were routinely accused of circumcising Christians; his role as circumciser would be all too familiar to audience members bred up in stories of Jewish ritual murder.[24] And if Shylock—or Shylock's audience—understands the story of his daughter's theft partly through the analogue of Dinah, his proposed punishment of Antonio would make a peculiarly appropriate ending to that story.[25] Solanio thinks that Antonio shall "pay" for Jessica's flight (2.8.26), and many have agreed that Shylock becomes more obdurate in his determination to cut off Antonio's pound of flesh after his loss of Jessica;[26] certainly he uses the prospect of revenge against Antonio—"I am very glad of it. I'll plague him, I'll torture him. I am glad of it"—to console himself for his inability to take more direct revenge for Jessica's theft (3.1.96–97, 78–79). Jacob's sons avenged Dinah's rape by mockingly offering to become "one people" with the Shechemites; from Shylock's point of view, then, there would be a nice tidiness in the revenge that made Antonio into one of the "circumcised Race" as repayment not only for his taunting and his economic competition but also for the theft that made Shylock's daughter a Christian. And the phantom ship that appears under Shylock's eaves as his daughter is being stolen eerily predicts just this outcome. That "prodigal" ship, "lean, rent, and beggared," anticipates both Shylock's characterization of Antonio as "a bankrupt, a prodigal, . . . a beggar" (3.1.37–38) and the rending to which Antonio's bankruptcy would subject him—a rending already implicit in the *ruptus*/rupture of "bankrupt."[27] The ship that appears under Shylock's eaves is thus not only an anticipation of but also a metonymy for Antonio's rent body.

Insofar as that rending would play out the logic of the Dinah story, with Shylock in the role of Jacob's vengeful sons, it makes sense for Graziano's metonymic ship to turn up under Shylock's eaves just as Shylock's daughter is stolen. But although Graziano's metaphor predicts the outcome of the Dinah story and anticipates Shylock's intended revenge, it does not account for the conjunction that makes Antonio's rent ships a figure for the perils of bodily desire—a conjunction that simultaneously raises the question of Antonio's own dangerous desires, and indirectly returns us to the story of the deacon. For if the danger of intermarriage in that story is that the Jewess will be able to reproduce her condition in the non-Jew, Antonio—it turns out—has already embraced that condition: in the trial scene, he famously characterizes himself as "a tainted wether of the flock" (4.1.113), registering his affinity with the circumcised/castrated body[28]—and with the rent and feminized body of his ship—even before Shylock begins to whet his knife. And if Antonio thus registers in his body the fate of the self-circumcising deacon, some bizarre accretions to the deacon's story are in fact hauntingly resonant with the Antonio of 4.1.

The continuing power of the deacon's story is suggested by the evidence that people could not let it alone: over time, the deacon who circumcised himself for love acquired as companions not only one or more women claiming to be Saint Mary but also "a youth who had given himself out to be Christ, and had pierced his own hands, sides, and feet," and a hermaphrodite.[29] Holinshed himself gives two versions of the story, which allows him to keep both of these latter accretions in play. In his first account, "two naughtie felowes were presented . . . either of them naming himselfe Christ. . . . Moreouer, to prooue their errour to haue a shew of truth, they shewed certeine tokens and signes of wounds in their bodies, hands and feet, like vnto our sauiour Iesus that was nailed on the crosse. . . . The one of them was an Hermophrodite." But he then adds, "Ralfe Coghshall sheweth this matter otherwise, and saith, that there were two men and two women . . . of the which one of the men being a deacon, was accused to be an apostata, & for the loue of a woman that was a Iew, he had circumcised himselfe."[30] Whether or not Shakespeare and his audience knew of these various accretions, they are useful in suggesting the extent to which the image of a Christian turned Jew through circumcision becomes the site for a set of related anxieties: the man who would display his wounds as Christ and the hermaphrodite attach themselves to the deacon as though they were exfoliations of his newly Jewish self-circumcised body. I suggest that in 4.1 Antonio's body becomes the site for a similar set of anxieties—about circumcision, desire, gender, and religious self-display—and that it is the business of the play, and especially of Portia, to keep those anxieties at bay and thus to ward off his resemblance to the Jew. For although Portia may be temporarily uncertain when she enters the courtroom, by the time she is finished there will be no mistaking which is the merchant and which the Jew.

⟨✸⟩

Theologically, of course, Shylock's attempt to circumcise Antonio should once again confirm his bondage to a superseded law and thus reinforce the distinction between Christian and Jew. When he says, "I stand here for law" (4.1.141), he might as well say, "I stand for circumcision," not only because that appears to be the ritual act that the letter of the Venetian law will allow him to perform on Antonio but also because circumcision is a familiar metonymy for the fleshly Mosaic Law: the Geneva Bible's gloss to "circumcision" in Romans 4.9, for example, notes that Paul "comprehendeth the whole Law" under this sacrament.[31] And as everyone—or at least everyone Christian—knew, Abraham's circumcision "was perfected and consummated in the person of *Christ Jesus* [and] the vertue thereof was extinguished in Christ";[32] in Calvin's economical formulation, "where baptisme is, there is no vse nowe of circumcision."[33] If circumcision marks the bodily difference between gentile and Jew, it thus also marks what the Duke calls "the difference of our spirit" (4.1.363); whatever the quality of the Christian's mercy in practice, the theoretical opposition between the mercy Portia invokes and the law Shylock stands for unmistakably plays out the Christian understanding of the benightedness of the Jews, who insist on living according to the letter of the old Law, with its bondage to the flesh.[34] And Shylock's inscription of the letter of this Law on Antonio's body would—literally—kill (2 Corinthians 3.6), which perhaps accounts for Bassanio's odd transformation of the letter reporting Shylock's legal hold on Antonio into Antonio's wounded body itself ("Here is a letter, lady, / The paper as the body of my friend, / And every word in it a gaping wound / Issuing life-blood"; 3.2.262–65).

Since circumcision is the master trope for bondage to the old Law of the flesh, it is not surprising that Portia equates Shylock's legal bond with the pound of flesh that he would cut from Antonio: "take then thy bond. Take thou thy pound of flesh" (4.1.303), she says, as though the two were interchangeable terms. Nor is it surprising that Portia defeats Shylock by forcing him to embody the rigors of the law. "In the course of justice none

of us / Should see salvation" (4.1.194–95), Portia tells Shylock; but it is a
commonplace of criticism that she triumphs over him not via the mercy
she invokes but rather via her insistence that he adhere to the letter of the
law ("As thou urgest justice, be assured / Thou shalt have justice more than
thou desir'st"; 4.1.311–12). Her strategy is particularly apposite to Shylock
as representative of the Law of circumcision, since it tidily illustrates the
danger of his reliance on that Law. Paul testifies specifically "to euerie man,
which is circumcised, that he is bounde to kepe the whole Law" (Galatians
5.3); but since in practice no one can keep the whole Law, "as many as are of
the workes of the Law, are vnder the curse: for it is written, Cursed is euerie
man that continueth not in all things, which are written in the boke of the
Law, to do them" (Galatians 3.10).[35] Shylock's reliance on the exact letter of
the law of circumcision—he refuses to call for a surgeon to stop Antonio's
wounds because it is not "so nominated in the bond" (4.1.254)—binds him
to keeping the whole law; a moment later Portia orders him to take his
pound of flesh without shedding "one drop of Christian blood" because "this
bond doth give thee here no jot of blood. / The words expressly are 'a pound
of flesh'" (4.1.305, 301–2). Bound by his own allegiance to the bond, Shylock
embodies the Pauline inadequacy of the Law with an almost comic efficacy.
In his attempt to circumcise Antonio, he is defeated by his incapacity to
follow the fleshly law completely, in this instance to circumcise Antonio's
flesh without shedding the blood not nominated in the bond.

As the word "bond" and its derivatives toll through the play,[36] it thus
comes to mark not only the temporal law of Venice but also the fleshly
Law of circumcision for which Shylock stands—and therefore, by implication, Shylock's status not as Isaac but as Ishmael, son of the bondwoman
Hagar in Paul's trope for the difference between Christian liberty and Jewish
bondage to the Law in Galatians 4.22–31.[37] But if Antonio thus inherits the
position of Isaac, son of the free woman, the difference between these sons
of Abraham is not thereby absolutely secured. Paul in fact concludes his
trope of the two sons specifically with a warning against a return to bondage, for which circumcision is the trope: "stand fast therefore in the libertie
wherewith Christ hathe made vs fre, and be not intangled againe with the
yoke of bondage. Beholde, I Paul say vnto you, that if ye be circumcised,
Christ shal profite you nothing" (Galatians 5.1–2). The circumcision that
Shylock would reproduce in Antonio is thus doubly dangerous to Antonio,
for it would undo the distinction between the sons and become the mark
of his own subjection to the flesh. Paul's warning against circumcision in
Philippians 3.2—"Beware of dogges: beware of euil workers: beware of the
concision," where "concision" is glossed as "cutting of"[38]—is particularly

resonant for *Merchant:* "dog" is a standard epithet for Shylock (see 1.3.107, 117, 123; 2.8.14; 3.3.6, 7; 4.1.127), and the threat of circumcision, or "cutting off," provides the climax of the plot. And although Portia may easily triumph over Shylock, Paul suggests that the threat to the free children of the promise is perpetual: "we are after the maner of Isaac, children of the promes. But as then he that was borne after the flesh, persecuted him that was borne after the spirit, euen so it is now" (Galatians 4.28–29).

The trial scene of *Merchant* is in effect a dramatization of the danger Paul warns against, "now," in the present; it allows Shakespeare's Christian audience to feel the delightful *frisson* of horror that unites them with martyrs of the early church. And even as the Jew's knife takes on the threat of the obsolete fleshly law that still threatens to ensnare the children of the promise, converting them into children of the flesh, it also recalls other forms of bondage and other ritual wounds. The Antonio of 4.1 is like Isaac insofar as he is a child of the promise subject to persecution by a child of the flesh, but the thrice-repeated phrase that opens 1.3—"Antonio shall be bound"; "Antonio shall become bound"; "Antonio bound" (1.3.4, 5, 8)—shortly before Shylock invokes father Abram (1.3.68, 156) anticipates Isaac in another guise: an anticipation confirmed by Antonio's own allusion to a ram just before Shylock whets his knife (4.1.113).[39] And as Antonio becomes the Isaac who is bound and must (to borrow Portia's phrase) "stand for sacrifice" (3.2.57), Shylock becomes a terrifying version of Abraham, the patriarch with the knife in his hand. For the vexed figure of Abraham always has the potential to exceed the meaning officially accorded him and thus to encode the double status of the Jew within Christianity. Theologically Abraham is the fleshly father of Christ and the vehicle through whom the promise passes to all nations, and his willingness to sacrifice his son Isaac was routinely read as an instance of his perfect faith.[40] But the figure of the Jewish patriarch with the knife maps all too easily onto the figure of the circumcising Jews who were said to have killed Christ—especially since Isaac himself was routinely identified as a figure for Christ.[41] When Shylock refers to the thief freed in place of Jesus (4.1.291) and echoes the cry that Matthew attributed to the Jews at the crucifixion—"His blood be on vs, and on our children" (Matthew 27.25)—in his "My deeds upon my head!" (4.1.201), he stands not only for the fleshly law of circumcision and for Abraham's near sacrifice of Isaac but also for the definitively "Jewish" crime of deicide.[42]

Hence perhaps the spatial indeterminacy of the incision Shylock would make in Antonio, an indeterminacy that allows it the multiple meaning of a dream. Initially unspecified, located only in what part of Antonio's body pleases Shylock (1.3.146–47), it is first localized in the foreskin through the frequent repetitions of the word "forfeit" and Shylock's near pun as he whets his knife "to cut the forfeit from that bankrupt there" (4.1.121). But in the course of the trial the incision migrates upward. Portia tells the court that the Jew's bond entitles him to "A pound of flesh, to be by him cut off / Nearest the merchant's heart," and Shylock echoes, "'Nearest his heart'—those are the very words" (4.1.227–28, 249). When Shylock first says that he "will have the heart of him if he forfeit" (3.1.105–6), the phrase can be heard as metaphorical, but it is literalized in 4.1, as though Shylock would in fact replay the wound of the crucifixion—the wound that traditionally displayed Christ's heart—in Antonio.[43] But Portia's twice-repeated "cut off" (4.1.227, 297) works to keep the location of the incision equivocal, since (at least in a male) flesh can more easily be cut off from the genitals than from the area nearest the heart.[44] Simultaneously a wound in the genitals and nearest the heart, the incision that Shylock would make thus condenses circumcision with crucifixion, as in the ritual murders that sometimes allegedly combined the two.[45] He thus offers economically to reenact, now, in full view of the audience, both the threat of adherence to the fleshly law and the crime that confirmed Jewish guilt—and Jewish difference—in perpetuity.

Paul had suggested in Galatians that the danger from the children of the flesh is perpetual; *Merchant* suggests that, even in the absence of openly observant Jews, English Christians at the end of the sixteenth century still needed that sense of a specifically Jewish danger in order to confirm their status as children of the promise. Hence I think the rhetorical utility of Foxe's construction of the nonexistent Jews in his audience as though they had been present at the crucifixion and were still a clear and present danger,[46] and hence his bizarre exhortation—"englut therefor thy greedie guts with goare"—that they continue to enact their blood-guiltiness now, in the present, as though they were caught in a kind of temporal Möbius strip, doomed perpetually to repeat the defining moment of their Jewishness.[47] And before Portia's last-minute rescue, *Merchant* promises to obey this mandate, reproducing the bloodthirsty Jew in Shylock in order to satisfy its audience's need. I have so far avoided the question of whether or not the play is "anti-Semitic," both on the grounds that the question has anachronistic implications and on the grounds that any answer must be relative (anti-Semitic compared to what? Marlowe?). But insofar as the figure of the Jew with the knife draws on the ancient image of Jews as Christ-killers and ritual murderers, it will be anti-Semitic in effect, no matter how "humanized" Shylock is at certain moments—just as *Othello*'s final invocation of a violent sexualized act between a black man and a white woman will be racist in effect, no matter how much sympathy accrues to its protagonist. In fact *Merchant*, like Foxe's *Sermon*, illustrates a troubling dynamic between the "human-izing" of the Jew and his bemonstering.[48] The liberal hope is that seeing the "humanity" of our enemies—seeing that they are people like us—will make a difference in how we treat them, but both play and sermon suggest otherwise: in both, I think, it is exactly the guilt attendant on seeing that likeness that needs to be warded off by the reassurance that the Jew is not fully human after all.

But *Merchant* is not simply anti-Semitic. Though it creates a monstrous Jew as it reproduces the threat of circumcision and crucifixion in 4.1, it also allows us to see what needs that creation fulfills, for its characters as well as its audience. For at the same time as the play encourages us to read Shylock realistically, as though a "real" Jew, given such provocation, might become the monster of his legendary past, it also makes clear the extent to which he is merely a creature of the play, motivated by fantasies altogether outside his "character"—particularly those invested in the figure of Antonio. Shylock's threat to reproduce circumcision and crucifixion—in other words—turns on itself, exposing Antonio as well as Shylock: though Shylock is their exter-nal agent, both threats are generated as much from Antonio's needs as from Shylock. I have already noted that Antonio calls himself the "tainted wether of the flock" in 4.1, as though the wound that Shylock would make in him would only confirm what he already recognizes in himself. Circumcision may be the Jew's way of replicating himself in the Christian, but for Anto-nio, it would be the sign of an already-existing shame and sexual taint—a sign that he is curiously eager to display. And if Shylock makes a satisfying Christ-killer in 4.1, Antonio makes a rather odd Christ.[49] He may specialize in delivering men from forfeitures (3.3.22)—a word to which Isabella's "all the souls that were were forfeit once" (*Measure for Measure*, 2.2.75) gives the proper theological weight—and his willingness to sacrifice his life in order to satisfy Bassanio's debt may echo the language of Christ's sacrifice. But he is no sacrificial lamb: he is a ram, and a castrated one at that; according to the old laws, he could not stand for sacrifice.[50] And he is in any case a little too willing to embrace the knife, and too eager to have Bassanio witness his own private *imitatio Christi* ("Pray God Bassanio come / To see me pay his debt, and then I care not"; 3.3.35–36). His final words before Portia deprives him of the opportunity for sacrifice are these:

> Repent but you that you shall lose your friend,
> And he repents not that he pays your debt;
> For if the Jew do cut but deep enough,
> I'll pay it instantly, with all my heart. (4.1.273–76)

(No wonder he stands silent for ninety-nine lines—ninety-nine lines! what is an actor supposed to be doing during all this time?—while Portia works out the terms of his release: she deprives him of the chance to display his heart to Bassanio.) In his simultaneous shame and desire for exposure, he is a very imperfect imitation of Christ; he more closely resembles one of the figures that accrued to the story of the self-circumcising deacon in *Holinshed's Chronicles:* the hermaphrodite who would display his wounds as Christ.

When Shylock offers to incise Antonio simultaneously in his genitals and in his heart, he satisfyingly confirms his own bondage to the letter once again by enacting a grotesque literalization of the familiar Pauline trope with which I began this chapter, or rather of the pithier phrase from Deuteronomy 10.16—"circumcise therefore the foreskin of your heart"—on which it is based. The contrast between circumcisions of the foreskin and heart signaled the shift from the outward observance of the law to the inward observance of the spirit; thus Donne can say that "the Jewish Circumcision were an absurd and unreasonable thing, if it did not intimate and figure the Circumcision of the heart,"[51] and Foxe can taunt his imaginary audience of Jews with their literal-minded failure to understand this figurative shift ("You do vaunt your selues lustily in speach of the circumcision of your foreskinnes, and your vncircumcised hearts ouerflowe with spyderlike poyson"; *Sermon*, E4v). The double location of Antonio's wound in 4.1 apparently allows Shylock to try to collapse this distinction: knife in hand, he would literally circumcise the foreskin of Antonio's heart, as though he were incapable of understanding what the move from flesh to spirit meant.[52] So far, so good. But when Shakespeare gives us an Antonio who runs to meet the Jew's knife, he troubles the tidiness of this theological demonstration. For in his literalizing actions, Shylock acts as an alibi for needs interior to Antonio: circumcision of the foreskin would correspond to—and cover for—Antonio's identification of himself as a tainted wether of the flock, meetest for death; and circumcision of the heart would allow him to display his wounded heart to Bassanio, as though that incision could turn him into a replica of the fifteenth-century Christ who said "Lo! here my hert."[53]

Shakespeare—in other words—complicates the play's theological discourse by anticipating Shylock's intended outer wounds in Antonio's inward man. And in so doing, he oddly duplicates the logic of Paul's move from circumcision of the flesh to circumcision of the heart, but with an entirely different valence. In its original context, Paul's insistence that "he is not a Iewe, which is one outwarde: nether is that circumcision, which is outwarde in the flesh: But he is a Iewe which is one within, & the circumcision is of the heart, in the spirit" (Romans 2.28–29) works to universalize God's promise to his chosen people by spiritualizing—and thus enlarging—the category of the Jew. But that insistence opened up a potentially troublesome inward space (the Geneva Bible's gloss to "spirit" here is "in the inwarde man & heart") and, with it, a potentially troublesome new definition of the Jew. No longer marked by externals, Jewishness became an inner condition, a condition that anyone could share; and once its valance had changed from positive to negative, the idea of an unseen interior Jewishness could become both a handy polemical tool and a source of individual shame.[54] In the confrontation between Shylock and Antonio, Shakespeare plays out the potential of this troubling inner space: Shylock may demonstrate his "Jewish" literal-mindedness when he attempts to circumcise Antonio's heart, but his incision of Antonio threatens to expose what the play construes as the taint of Antonio's Jew within.

⟨∞⟩

When Shylock threatens to open Antonio up, he literalizes a discourse of interiority that is everywhere in *Merchant*, a play famously obsessed with interiors. The most obvious dramatic emblem for this obsession is the caskets; "I am locked in one of them," Portia tells Bassanio (3.2.40), and all three suitors engage explicitly with the problem of interiors as they make their choices.[55] But seen from the vantage point of Shylock's proposed opening up of Antonio, these interiors are curiously bloodless, and the lesson they teach—"so may the outward shows be least themselves" (3.2.73)—is too tame to require such extensive treatment. In the relation of its two plots, the play seems to me to enact a displacement of sorts, as though the fantasy-structure underlying the play required the reiterated image of a showing forth of what is inside, but only if it could be kept safely distanced from the Antonio-Shylock plot. With its reliance on safe aphorisms and its fairy-tale atmosphere, the casket-choice scenes could hardly be more distanced. But the fairy tale of Belmont becomes the nightmare of 4.1, and the language provoked by the casket plot insistently returns us to Shylock's knife, in effect undoing that distance after all. Morocco initiates the casket choices by offering to "make incision for [Portia's] love" (2.1.6); Bassanio's reference to cowards, "Who, inward searched, have livers white as milk" (3.2.86), similarly invokes the image of the knife.[56] Faced with the caskets, Aragon prides himself on his capacity to see beyond "the fool multitude . . . Which pries not to th'interior" (2.9.25–27); but the first—and last—interior the play invites its audience to pry into is Antonio's.

The play opens in the mysterious domain of Antonio's sadness; his—

and the play's—first words are "In sooth, I know not why I am so sad."
For the next one hundred lines, Antonio continues to fend off his friends'
attempts to pry into the causes of his sadness, and perhaps to fend off his
own self-knowledge as well: Antonio may, like Hamlet, have that within
which passes show, but unlike Hamlet (and *Hamlet*) Antonio takes no delight in self-analysis. He doesn't know "what stuff [his sadness is] made of,"
"whereof it is born," or how he "caught it, found it, or came by it" (1.1.4, 3),
and he apparently doesn't want to know; he interrupts his contemplation of
its origins with an extraordinary three-beat silence (l. 5), as though he would
like to curtail scrutiny—or perhaps as though there is nothing within him
to scrutinize.[57] When Graziano accuses Antonio of assuming a "wilful stillness" (1.1.90) like a death monument, his contrast between warm blood and
cold alabaster—"Why should a man whose blood is warm within / Sit like
his grandsire cut in alabaster?" (1.1.83–84)—images one of the desires that
seem to underwrite this melancholic silence: the silent man cut in alabaster
would (like Erasmus's "marble simulacrum of a man")[58] have no interior to
pry into, no warm blood and no messy passions within. And for the most
part, the play respects Antonio's silence: if it begins by opening up the space
of Antonio's interior, it almost immediately forecloses that space, terminat-
ing the conversation about his sadness and removing him from center stage
for much of the play. This is a very peculiar beginning: it makes his melancholy into a kind of prologue to or unacknowledged premise of a play apparently as determined as Antonio is to traffic mainly in exteriors—exteriors
that will give him ample excuse for his sadness in an ex-post-facto sort of
way. But those exteriors seem to lead inexorably to the opening up of his
messy interior after all: the danger of self-exposure that Antonio's silence
manages to deflect in the play's opening moments returns in graphically
literal form when he faces Shylock's knife.

Leslie Fiedler years ago called the Antonio of *Twelfth Night* the "'shaman-
ized' dreamer" of his play, and that resonant if somewhat mysterious phrase
seems to me to apply even more aptly to *Merchant*'s Antonio.[59] For the in-
nards concealed in the prologue in effect spill out dreamlike into the action
of the play, into a plot that threatens to open him up and a set of literalized
metaphors that express what he does not want to know that he has within.
Antonio responds to Solanio's speculation that he may be sad because he
is in love with "Fie, fie" (1.1.46), dismissing—rather than answering—the
question, but his interpreters have not been satisfied with his dismissal; it
has become a critical commonplace that his sadness is a consequence of his
homoerotically charged feeling for Bassanio, who is about to leave him, trad-
ing in their relationship for marriage.[60] (Solanio himself suggests as much

when he refers to Antonio's "embracèd heaviness" immediately after Salerio has described Antonio's tearful parting from Bassanio [2.8.52]: as though
Antonio welcomes his sadness as the residue of their relationship, embracing it in place of Bassanio.) And if what Antonio's silence in 1.1 defends
him against is knowledge of his desire for Bassanio, that desire everywhere
leaks out, not only in (for example) his melancholy insistence that he does
not mind dying as long as Bassanio is present at his death (3.3.35–36) or in
the contest he sets up with Portia in 4.1—"Commend me to your honourable wife. . . . Say how I loved you. . . . bid her be judge / Whether Bassanio
had not once a love" (4.1.268–72)—but also in plot elements that provide
a displaced and unacknowledged language for what is concealed within: a
language of ships and blood and wounds to the heart.

When Antonio's rent ship turns up under Shylock's eaves in 2.6, it serves
as a trope for the perils of desire satisfied; but beleaguered ships are also traditional tropes for the turmoil of love frustrated. Salerio sets this traditional
trope in motion when he speculates at the very beginning of the play that
Antonio's "mind is tossing on the ocean" (1.1.8)—a speculation that turns
Antonio's ships into allegorical figures for his mind, enabling us to read the
damage they suffer as an enactment of the storms of love, just as a Petrarch
or a Britomart might do.[61] (This figure for frustrated love does its work well:
the letter reporting on the loss of Antonio's ships reaches Bassanio immediately after he has won Portia, and it has the effect of forestalling their
wedding night. Score one for Antonio's buried fantasy life, though it is only
a temporary victory.) The blood that Antonio would shed in the plot has a
similarly figural relation to his desire. When Bassanio tells Antonio, "The
Jew shall have my flesh, blood, bones, and all / Ere thou shalt lose for me
one drop of blood" (4.1.111–12), he unintentionally mobilizes the language
of love-longing that underwrites Antonio's would-be blood sacrifice. Early
on, Graziano has reminded us that mortifying groans drain blood from the
heart (1.1.82);[62] if Antonio's sighs are any indication, he has already lost at
least one drop of blood for Bassanio. The two languages of blood—the blood
that Shylock would shed and the blood that Antonio's love-melancholy has
already cost him—collide in Bassanio's speech, as though Shylock's knife
would merely externalize the loss of blood that Antonio has already suffered
within. And in the most grotesque plot-externalization of Antonio's concealed emotion, Shylock's determination to "have the heart" of Antonio
(3.1.105) would put that heart on display, simultaneously exposing the
wound that Bassanio's voyage to Portia has made in him and the debt of
love that he would pay "with all [his] heart" (4.1.276).

"Lay bare your bosom," Portia instructs Antonio (4.1.247), deploying the traditional language for self-disclosure in a graphically literal register.[63] If Antonio refuses to confess to his friends in the play's opening scene, the plot confesses for him: as in a dream, it generates representations for the desire that Antonio cannot know or allow others to know, projecting it outward as though it had nothing to do with him. And yet these projections all return to Antonio's own body, in effect betraying their origins. Shylock's proposed exposure of Antonio's heart and his blood "warm within" (1.1.83) is the most obvious instance, but the ships enact the same return. I have already suggested that the rent ship that figures the danger of desire is tantamount to Antonio's own body; Bassanio in fact underscores this equivalence of ship and body when he responds to the news of Antonio's losses in words that transfer the touch of the rocks from the vessel to the body of the merchant ("not one vessel scape the dreadful touch / Of merchant-marring rocks?" 3.2.269–70).[64] The letter reporting on the loss of the ships thus becomes "the body of my friend," with every word "a gaping wound / Issuing life-blood" (3.2.263–65), as though the reported rupture in Antonio's ships were a rupture in Antonio himself. (Hence in part the quasi-magical fate of Antonio's ships in the fantasy that undergirds the plot: once Portia has succeeded in forestalling the rupture in Antonio, she can return his ships to him intact as well.) And if Antonio's ships betray their origins as projection, they also betray the complex of emotions that necessitates projection as an expression of a concealed inwardness, for they concretely embody not only the dangers of desire but also the dangerous pleasure of display. Almost as soon as we learn that Antonio has ships, we are asked to imagine them as ruptured, their contents spilling out:

> Should I go to church
> And see the holy edifice of stone
> And not bethink me straight of dangerous rocks
> Which, touching but my gentle vessel's side,
> Would scatter all her spices on the stream,
> Enrobe the roaring waters with my silks,
> And, in a word, but even now worth this,
> And now worth nothing? (1.1.29–36)

This is a gorgeous image—virtually the only moment of visual beauty permitted in Venice—but it terminates in "nothing." And though Salerio's image perfectly anticipates the fate of Antonio's ships, it is (I think) driven less by the romance of mercantile risk than by a fantasy of the personal annihilation—the "nothing"—to which such a gorgeous spilling out of inner contents would lead.

Graziano calls attention to the warm blood within the gentle merchant shortly after Salerio's image of gorgeous annihilation; that image of spices and silks pouring out of the "gentle" vessel seems to me to anticipate the potential flow of that warm blood.[65] For the image functions, I think, as something like an aestheticization of Antonio's inner contents: both the desires hidden in his bosom and the blood that would figure their exposure. As such, it may serve in part as a substitute satisfaction for the audience's desire to see what is inside him—the desire thwarted both here in 1.1 and in 4.1, when Portia forbids the flow of his blood. And if it suggests the dangers of self-exposure—the "nothing" Antonio risks becoming—it also encodes Antonio's own ambivalent desire for such an opening up. Salerio's image is placed in response to Antonio's attempt both to call attention to and to deny access to his insides because it so perfectly expresses the dread and desire bound up with that outpouring: it images Antonio's body as a container of riches—its own variant of infinite riches in a little room—made visible only by the touch that would annihilate him. In its evocation of a distinctly human agency and a distinctly animate sensation, Salerio's word "touching"—oddly gentle for the action of rock upon ship and echoed in Bassanio's "touch / Of merchant-marring rocks"—may gesture toward Antonio's desire for this rupturing touch,[66] for Antonio in fact imagines himself being opened up in extremity for his friend not long after Salerio invokes his gorgeously ruptured ship. Bassanio has just approached him to ask for the money to woo Portia, carefully reassuring Antonio that his love is still directed toward him, not her: "To you, Antonio, / I owe the most in money and in love" (130–31). Money has apparently long been the currency of love in their relationship; in response, Antonio registers his longing to be opened up to—or by—Bassanio in the only terms available to him:

> Be assured
> My purse, my person, my extremest means
> Lie all unlocked to your occasions. (1.1.137–39)

My purse, my person: the equivalence simultaneously underscores Antonio's erotic fantasy and marks its limits: spending his wealth appears to be the only form of spending himself that he can articulate, and unlocking his purse the only form of unlocking his person.[67] No wonder the merchant and his ships tend to become indistinguishable.

If being ruptured and spilling one's inside contents make one "nothing," that is also a consummation devoutly to be wished, or so the proximity of Salerio's gorgeous image with Antonio's offer to unlock himself purse and person to Bassanio suggests. Blood, semen, silk, spices: all seem to me to flow together in the fantasy that equates the emptying of gentle ship and gentle merchant. And because the play uses the language of the body to express the inwardness of the self, this prodigal outpouring seems to me to express not only the sexual desire to be opened up but also the desire to be known inwardly after all, as though that desire were the undertow to Antonio's determination both to display his sadness and to deflect inquiry into its causes. Or at least to be known inwardly by Bassanio. When Bassanio responds to Antonio's offer to unlock himself purse and person with his extended arrow metaphor, as though he has not really understood the offer,[68] Antonio accuses him of doing him wrong, allowing himself his only moment of anger with Bassanio in the play:

> You know me well, and herein spend but time
> To wind about my love with circumstance;
> And out of doubt you do me now more wrong
> In making question of my uttermost
> Than if you had made waste of all I have. (1.1.153–57)

What Antonio wants Bassanio to know is his willingness to be in extremity for him (1.1.138), to spend himself to the uttermost (1.1.156, 181); such self-spending is in fact his only means of making himself known. Bassanio's casual refusal of this knowledge[69]—he does not want to hear what Antonio has just said; he winds about Antonio's love with circumstance, treating him as though he were any rich man to be cajoled—is worse for Antonio than if Bassanio had made waste of all he has: worse, because it transforms the nature of the offer, making Antonio's fantasy-gift of his uttermost, his unlocking of purse and person, into a merely financial transaction.

In the relation between its two plots, the play literalizes the emotional equivalence that turns a failure of acknowledgment into absolute ruin in this passage. The greater Bassanio's emotional distance from Antonio—he apparently does not give him a moment's thought in Belmont—the more the ships that Antonio has mortgaged for him founder, right up until 3.2, where the two plots cross. And there, Bassanio's successful wooing of Portia is followed immediately by the news of Antonio's disastrous losses, as though the one were magically the consequence of the other: as though Bassanio's unknowing of Antonio had in fact succeeded in making waste of all Antonio has. But with Shylock's help the play reverses this trajectory, turning ruin back into a form of acknowledgment after all. For if Antonio wants to put himself—his body, not only his money—at the uttermost extremity for Bassanio in order to be known by him, Shylock's bizarre offer to substitute flesh for money comes as though in answer to this desire.[70] No wonder Antonio embraces the bargain so willingly: Shylock both literalizes and gives an alibi for Antonio's initial desire to be unlocked purse and person for Bassanio, to be known inside out by him. From the beginning, Antonio's desire to be at his uttermost has expressed itself in the language of judicial torture: "Do but say to me what I should do . . . And I am pressed unto it," he tells Bassanio (1.1.158–60); "Try what my credit can in Venice do; / That shall be racked even to the uttermost" (1.1.180–81). And confession is familiarly the end of such torture: when Bassanio later tells Portia that he "live[s] upon the rack," she responds, "Upon the rack, Bassanio? Then confess . . ." (3.2.25–26). Shylock may imagine his bargain with Antonio as a form of torture—"I'll torture him," he says when he hears of the lost ships (3.1.96)—but Antonio himself generates the presence of the torturer well before Shylock appears onstage, as though only torture could extract the confession that Antonio wants both to conceal and to make, the confession displaced into the Bassanio-Portia plot when Bassanio says, "'Confess and love'" (3.2.35). Shylock thus becomes the agent of Antonio's ambivalent desire for self-disclosure. "Lay bare your bosom," Portia says, echoing the implicit instruction not only of the priest but also of the torturer who would extract a confession; and Antonio finally complies, undressing himself onstage before Bassanio and the audience, preparing for the ultimate disclosure of Shylock's knife.

This is an extraordinary moment. After what amounts to the scene's— and the play's—slow striptease, the man who would not disclose himself in 1.1 stands half-naked on stage for at least seventy long lines while Shylock prepares to make incision into him.[71] Shakespeare is much more restrained here than Nashe, whose protagonist, similarly faced with the Jew's knife, dreams of the "smooth-edged razor tenderly slicing down my breast and sides,"[72] but his scene is similarly erotically charged: it simultaneously feeds the audience's voyeuristic bloodlust and promises Antonio masochistic satisfaction of his desire to unlock himself to Bassanio. Better: in one economical gesture, it promises to provide both satisfaction of and punishment for the desire that would rend him. For insofar as Shylock's proposed circumcision is of both heart and foreskin—insofar as it fuses the two organs in grotesque fulfillment of the command to circumcise the foreskin of the heart—it would simultaneously serve to open up his heart for inspection and to punish the offending organ for the desire thus revealed.[73] Or rather to externalize the punishment that Antonio already feels within, for Shylock's circumcision/castration of him would come as a kind of objective correlative to his internal state as the wether of the flock, already tainted, and unmanned by his desire.[74] In that sense, Shylock's punishment of him would be tantamount to his own confession: it would in effect inscribe his inside on his outside, making his desire and his shame visible to all.

But I think it would be a mistake to read this scene of exposure only in terms of the particulars of Antonio's sexual desire. If the caskets' disclosure of interiors at the center of the play (3.2) rather patly instructs us not to judge insides by outsides, the trajectory from 1.1 to 4.1 unfolds a much more troubled discourse about interiors. Antonio's—and the play's—first words are "In sooth I know not why"; through him, the play seems to me to express the deep pathos of a man who cannot fully know his own desires and cannot allow others to know them, for whom being known would be tantamount in fantasy to being excruciatingly opened up to view—and who nonetheless wants nothing more than to be known. Let me be clear that I would not consider this ambivalence only the product of Antonio's "closeted" subjectivity even if a fully formed subjectivity founded on sexual desire were not in all likelihood an anachronism. The direction of Antonio's desires may complicate his self-exposure, but it does not entirely determine the fantasies through which it is represented; at a time when one's innermost self was increasingly available to be construed as one's own inviolable private space, subjectivity itself may begin to take on the aspect of the closet.[75] In its representation of Antonio's concealed inwardness and his ambivalent desire for exposure, Merchant seems to me to anticipate not only Hamlet's noisier insistence that he has something inaccessible within but also this developing sense of the self; and Antonio's ambivalent desire for self-exposure catches exactly the dilemma of this private self in its most painful form. One of the foremost modern theorists of selfhood suggests that our most private selves are by definition closeted, by definition subject to the beauty and terror of being known: in his view, we are all subject to the "inherent dilemma, which belongs to the co-existence of two trends, the urgent need to communicate and the still more urgent need not to be found"; and although "it is joy to be hidden," it is "disaster not to be found."[76] Salerio's gorgeous image of Antonio's ship spilling its contents seems to me the condensed expression of this beauty and terror: its prodigal outpouring of inner contents enriches the world—it scatters spices like seeds and dresses the waters in silk robes—but it ends in inner impoverishment and annihilation, in "nothing."

For things can be opened up—can have their insides disclosed—without shedding blood; people can't. At least they can't in this play, where Antonio's body provides the language of disclosure, and Shylock provides the means.

Shylock provides the means: for Antonio gets the Shylock he needs to express his ambivalent desires, including the desire not to know what he knows. In this sense, Shylock is the largest and most effective of Antonio's projections: he comes as though in answer to Antonio's dream of being at his uttermost for Bassanio, being opened up for and to him. Shylock is in effect the literalist who enables the plot's enactment of Antonio's desire: through him, the play that initially appears to be about Antonio's mysterious sadness turns into a play about the bloodthirstiness of the Jew, bound to the law of the body; and in this play, Antonio can imagine himself—and his audience can imagine him—as a pure sacrificial victim on the analogue of Christ, without ever having to acknowledge his desires. And Shakespeare? Dramatic characters are all to some extent partial authorial projections, insofar as they give satisfyingly concrete outer expression to internal phenomena, externalizing the theater of the inner world. But the extent to which the Antonio-Shylock plot—the lost ships, Shylock's bargain, and the ambiguous location of Shylock's incision—appears to be generated out of the unacknowledged fragments of Antonio's desire, and the recurrence in the Portia-Bassanio plot of phrases more resonant for the Antonio plot—"I stand for sacrifice"; "Confess and love"—suggest Shakespeare's unusual complicity in Antonio's ambivalent unknowing: as though he too wanted to find a way of simultaneously making himself known and concealing himself onstage through this collaboration of victim and victimizer.[77]

For all this, the Jew with the knife is both the agent and the scapegoat, the figure who must be punished for his proposed enactment of Antonio's unacceptable desire to be opened up and known. Shylock is ideally suited to perform this function, and to be punished for it: in him, older anxieties about the Christ-killing Jew who allegedly circumcises and performs ritual murders are conjoined with newer anxieties about the Jew who can (in Aragon's resonant phrase) pry to the interior. In a particularly contemporary twist to the worry that the Jewish physician has a special and dangerous access to the insides of bodies, the Jew who wields that eroticized knife in *The Unfortunate Traveller* is an anatomist, and—at least in Jack Wilton's fantasies of death by bleeding—an anatomist who practices his craft specifically on live bodies.[78] The image of Shylock poised with his knife seems to me to be a version of the same figure: even as he acts to fulfill Antonio's unacknowledged desire, he provides a locus for the terror that one's insides could be literally exposed against one's will, like those of the coward who is found out when his milk-white liver is "inward searched" by the surgeon-anatomist that Bassanio imagines (3.2.86). When Lear imagines the "trial" of his daughters, he invokes the figure of the anatomist—"Then let them anatomize Regan; see what breeds about her heart" (3.6.32, 70–71)—as though opening her up could give him all the evidence he needs.[79] Although it is never clear exactly who or what is being tried, 4.1 of *Merchant* is similarly structured like a trial, with Antonio as the subject to be opened up and Shylock as the anatomist.

Or rather as the anatomist-inquisitor. I argued in the last chapter that *Merchant*'s concern with the status of converts (forced or not) and with purity of blood invokes the offstage presence of the Inquisition; the play's allusions to racking and confession—in Protestant accounts the standard juridical procedures of the Inquisition[80]—similarly prime the audience to sense its shadowy presence. And in 4.1, one of the anxieties that attach to that presence is given substantiation onstage: when Shylock offers to anatomize Antonio, prying into his interior in the most literal way possible, he fuses with the terrifying figure of the Inquisitor, the anatomist of souls who would—in Bacon's memorable phrase—"make windows into men's hearts and secret thoughts."[81] For the Inquisitor threatens to breach the barrier of the self, demonstrating that one's interior can be exposed against one's will, that one can be known as it were inside out. William Warner thus warns that the Inquisitors "will exact by Torture what thou thinkest, and hast thought"; Montanus, that the victim of the Inquisitors "must nedes vtter himselfe, and playnly shew what he is in conscience and belief."[82] This is, I think, the fear given a local habitation in *Merchant*'s anatomizing Jew, whose ambiguously located circumcision would literally cut a window into Antonio's heart, in effect making theater out of his self-display. The Inquisition was in fact accused of making theater out of just this kind of exposure. Foxe describes the "three mighty Theatries or stages" erected for the sentencing of thirty prisoners brought before the Inquisition in 1559, along with the "infinite multitude of all sorts of the world there standing, and gazing out of windows and houses to hear and see the sentences and judgments of this inquisition," and the marginal note enthusiastically adds "Three stages."[83] And for Montanus, the Inquisitorial trial itself is a combination of anatomy and theater:

there is a scaffold reared, where the Inquisitour, the Prouisor, & the
Clearke do sit, to see the Anatomie made of him that is brought the [sic]
them. Then the linkes being lighted, and al the players entred that haue
partes in this tragedie, the Executioner . . . commeth also at the length,
and of him selfe alone maketh a shew worthy the sight . . . being wholy
arayed all ouer from the toppe of hys head, to the soule of his foote in a
sute of blacke canuas . . . much like that apparell that the deuils in stage
playes vse here with vs in England.[84]

Here with us in England: part of the power of 4.1, I think, lies in its oblique
re-creation of this "Inquisitours Theatre,"[85] in which the interior self could
be anatomized and "playnly shew[n]." In Antonio's long striptease and Shylock's whetting of the knife, the scene seems to me calculated to invoke both
the terror and the scandalously pleasurable theatricality of this involuntary
self-exposure.

It may seem bizarre to associate the Jew Shylock with the figure of the
Inquisitor, especially given that Jews were known in England to have been
among the Inquisition's first victims in Spain.[86] But Protestants often accused Catholics of Judaizing, the Spanish were familiarly considered at least
half Jewish, and the Spanish Inquisition itself was routinely considered a
"Jewish" institution, a "popish Sinogoge" in which the Inquisitors and their
associates were routinely branded as Jews.[87] The apparent complicity of the
Jew Lopez with the Spanish—"that *Spanish-Iewish Atheist*," Warner calls
him[88]—would have recently shored up the association; and the ravenous
wolfishness that links Shylock to Lopez in name—his desires are "wolfish,
bloody, starved, and ravenous," according to Graziano (4.1.137)—echoes one
standard trope for the Inquisitors, who are "woluish & rauening" throughout
Montanus's *Discouery*.[89] The complex of avarice and cannibalism associated
with Shylock would similarly link him with popular representations of the
Inquisitors, who "haue drawen the very bloud to deuoure it" and who "seeke
to sucke [their victims'] bloud," "like bloudy butchers, [who] continually
thirst after bloud";[90] as expected, the servants of the Inquisitorial idol in *The
Faerie Queene* "sacrifice / The flesh of men . . . And [pour] forth their bloud
in brutishe wize" to him, and the monster beneath the idol "deuoures" these
sacrificial victims, "both flesh and bone" (5.10.28–29). And like the Inquisitors, Shylock stands specifically for a bloody perversion of law: according to
Montanus, the Inquisitors "vnderstand by this word law extreme tormenting
and mangling of men"; according to Warner, "A bloodier Law vsde bloodi-
erly was neuer heard or shall."[91] As Shylock prepares to make his incision
into Antonio, he is therefore ideally suited to represent this "Inquisitours

Theatre": Inquisitor and historical victim of the Inquisition change places as Shylock prepares to make a window into the heart of Antonio, forcing him—or is it enabling him?—to "utter himself" in the flow of his blood.

Portia forestalls this flow, and specifically in the name of Christian blood: she tells Shylock "if thou dost shed / One drop of Christian blood, thy lands and goods / Are by the laws of Venice confiscate / Unto the state of Venice" (4.1.304–7). But why this specification? Portia has already told Shylock that the bond gives him "no jot of blood" of any kind (4.1.301); the absence of generic blood in the bond presumably would have served to best Shylock in his own domain of law without further specification, as it does in the source tale. So why is "Christian" necessary? Perhaps because an unspoken anxiety about the blood that Antonio would shed dominates 4.1. When Bassanio tells Portia that all the wealth he has runs in his veins (3.2.253–54), he makes a claim to inner riches—and to an aristocratic blood difference—that legitimizes his claim to her, despite his outer poverty. But what wealth runs in Antonio's veins? If I am right in reading Salerio's gentle vessel as a trope for Antonio's gentile body, then the play enables the fantasy that Antonio's inner contents would enrobe—and ennoble—the world (1.1.34), that his blood would be salvific in a secular vein. But what if the wealth that runs in Antonio's veins is no different from the Jew's wealth? This is the possibility that Shylock himself insists on (3.1.54) and that the play comes dangerously close to exhibiting in 4.1. That scene famously worries the signs of difference between Christian and Jew: Portia's opening question—"Which is the merchant here, and which the Jew?"—comes in response to the Duke's asking her if she is "acquainted with the difference / That holds this present question in the court" (4.1.169, 166–67), a formulation that exceeds its application to the legal dispute between Shylock and Antonio, turning the difference between them itself into the question in the court. And if at the end the Duke can happily reify "the difference of our spirit" (4.1.363), he can do so I think exactly because Portia has reinstated the blood difference that subtends all other differences in the scene.

Taken together, the most common bodily marks of the Jew—circumcision and the blood taint of hemorrhoids and male menstruation—encode a set of anxieties about genital damage and feminization that are registered through his blood: already set apart by the incision of his genitals, the Jew bleeds like a woman.[92] But those anxieties are localized not in Shylock but in the Antonio who would spill his contents. His desire to be unlocked to Bassanio would merely find its externalization in Shylock's bloody incision of him; internally, he tells us, he is already a circumcised/castrated and thus feminized Jew (4.1.113). (No wonder his female ship—another stand-in for his ruptured body—appears under the Jew's eaves as a trope for the perils of bodily love.) And if the shape of his desire would put him in proximity to the feminized Jew, the flow of his blood would underscore the likeness, and not only because it would give him the Jew's "leaky" body.[93] The very quality of Antonio's blood would undo his difference from the Jew, for all men can bleed like a woman when they are subject to melancholy blood. Here, for instance, is *The Problemes of Aristotle*—a popular compendium of beliefs largely about the humoral causes of various diseases and conditions—on the subject of hemorrhoids:

> Question. *Why haue some men the piles?*
> Answer. Bicause they are cold and melancholike [which causes an over-abundance of melancholy blood to reach certain veins in the back.] And when those vaines are very full of melancholy blood, then the waies and conduits of nature are opened, and that blood issueth out once a moneth like a womans tearmes or flowers.[94]

As though to reinstate the difference that this passage threatens to obscure, *Problemes* immediately goes on to specify that monthly bleeding does have a special relation to Jewish men after all:

> Question. *Why are the Iewes subiect vnto this disease very much?*
> Answer. The Diuines do say, bicause they cried at the death of Christ, *Let his blood fall vpon vs and our children.*[95]

But this reassuring difference dissolves as *Problemes* turns back from the theological to the humoral frame of reference on which it habitually draws:

> Another reason is, bicause the Iewes do eate much fleugmatike and cold meats, which doth breed melancholy blood, which is purged by this fluxe of blood. Another reason is, bicause moouing doth cause heat, & heat digestion . . . but the Iewes do not mooue nor labor, nor conuerse with men. Also they liue in great fear, lest we should reuenge the death our Sauiour [sic], which doth also breed a coldnes in them, which doth hinder digestion, which doth breed much melancholy blood in them, which is by this meanes purged.[96]

In this final mix of dietary, social, and psychological causes for the Jews' subjection to this disease, Jewish blood turns out to look very much like Christian blood—in fact to look specifically like Antonio's blood, made melancholy (1.1.101), his friends speculate, by his fear, his "wilful stillness" (1.1.90), and his withdrawal from the conversation of men.

Merchant recuperates blood difference, I suggest, exactly by locating it in the theological domain that *Problemes* invokes and then obscures. When Shylock echoes the cry routinely attributed to Jews at the Crucifixion, he invokes not only the Jews' status as Christ-killers but also the set of blood diseases that were widely believed to originate in that blood curse: not only bleeding hemorrhoids (as *Problemes* would have it) but male menstruation, the monthly appearance of the bloody sores that cause *foetor judaicus,* and such oddities as the birth of all Jewish children with bloody fingers affixed to their foreheads.[97] These diseases marked Jews specifically as Jews in their blood, not proto-racially, through inheritance, but theologically, as a consequence of their killing of Christ; and they provided a rationale for the alleged ritual murders in which the Jews compulsively repeated that act. For the primary object of those murders was the acquisition of Christian blood: blood that the Jews needed not only for their Jewish ceremonies—circumcision, the anointing of rabbis, the making of matzah, and the like—but also to cure the blood diseases that marked them as Jews.[98] The ritual-murder accusations of the blood libel thus depended conceptually on the belief that Jewish blood was entirely distinct from Christian blood: when the Jew replicated the Crucifixion in those murders, he thereby replicated the originating moment of his own blood difference, the very blood difference that (circularly) required such a murder for its cure.

When Portia prevents Shylock from shedding Christian blood, she reminds us that the difference between Jewish and Christian blood is the subtext of the ritual murder that Shylock would enact onstage: prosecutors of alleged murderers in the ritual-murder trials routinely plagued their victims until they confessed that they needed specifically Christian blood, and guidelines drawn up for the interrogators routinely asked, "To which Jews was the blood given? What was the blood used for? Do they need blood from a Christian child every year and why?"[99] Shylock may have earlier claimed that Jews are "subject to the same diseases, healed by the same means" (3.1.52–53), but at least some in his audience would have known better: they would have felt the special *frisson* of self-confirming horror when he disingenuously asks, "If he should break his day, what should I gain / By the exaction of the forfeiture?" (1.3.159–60). (The response of the Shylock-figure in *The Orator* would have confirmed their worst suspicions: "I might also say that I have need of this flesh to cure a friend of mine of a certaine maladie, which is otherwise incurable.")[100] And in the context of Shylock's would-be ritual reenactment, Portia's invocation of specifically Christian blood underscores his covert purpose, in its own way echoing the standard formulas used in the prosecution of ritual murder.

Portia's addition of "Christian" to the blood specification is not incidental or trivial in this scene of inquisition: it crystallizes the difference between merchant and Jew just when it is most in danger of disappearing. For Shylock as inquisitor threatens in effect to uncover the "Judaizing" tendencies hidden within Antonio:[101] not Paul's spiritualized Jew within but its literalized contemporary avatar, the feminized and sodomitical Christian.[102] And the self-disclosing flow of Antonio's blood would be both the medium and the trope for this display: if Shylock were to prick him, he would bleed—and his blood would be no different from the Jew's. But even as Shylock threatens to reveal blood likeness in one domain, he reinforces blood difference in another, for his double enactment of Crucifixion and ritual murder in itself reassuringly recalls the founding moment of Jewish blood difference. Hence the necessity—and the perverse brilliance—of Portia's last-minute invocation of Antonio's Christian blood: it simultaneously manages to prevent the display of blood likeness and to ground the fiction of blood difference firmly in the theology that underwrites the play. And by implication it forestalls any residual doubts left over from 3.5, the scene that immediately precedes the trial, in effect reifying the sins of the father (3.5.1) that Jessica inherits in her blood. Critics sometimes imply that a difference that is merely theological should be somehow better for the Jews, but the relation between the Jessica plot and the Shylock plot suggests otherwise. For the racialized blood distinction between Jew and gentile that Lancelot and others would locate in Jessica is never entirely secure; it is potentially destabilized both by the discourse of the dispersal of nations and by Paul's "one-blood" claim. But the blood distinction in 4.1 is founded securely on the theological moment—the killing of Christ—that decisively and permanently separates Jews from Christians.

The closure both of the scene and of the play as comedy depends on reestablishing the distinction threatened by Antonio's Jew within: it depends thus on the closure of Antonio's Christian body, which repositions that body as not leaky, not feminized, not Jewish. And the representation of Shylock in 4.1 is essential to that closure. Initially created a monster in order to justify Christianity's abandonment of its "father Jew," Shylock must here play out his theologically determined role in order to cover over the threat of the Jew within the Christian. If Antonio feels himself tainted and castrated—and hence "Jewish"—because of his unspeakable desires, then the play shifts the burden of making him a Jew onto Shylock, who would circumcise him, open him up, make him bleed. Forced to become the Christ-killer and ritual murderer to enable Antonio to hide his desires from himself, Shylock is then forced to pay the price for what the play has made him: for those roles reify the very distinction that incising Antonio would threaten, and reify it precisely in the Christian blood that Shylock must not shed—the blood that he by definition can never have. And with that distinction securely in place, the play can return Shylock to his proper place as victim—not anatomist-inquisitor—of the Inquisition taking place in the Duke's courtroom. By the end bereft of both lineage and livelihood—both losses predicted by the "stones" that Jessica takes from him—Shylock is thus indelibly marked as the castrated and feminized Jew, reabsorbing into himself the taint that he had threatened to reveal in Antonio.

⸙

But why Portia? Why should she be the one to seal off the potential wound in Antonio's Christian body? And why in transvestite disguise? Although her role as Balthasar is an inheritance from *Il Pecorone*, Shakespeare—as is his wont—justifies it not only as a necessity of the plot but also from within her character, grounding it on the particulars of her relationship to Bassanio: her role as Balthasar fulfills both her desire to test the nature of Bassanio's commitment to Antonio (perhaps that is one way of understanding why she waits so long to pull the "no-blood" clause out of her legal hat: how far will Bassanio go to demonstrate his love for Antonio?) and her desire to put her new master Bassanio as well as his beloved Antonio in her debt, in effect replacing Bassanio's debt to Antonio with one to herself. The disguise she adopts for her rescue mission serves both her own interests and the mandatory heterosexual closure of the play in Belmont well, even while permitting the muted and displaced expression of homoerotic desire in Bassanio's "Sweet doctor, you shall be my bedfellow" (5.1.283). (Muted because Portia's transvestized body is so severely removed from the domain of desire: she is nearly unique among Shakespeare's transvestized heroines in not stirring up desire as she crosses genders. And displaced because it offers Bassanio rather than Antonio this satisfaction; for Antonio it might well be salt in the wound.) But what in the terms that I have been elaborating might make Portia the specific antidote to the wound that Shylock would make in Antonio?

Perhaps she can take on this role because she is held partially responsible for the wound in the first place. Though Shylock and Portia are construed as opposites in the trial scene, the play nonetheless gestures toward an odd collaboration between them. This collaboration has some basis in the plot:

insofar as Portia is the motive for the debt Antonio assumes for Bassanio, she is the proximal cause of his self-mutilating bargain. And it may have some basis in Antônio's character: when she wins Bassanio away from Antonio, she leaves him subject to the melancholy sense of self-loss that is eventually externalized both in the loss of his ships and in the wound that their loss nearly entails. But the strange alliance between Portia and Shylock emerges less in these comparatively naturalistic domains than in the fantasy embedded in the metaphor of the rent ship that turns up under Shylock's eaves. Graziano's trope for desire predicts both the loss of Antonio's ships and the rent in his body that Shylock would make; but it attributes those wounds not to the Jew but to the embrace of a decidedly female figure who emasculates as she embraces. That figure seems to me the portal through which an apparently discarded element of *Il Pecorone*—an element that links the lady with the Jew—leaks back into *Merchant*.

In Shakespeare's source text, the loss of the ships that nearly costs the Antonio-figure his life is caused not by the strumpet wind but by the strumpet Portia-figure, who seizes the ships of would-be lovers—the Bassanio-figure among them—who fail to stay awake during their nights with her. *Merchant* elides Portia's responsibility for the loss of the ships when it transforms the Bassanio-figure's three attempts to win the lady—the last of them successful—into the triple trial of the casket plot. But the memory-traces of that lady's emasculating power nonetheless emerge at discordant moments in the play: in the anxious references to Portia as Medea (1.1.170–72, 3.2.240), in the image of spidery entrapment with which Bassanio greets her portrait in the casket (3.2.120–24), in the ban on marriage that is the fate of her failed suitors[103]—and in the strumpet wind metaphor. For the dangerous lady apparently elided in *Merchant* returns in the metaphor that reads Antonio's wound as the sign of his subjection to a sexualized female force: a force that has the power to rend his body and thus anticipates the action of the Jew's knife. And a web of associations implicates Portia in that metaphor: she herself is associated with the destructive ocean in the chain that links the mesh of her golden hair (3.2.120–22) to the ornamental golden locks that are "but the guilèd shore / To a most dangerous sea" (3.2.92, 97–98); and her figuration as Medea associates her both with ships and with rent male bodies—and with the witch's familiar power to raise storms. And if the wind in Graziano's metaphor serves as a figure for fortune—traditionally figured by storms at sea and traditionally a strumpet[104]—Portia herself plays the role of fortune when she magically restores Antonio's ships to him, as though she, like the lady of *Il Pecorone*, has been in possession of them all along.[105]

In the fantasy elided in the plot of *Merchant* but vividly present in the strumpet-wind metaphor, Portia is complicit in the loss of Antonio's ships, and therefore complicit with the Jew, who would merely reiterate the rent already made by the strumpet wind. But why should the agent of that wound be coded female? And how does Portia's drag serve to seal it up? Insofar as that metaphor localizes the vague sense of threat that accrues to Portia throughout the play, it pinpoints not only the extrusion of *Il Pecorone* into *Merchant* but also the familiar scapegoating of women for the feminizing wound of desire, for it codes the damage of desire—whatever its object—as a form of female contagion: hence the transformation of the male younker into the female ship embraced by the strumpet wind. No wonder, then, that the agent of a bodily rupture coded as female—itself a figure for the feminizing desire that would open Antonio up—should herself be female. And perhaps no wonder that she should foreclose that bodily rupture in drag, for her disguise answers precisely to the fantasy registered in Graziano's metaphor and to the wound in Antonio's body: it undoes the threat of man-as-woman by presenting us with woman-as-man, as though the sealing up of Portia's femaleness in a male disguise could in itself seal Antonio up and ward off the Jew's wound in him. Or perhaps as though it could do away with the conundrums of gender altogether. Portia's drag can assuage Antonio's wound, I suggest, in part because it bizarrely literalizes Paul's wished-for state beyond gender: in her masculinized body, his "there is nether male nor female: for ye are all one in Christ Iesus" (Galatians 3.28) is given a local habitation and a name. And just here, I think, the religious and the psycho-sexual discourses of the play cross: for Portia's drag can provide a solution not only to the feminizing desire that Shylock's wound would reveal in Antonio but also to the vexed economies of gender that attach to Christian and Jew in the play.

It's worth remembering, first of all, that Portia's is not the only instance of transvestite disguise in the play: Jessica too disguises herself as a boy as she prepares to trade in her Judaism for Christianity. But why should both these moments of differentiation between Christian and Jew be framed via transvestite disguise? To what problem in the relation of Christian to Jew is transvestite disguise the imagined solution? I have been arguing that the Jew is a feminized figure, but that is most of all true of the Jew that Shylock threatens to reveal within Antonio. For Shylock himself is emphatically coded masculine: he is the avatar of the terrifying patriarch with the knife, the ur-father not only of Jessica but of Christians and Christianity; and in a world that identified the closed body with the masculine body, his sloganistic "Shut doors after you. / Fast bind, fast find" (2.5.51–52)—a motto for himself as well as for his house—identifies him as a kind of hyper-male.

Although he plays with the codes of femaleness when he tells Antonio that he has borne abuse "with a patient shrug, / For suff'rance is the badge of all our tribe" (1.3.105–6), we know that he is in fact contemplating murder. But if Shylock merely mimes the codes of femaleness, Antonio enacts them in 4.1—and enacts them just as he prepares to take on the role of Christ. The fears of feminization that attach to Antonio are, I suggest, not his alone; they play out fears that attach to Christianity itself: fears that derive both from the multiply penetrated body of Christ and from Christianity's valorization of patient "suff'rance" rather than manly anger. Insofar as *Merchant* forecloses the display of Antonio's feminized Christian body and rewrites Shylock as feminized after all, it assuages those fears. But it also suggests that the construction of the feminized Jew is itself a defense formation, a means through which the Christian can deflect his own anxieties about feminization onto the Jew's body.[106] And the play's doubled transvestite disguise seems to me to play a crucial role in this fantasized transfer of feminization from Christian to Jew.

Portia's disguise as Balthasar alludes to the supersession of Jew by Christian and thus predicts Shylock's end: the name she takes alludes to the Daniel—also called Belteshazzar or Balthazar—who read the writing on the wall and thus predicted the end of King Belshazzar's reign (Daniel 5.1–29).[107] But in taking on this male role, Portia-as-Balthasar does not simply predict the triumph of Christianity; she also rewrites Jessica's earlier disguise, complexly inserting gender into this story of supersession. I argued earlier that Jessica's transvestism makes her a stand-in for the gelded and effeminized figure of her father, and as such it underscores the femaleness of the Jew, as though a male Jew were really only a woman after all. In that sense her disguise serves to anticipate the femaleness that Portia's manipulations will inscribe in Shylock. Hence I think the odd set of puns that makes use of Jessica to gesture toward Shylock's castration/feminization: she famously steals his stones (though she herself remains female even when "she hath the stones upon her"; 2.8.22); and in Salerio's play on Shylock's "flesh and blood," she herself becomes a kind of equivalent to her father's feminized penis (3.1.30–31). But Portia's disguise seems to me to function in exactly the opposite way.

Portia's disguise comes as a kind of interruption to the consummation of her marriage, at the moment when her still-closed body marks her as not-yet-fully-female. When she takes on male disguise, she carefully directs the audience's attention to what she lacks (3.4.62) and therefore to the body of the boy actor beneath her ostensible womanhood; and the final byplay with the ring—in which she is simultaneously herself and the male doctor—simi-

larly reminds the audience of her male body.[108] In other words: her use of
her disguise makes her femaleness an illusion suspended between the boy
actor who plays her and the boy lawyer whom she plays. In this state, femaleness vanishes, as in Paul's "there is nether male nor female: for ye are
all one in Christ Iesus," where the default position that remains once we are
beyond gender will inevitably be imagined as male: the Geneva Bible's gloss
to Paul's "one" is, tellingly, "as all one man." And if Jessica's disguise reinforces the fantasy that even Jewish men are women after all, Portia's disguise
repairs the suspicion that there is something too feminine in Christianity:
by enabling the fantasy that even its women are men, Portia can undo the
damage that Shylock threatens to display in Antonio, since "she" really is
accomplished with what he fears to lack. Who better, then, to secure the
closure of Antonio's body and to assign the threat of an obsolete femaleness
to the Jew?

With Portia's triumph, the potential wound in Antonio's body—and in the
smooth Christian surface of the play—is sealed off, and the play can retreat
to its nearly impenetrable Christian domain of Belmont. There, Portia's satisfyingly disembodied father can replace the all-too-bodily father-Jew, who
is present only in the feminized fleshly residue that is his daughter Jessica.
But the retreat is uneasy, for *Merchant* seems to me everywhere haunted by
what it cannot allow itself to know. In its play of glib surfaces, *Merchant*
represents self-knowledge as a wound, and one that must be forestalled. In
that sense, Antonio is the play's epitome, and the epitome of the relationship that the play unwittingly discloses between Christian and Jew. For the
play cannot know its own fear and guilt about Christianity's relation to the
Jews—its ancestry in a Judaism it has disavowed, its bloody persecution of
the Jewish remnant, its continual need to find a justifying difference from
the Jew—and so it creates the figure of the monstrous Jew to seal off that
knowledge. And once that knowledge has been foreclosed, the debt to the
Jew—the debt the play encodes as three thousand ducats for three months—
need never be repaid.

NOTES

CHAPTER ONE

1. E. Baker, *Bardolatry*, 29–30. Coppélia Kahn, who first directed me to this passage, notes that "the joke's on him—*I'm* one of those 'ringers from inter-marriages.'"

2. Ibid., 31, 3, 6, 17. Shapiro usefully sets Baker in the context of others who worry the question of "Shakespeare, Englishness, and the Jews" from either a philo-Semitic or an anti-Semitic perspective; oddly, his account of Baker's "devotion to the purity of Shakespeare" does not consider the complication that Baker's anti-Stratfordian stance makes him read Shakespeare himself—and not only contemporary Shakespeareans—as contaminated by Jewishness (*Shakespeare and the Jews*, 81–82).

3. E. Baker, *Bardolatry*, 37, 49. Though I dislike the form that Baker's implied question takes, I find the question itself fascinating. At the time I would have said that my initial attraction to Shakespeare was both natural and inevitable, but now I wonder why so many Jewish literary scholars roughly of my generation were attracted to the study of Shakespeare. Perhaps—as with the generation of Anglo-Jewish Shakespeareans like Sidney Lee—because Shakespeare represented an access to the cultural center otherwise only marginally available to us? Perhaps because his works so richly reward the kind of textual study traditionally practiced on Jewish religious texts and therefore can function as a legitimized Torah for secularized Jews?

4. In this fantasy, the critic Leah Marcus is Baker's chosen Jessica: "I'll meet her at any Ramada Inn of her choice, with the sole evil intention of swaying her toward the insurgents. Oh Leah . . . Leah S. . . . if ever Yeshiva University has a football team I hope you coach it" (ibid., 33).

5. This normative Christian reader—a reader who in fact need not be Christian and is to be sharply distinguished from any number of actual Christian readers of the play— would presumably see nothing to trouble the play's illustration of the easy triumph of Christian values over Jewish ones. In that reading, Shylock simply plays bad Jewish Law to Portia's and Antonio's good Christian Mercy, as in Frank Kermode's famous formulation: "*The Merchant of Venice*, then, is 'about' judgment, redemption and mercy; the supersession in human history of the grim four thousand years of unalleviated justice by

the era of love and mercy. . . . And all the time it tells its audience that this is its subject;
only by a determined effort to avoid the obvious can one mistake the theme" ("Mature
Comedies," 224). Lewalski remains the most powerful exponent of this Pauline reading of
the play; see also works by Coolidge and Danson. Though Danson claims to emphasize
the "dynamic, dialectical nature of the debate" between justice and mercy (*Harmonies*,
70), in practice he often proceeds by disabling those elements in the play that might
interfere with his vision of *Merchant* as a harmonious romantic comedy based in Pauline
supersessionist doctrine (see, e.g., 117–19, 131–33, 137–38). For more extreme and
tendentious versions of this tendency, see, e.g., Wortheim, "Treatment of Shylock," and
Morris, "Judgment Theme." One answer to the rhetorical question I pose here has been
provided by the recent spate of Jewish critics—chief among them Shapiro and Metzger—
who focus on issues of identity and therefore on Jewishness as a threat to the idea of
Englishness; see also Kaplan's exceptionally useful edition of the play. I shall have
occasion to cite each of these critics elsewhere, but let me say here that some of the
material Shapiro provides and several of his conclusions in *Shakespeare and the Jews*
anticipate aspects of my own work. Like many who had been working in this area before
publication of Shapiro's book, I initially greeted it with some ambivalence; although our
methods and emphases are ultimately different, I have since come to find it a wonderful
resource, both because of his magisterial mustering of evidence and because of his skill as
a cultural critic.

   6. The phrase is Coolidge's ("Law and Love," 243).

   7. I find Ruether's *Faith and Fratricide* the most sustained and useful—as well as the
most courageous—account of this simultaneous dependence and disavowal. In her view,
the development of a Christological hermeneutics that could legitimate Christian
revelation only by appropriating Jewish scriptures for its own purposes had the effect of
rendering Judaism obsolete and demonizing Jews, hence providing the foundation for
racial anti-Semitism (see esp. 94–95, 116). M. Cohen similarly attributes the fact that
Jews were treated more harshly in Christian countries than in Islamic ones in part to the
psychological proximity of Christianity to Judaism, which made anti-Judaism "from the
outset, an essential ingredient of Christian self-definition" (*Under Crescent and Cross*,
17–29, 139). Hamilton's warning—"scholars who suggest that representations of Turks,
Moors, and Jews in Shakespeare's plays indicate that his subject is Turks, Moors, and Jews
need also to be aware of how such terms function in the religious discourses of Catholics
and Protestants"—is well taken ("Shakespeare and Religion," 194). But understanding the
functions that references to Jews could take on in these religious discourses should not be
the same as dissolving the "subject" of the Jew: the term "Jew" works in these polemics
exactly because it carries the weight of the foundational distinction between Christian
and Jew that Ruether and Cohen explicate.

   8. Alter's seems to me the most elegant and economical recent account of the
"hidden affinities between self and other" in *Merchant* ("Who Is Shylock?" 31–34). But
the uneasy sense that the Christians are more like Jews—or more narrowly, that Antonio
is more like Shylock—than they would like to admit has long been a feature of *Merchant*
criticism. In 1951, Goddard argued that "Antonio abhors Shylock because he catches his
own reflection in his face" (*Meaning*, 88); in 1959, Barber characterized Shylock as "an
embodied irony, troublingly like" the Christians (*Festive Comedy*, 168); in 1964, Moody

elaborated on the "essential likeness of Shylock and his judges" (*Shakespeare*, 10). Girard seems delighted rather than troubled by the play's display of the paradox of "undifferentiation"—the "obsession with displaying and sharpening a difference that is less and less real"—which he finds characteristic of all of Shakespeare's works ("'To Entrap the Wisest,'" 104); see Halpern for an incisive critique of Girard—and by implication other "likeness" critics—partly on the grounds of his "credulous reliance on irony as an antidote to prejudice" (*Shakespeare among the Moderns*, 177). Although some locate this likeness in Antonio's harshness toward Shylock (in Danson's account, e.g., Antonio's malice toward Shylock "convicts him of being . . . himself spiritually a 'Jew'"; *Harmonies*, 32), most locate it in the domain of the economic, especially in the anxieties about developing capitalism that are reflected in the play's—and Antonio's—attempt to make a sharp distinction between Christian merchant and Jewish usurer. Auden is the spiritual grandfather of this line of thought, as of much else in contemporary criticism; Hinely, Shell, W. Cohen, and Engle seem to me particularly noteworthy among his progeny. But Halpern reads Shylock's mirror function less as a consequence of a particular stage in capitalism than as a consequence of his—and more broadly the Jew's—status as representative of the emptied-out money-form itself (*Shakespeare among the Moderns*, 184–210). For a reading of the likeness between Shylock and Antonio as part of the play's critique of "the illusion of subjective autonomy," see Oz, *Yoke of Love*, 158; in Oz's view, Shylock can serve as a reflector of others because he is a "composite construct" of contradictory materials, a "bigger than life stereotype [who] may represent no one and everyone" (102).

9. Shapiro argues that the spectacle of Jewish conversion problematizes religious identity both because the Inquisition's forced conversion of the Jews complicated the question of what a Jew—or a Christian—was and because recent English religious history had already problematized it (*Shakespeare and the Jews*, 5–8, 14–17, 134–35).

10. Both Shapiro and Metzger write powerfully about the conversos. My formulation here refers not only to the length of time between the widespread admission of Jews into the profession and the relatively recent legitimizing of what might be called a Jewish perspective on this play by these and other critics, but also to my own vexed history with it. For years I taught the play as infrequently as possible and wrote about it only in the context of gender relations, e.g., in my "Male Bonding in Shakespeare's Comedies," 79–80; both in that essay and in *Suffocating Mothers*, I was willing to risk asking "new" questions as a woman well before I was willing to ask them as a Jew. (For an incisive—and well-deserved—critique of the unintended heterosexism of my early essay on "male bonding," see Sinfield, *Shakespeare, Authority, Sexuality*, 57–58.)

11. See Shapiro's compelling account of the struggle of Anglo-Jewish historians from 1888 on to establish acknowledgment of a Jewish presence in England between the 1290 expulsion and the so-called Readmission in 1656 (*Shakespeare and the Jews*, 62–67); in his view, what was at stake was "whether Jews should be recognized as belonging to England's past," particularly given the "nostalgic view of the Elizabethan world . . . that fixes in Shakespeare's age a pristine, unsullied notion of Englishness" (62–63, 77). Shapiro answers that question with an emphatic "yes" (67–76).

12. London's Domus Conversorum was established in 1232; see Stacey's "Conversion of Jews" for its founding and continued maintenance. Christian eschatology in fact

required the presence of the Jews, whose wholesale conversion was one of the precursor signs of the end of days; the need to keep some Jews alive long enough to convert them partially accounts for the protection sometimes accorded Jews in Europe (see, e.g., Stacey, "Conversion of Jews," 263; Edwards, *Jews in Christian Europe*, 17–18), as it accounts for some odd alliances with the Christian Right today. Marvell's "I would / Love you ten years before the Flood, / And you should, if you please, refuse / Till the conversion of the Jews" ("To His Coy Mistress," ll. 7–10)—probably written in proximity to the millenarian hopes that accompanied the Readmission debates—wryly predicts the chronic frustration of those hopes.

   13. See, e.g., the communities and individuals described by Roth (*History of the Jews in England*, esp. 132–42) and Hyamson (*Sephardim*, esp. 1–9). In addition to these converted Jews, there are occasional accounts of unconverted Jews living in England after the expulsion; see, e.g., Roth's account of Henry IV's Italian Jewish doctor, who arrived in England in 1410 accompanied by ten followers to form a minyan (133).

   14. Wolf located eighty to ninety members of the Sephardic community and listed their names in his "Jews in Elizabethan England" (33–35); Furness included a section entitled "Jews in England" in his *New Variorum Edition of Shakespeare: The Merchant of Venice* (395–99). In addition to this Sephardic community, Prior claims to have found evidence of a community of Italian Jews, initially brought to England as musicians in the time of Henry VIII and living in Shakespeare's London ("Second Jewish Community"). According to Prior, this community included the family of Emilia Lanyer, aka Emilia Bassano, Rowse's (and Prior's) discredited candidate for Shakespeare's dark lady; see Bevington, "A. L. Rowse's Dark Lady," for a particularly elegant demolishing of that candidacy. Though Prior's argument for this identification is not convincing, his evidence that the Bassanos were part of an Italian Jewish community has proved to be at least partially persuasive: Hutson's entry on Lanyer in the *Dictionary of Literary Biography: Missing Persons* identifies her as a member of "a family of Italian Jews" (388); Woods calls the evidence for Lanyer's Jewish heritage "circumstantial but cumulatively possible" (*Lanyer*, 180n48); and Barroll thinks that she was "probably a Jew" and considers her Christian baptism "part of the vexed context of Jewish assimilation in Tudor England" ("Looking for Patrons," 29, 44). Woods, moreover, comments that "Shakespeare could hardly have avoided" several of the Bassanos, who were musicians associated with the court in the 1590s (*Lanyer*, 181n49). Given the centrality of conversion and intermarriage to *Merchant*'s Jews, it seems to me not altogether implausible to imagine that Shakespeare might have been influenced in his choice of the name Bassanio (in place of the Gianetto of his main source, *Il Pecorone*) by the presence of this family.

   15. Brown, *Arden Shakespeare: Merchant of Venice*, xxxi.

   16. Hunter, "Theology," 215. Hunter cites Jacob Lopes Cardoso's 1925 *The Contemporary Jew in Elizabethan Drama* as the basis for his claim; oddly, his footnote to Cardoso's claim also cites Lee's and Sisson's accounts of the Jewish colony in England without comment.

   17. See Hunter, "Theology," 215, for this caution. Sisson similarly seems to have had the Nazis in mind when he concluded that "the Jewish problem was, in truth, no problem in London in the reign of Elizabeth" ("Colony of Jews," 50). Shapiro is less willing to give Hunter the benefit of the doubt than I am. He attributes the repudiation of Nazi-style

NOTES TO PAGES 5-6

racial thinking to Hunter's source, Guido Kisch, rather than to Hunter himself, and he points toward the anti-Semitic tinge in Hunter's writing (*Shakespeare and the Jews*, 83–85).

18. For Jerome, see Morrison, *Understanding Conversion*, 73; for early traces of "an irreducible element to Jewish identity in the eyes of many Christians, which no amount of baptismal water could entirely eradicate," see Stacey, "Conversion of Jews," 278. Elukin warns against confusing medieval attention to ethnic identity with "the biologically defined racism of modern Europe" but gives a good deal of evidence for the persistence of physical elements identified as "Jewish" in medieval converts and adds that "this perception of immutability, when combined with the emphasis on lineage and the embryonic ideas of the physical distinctiveness of the Jews through which lineage was expressed, made it easier for Christians to imagine that Jews were incapable of being assimilated into Christian society" ("From Jew to Christian?" 184). For additional examples and a reading of medieval racial anti-Semitism specifically in relation to *Merchant*, see Kaplan, "Jessica's Mother."

19. For Añes, see Hyamson, *Sephardim*, 5. For Fernandes, see Hyamson, *Sephardim*, 6; and Wolf, "Jews in Tudor England," 87. For the testimony to the Inquisition, see Katz, *Jews in the History of England*, 11. According to Hyamson, Fernandes was so strictly observant that, "when she occasionally travelled to London, she arranged with the innkeepers on the way to provide new cooking utensils so that she should not run the risk of having to eat forbidden food [i.e., food prepared with non-kosher utensils]. The *seder* was observed in her house every year, and she herself baked the unleavened bread for the whole community" (*Sephardim*, 6).

20. See Wolf, "Jews in Elizabethan England," 7, 21, for the deposition to the Inquisition and Barton's letter; the full text of the letter is quoted on 68.

21. Sisson, "Colony of Jews," 41–51. The case involved a suit by Mary May, the widow of an English merchant who had entered into a partnership with two Portuguese conversos living in London, Ferdinand Alvares and Alvaro de Lyma, in order to carry on covert (because forbidden) trade with Lisbon. The widow's claim was that her husband's share of the profits had been unfairly charged for expenses—mainly the bribes the conversos' agents had paid to avoid denunciation to the Inquisition—that had accrued to the expedition solely because his partners were Jews. Since the case depended partly on the conversos' covert Jewishness, their servants were called into court to testify. One of them (William Wilson) reported that everyone in Lisbon knew about the secret Jewish practices in London and that both he and his son Thomas had seen those practices. The description of the secret ceremonies that Thomas gave turned out to be based on observations by the "blackmore" servants in the household rather than on his own observations, but his description of Shabbat is relatively accurate ("they during that tyme did make Saterday their Sunday being fyne and best apparelled on Saterdayes and wold not worke nor do any busynes on Saterdayes but contrarywise on Sunday they wold go and do as if any workeyday"; 45). But his description of the conversos' Easter, "which they did use to keep a week before our Easter," is hopelessly confused ("they did comonly . . . light a great wax candle and sett the same in a basen with 4 white loaves about the Candle in the myddest of a great roome . . . and that done and the window curtens spredd wold come or steale secretly into the room barefoote and there stay a certen tyme looking

for Christ"; 45); Sisson finds in this description misunderstood representations of elements of Shabbat, Passover, and Yom Kippur (46–47). This confusion in itself may make it more plausible that Thomas was reporting on something suspiciously "Jewish" that the household servant did in fact see; one would expect a suborned witness to have been better coached.

22. For the will, see ibid., 48. For contributions to the Antwerp synagogue and Lopez's visit to Venice, see Wolf, "Jews in Elizabethan England," 9, 10, 20, 31.

23. Wolf, "Jews in Elizabethan England," 21. Katz similarly concludes that "the so-called secret community of Marrano Jews in Elizabethan London was . . . hardly secret at all" (Jews in the History of England, 65).

24. Cited in Gwyer, "Case of Dr. Lopez," 181.

25. For Barton, see Wolf, "Jews in Elizabethan England," 89; for the summary, see Katz, Jews in the History of England, 91. The equation of Judas and Jew is virtually axiomatic: see George Herbert's "Self-condemnation," where anyone who loves "This worlds delights before true Christian joy, / Hath made a Jewish choice"; since he has "sold for money his deare Lord," he "is a Judas-Jew" (cited in Hunter, "Theology," 213–14). See Kaplan, Merchant of Venice: Texts and Contexts, 306–7, for another contemporary instance of the equation of Lopez with Judas, and Glassman, Anti-Semitic Stereotypes, 58, for a broadsheet that made the same equation a few years later.

26. For Judas as the apostolic type of the wavering convert, see Morrison, Understanding Conversion, 74.

27. Ibid., viii–ix.

28. Katz (Jews in the History of England, 106), Orgel ("Shylock's Tribe," 42–43), and Alan Stewart (in a paper delivered at the Shakespeare Association of America meeting in 2004) have argued that Lopez's Jewishness did not figure largely in the legal proceedings against him. (Stewart argues specifically that Lopez was tried and convicted more as a Portuguese than as a Jew. But see n. 37 below; these categories may not have been altogether distinct.) Moreover, whatever the status of Lopez's covert Jewishness in the legal proceedings, the citations in this paragraph suggest that in many quarters it was inescapably tied to the presumption of his guilt. Years earlier, Gabriel Harvey had already suspected that only Lopez's Jewishness could account for his suspicious success as a physician: he was, according to Harvey, "descended of Jewes," though now a professed Christian, and "none of the learnedest, or expertest Physitians in the Court: but one, that maketh as great account of himself, as the best: & by a kind of Jewish practis, hath growen to much Wealth, & sum reputation: as well with the Queen herself, as with sum of the greatest Lordes, and Ladyes" (Katz, Jews in the History of England, 58). Immediately after the trial, Cecil associated Lopez's guilt with his status as a "vile Jew" (Katz, Jews in the History of England, 92), and in William Warner's Albions England (1612), Lopez is "that Spanish-Iewish Atheist" (242). The account of Lopez's last words and the derision they produced occurs first in 1625, in William Camden's Annales rerum Anglicarum et Hibernacarum (see Katz, Jews in the History of England, 96); whether or not the account is accurate, the extent to which it became part of Lopez lore suggests the power of the equation between crypto-Judaism and treachery. Greenblatt notes that the Jewishness ascribed to Lopez would have served to "reinforce the sense that the queen had been miraculously saved by divine intervention"; see especially his wonderful historical

fantasy about the effect on Shakespeare of the crowd's derision, registered in the queasiness of the laughter in *Merchant* (*Will in the World*, esp. 275–80).

29. Sisson, "Colony of Jews," 51.

30. The probability that Shakespeare was the "Hand D" who wrote this scene was established in *Shakespeare's Hand in the Play of Sir Thomas More*, ed. Pollard; this 1923 volume contained papers by a set of leading Shakespeareans—Pollard, W. W. Greg, E. Maunde Thompson, J. Dover Wilson, and R. W. Chambers—arguing for that attribution. That probability is strongly endorsed in the most recent collection of essays on the play, *Shakespeare and "Sir Thomas More*," ed. Howard-Hill; see, e.g., Metz's summary of prior scholarly consensus that Shakespeare is Hand D ("'Voice and Credyt,'" 22) and Howard-Hill's summary statement that "the evidence for Shakespeare's authorship is stronger now than it was before" (Introduction, 3). As far as I have been able to ascertain, Kinney is alone among recent scholars in contesting Shakespeare's identity as Hand D ("Text, Context, and Authorship").

It is generally assumed that the original text of *Sir Thomas More* was written in the early 1590s in response to the outbreak of anti-alien sentiment (see, e.g., Howard-Hill, Introduction, 1; Long, "Occasion"). Pollard reproduces accounts of the stranger riots of 1593 and 1595 from contemporary documents (*Shakespeare's Hand*, 23–27, 33–40). Dating of the additions to the play, among them the contribution of Hand D, is somewhat more vexed. Gabrieli and Melchiori assume in their edition of the play that Hand D's contribution was written in 1593–94, specifically in response to the anti-alien rhyme posted on the wall of the Dutch Cemetery at the height of the troubles in 1593 (*Sir Thomas More*, 26; see also Melchiori, "*Book of Sir Thomas More*," 93; Melchiori, "Master of the Revels," 176). That dating is challenged by Taylor ("Date and Auspices," 119–21) and Forker ("Webster or Shakespeare?" 160), both of whom place the additions between 1601 and 1605 largely on stylistic grounds. But according to Metz, assigning the additions to a year or two after the original text is still the "mainstream" view ("'Voice and Credyt,'" 28), and that view is endorsed by Long ("Occasion," 47–50). For the repeated censorship of the term "stranger" in *The Book of Sir Thomas More* by Master of the Revels Edmund Tilney, see Pollard's introduction to *Shakespeare's Hand* and his reproduction of portions of the text (4, 200) and McMillan, "*Book of Sir Thomas More*," 58.

31. Citations of *Sir Thomas More* are to the Gabrieli and Melchiori edition. The play specifically identifies its strangers as French and Dutch, e.g., at 2.1.51 and 67. Pollard reproduces a variety of contemporary documents that identify the French and Dutch strangers as the rioters' targets in 1586, 1593, and 1595 (*Shakespeare's Hand*, 36–38); see also Shapiro for libels and anti-alien riots directed at French and Dutch aliens throughout the sixteenth century, particularly in the 1590s (*Shakespeare and the Jews*, 182–87).

32. In fact, the Dutch Cemetery libel to which Melchiori thinks Hand D was responding in *Sir Thomas More* (see n. 30 above) explicitly associates the Dutch strangers with Jews ("And like the Jews you eat us up as bread"), as Shapiro notes in his excellent account of the ways in which anti-alien discourse often mapped onto anti-Jewish discourse (*Shakespeare and the Jews*, 184–85). If a later report of another of the 1593 libels can be trusted, the Protestant strangers were also like the conversos in their susceptibility to suspicions of religious hypocrisy: according to John Strype's 1731 *Brief Annals of the Church and State under the reign of Queen Elizabeth*, one libel claimed

that the Belgian, Flemish, and French strangers "have by a feigned Hypocrisy, and counterfeit shew of Religion, placed yourselves in a most fertile Soil" to the detriment of England's "own natural Subjects" (quoted in *Shakespeare's Hand*, 39). Shapiro argues persuasively that *The Merchant of Venice*, like *The Jew of Malta*, takes advantage of the convergence of alien with Jew: in his view both plays function partly to allow the safe expression of anti-alien feeling by making their dangerous aliens into Jews (*Shakespeare and the Jews*, 186–89).

33. "The Translatour to the Reader," in Montanus's *A Discouery and Playne Declaration of Sundry Subtill practices of the Holy Inquisition of Spayne*, A2r; all references to *Discouery* are to the 1568 edition unless otherwise noted. "Montanus" was a pseudonym, though for whom is not entirely clear; Hillgarth thinks that he was probably a Spanish friar turned minister of a Calvinist congregation (*Mirror of Spain*, 313). Montanus's work, originally published in Latin in Heidelberg in 1567, was translated into French, German, Dutch, and English and is considered by some to have been the major influence on representations of the Inquisition before the nineteenth century (see Hillgarth, *Mirror of Spain*, 233, 313). The 1568 English edition—published in a cheap format that suggests its popularity—was followed by another edition in 1569, this time dedicated to the archbishop of Canterbury with the explicit hope that it would help "the multitude of the ignoraunt people [who were] in so great a perplexity and doubt of two religions" (A3r).

34. In his monumental work of Protestant propaganda, John Foxe similarly notes that the Inquisition was initially "instituted against the Jews," and he compares their fate to that of the Protestants (*Acts and Monuments*, 4:451; see also Achinstein, "John Foxe and the Jews," 99).

35. Rather than attributing Jewish intransigence to their perfidy or the stiff-neckedness traditionally assigned to them, Montanus attributes it to the Inquisition's tactics, chief among them conversions of the kind that the Venetians would force on Shylock: instead of being provided with "godly instructors, pastours and teachers, to win and allure the counterfait christians, (as it becomed them) by charitie and gentlenes, labouring withall diligence to withdraw them from their errours to embrace true christianitie sincerely and without dissimulation," the "poore wretches" were put under the jurisdiction of the Inquisition, where they were "robbed and spoiled of all their goodes and possessions, and either put to most cruell death, or suffer most intollerable tormentes by whippe or otherwise, leading the rest of their life in perpetuall obloquie and ignomi-nie, and sustaining extreme pouerty by losse of landes and goodes" (*Discouery*, B3r–v).

36. In the course of his argument for editing (and reading) across "hands," Masten notes this handy-dandy and persuasively locates it in the context of the play's "massive complication of . . . boundaries," including its "radical denaturalization" of the category of the stranger ("*More* or Less," esp. 117–21).

37. Katz cites Bishop Godfrey Goodman's comment that "at that time there were many Portugal physicians here, and we did suspect them all to be Jews, as I knew one was" (*Jews in the History of England*, 77).

38. The relative infrequency of "whet" in Shakespeare's works—it occurs only thirteen times outside these two plays—underscores the resemblance between the gestures. *Merchant*'s echo of *More*'s spurned dog has often been noted (see, e.g., Brown's

Arden Shakespeare: Merchant of Venice, xxv; Gabrieli and Melchiori, *Sir Thomas More,* 104), usually as evidence for Shakespeare's presumed sympathy to strangers and therefore to Shylock (see, e.g., J. Wilson, *Shakespeare's Happy Comedies,* 110–12). Matchett is unusual in noting the echo of both dog and knife; he reads it as evidence of Shakespeare's capacity "to achieve fullness of character through portraying unresolved contradictions" ("Shylock, Iago, and *Sir Thomas More,*" 220–21).

39. For Hooker, see V. Olsen, *John Foxe and the Elizabethan Church,* 177; Olsen considers Hooker's formulation "the common view of the Anglican Fathers" and claims that Foxe shared the same concept of church and state as "homogeneous" (177). Helgerson, who cites the same passage from Hooker, would agree ("Foxe, too, had thought of church and state as ideally congruent"), but he adds the caveat that "some Englishmen might not belong"; and he brilliantly depicts the differences between Hooker's and Foxe's conceptions of both church and nation (*Forms of Nationhood,* 277, 284). Others note the considerable tension between the idea of the church as a persecuted remnant of the elect and the idea of the church as coextensive with the nation: see, e.g., McEachern, Introduction, 4, 7; Parry, "Elect Church or Elect Nation?" 171; Loades, "Afterword," 283; Collinson, "Biblical Rhetoric," 20, 27. Collinson concludes that "we can no longer elide the godly Protestant community with the national community, as if they were one and the same thing" but also that "the inclusive unity of the whole Protestant nation was something [Foxe] chose, or, dare we say, pretended to believe in" ("John Foxe and National Consciousness," 25). But the Jews, converted or not, would be a special case: Achinstein notes that *Acts and Monuments* is "shot through with a concern about the Jews as an alien *nation* living within England's midst" ("John Foxe and the Jews," 96); and questions about the relation of the Jews both to the English nation and to the Church of England are at the heart of Shapiro's *Shakespeare and the Jews* (see esp. chap. 6, "Race, Nation, or Alien?"). For the afterlife of these questions in the nineteenth century, see Ragussis, *Figures of Conversion,* esp. 15–26; Ragussis understands the revisionist tradition that separates English "tolerance" for Jews from the requirement that they be converted as a rewriting of *The Merchant of Venice,* "the English mastertext for representing the Jew" (58).

40. See, e.g., Shapiro, *Shakespeare and the Jews,* 21–22. For some specific instances of John Foxe's equation of Catholics with Jews, see n. 63 below and Achinstein, "John Foxe and the Jews," 93–94, 100.

41. See Shapiro's citation of Privy Councillor John Wolley's argument against a 1593 bill limiting the activities of merchant strangers: the bill "should be ill for London, for the riches and renown of the City cometh by entertaining strangers, and giving liberty unto them. Antwerp and Venice could never have been so rich and famous but by entertaining of strangers, and by that means have gained all the intercourse of the world" (*Shakespeare and the Jews,* 183).

42. *The Three Ladies of London* was printed in 1584 with the title-page notation that it had been publicly played, perhaps by Leicester's or the Queen's Players, since Wilson was for a time an important member of both companies (see Mithal, *"Three Ladies,"* lxv, lxx–lxxx; citations of both plays are to this edition). Probably written in 1581, *Three Ladies* was popular enough to have been attacked by Gosson; it was probably revised and remounted in 1588, when its sequel—*The Three Lords and Three Ladies of London*—was

written, and it was published in a second quarto in 1592 (see Mithal, "Three Ladies," xxi, xxiii–xxiv, civ).

Although Bullough considers Three Ladies "part of the background against which [Shakespeare] wrote" rather than a source (Narrative and Dramatic Sources, 451), the conviction that Shakespeare's Shylock was influenced by Wilson's Gerontus has been growing. Cartelli mentions Three Ladies as a possible influence on Shakespeare ("Shakespeare's Merchant, Marlowe's Jew," 259); Mithal assumes that Shakespeare knew the play, since Merchant echoes both the sum and the duration—three thousand ducats for three months—of the Jew's bond in Three Ladies (xix); and Kaplan thinks that "Shakespeare almost certainly knew" it (Merchant of Venice: Texts and Contexts, 154).

In addition to the repetition of the amount and duration of the bond noted by Mithal and others, I would add a set of other minute but teasing resemblances. Both Shylock and Gerontus bargain to retain the principal of their loan, and Shylock's "Give me my principal, and let me go" (4.1.331) initially echoes Gerontus's "Pay me the principall, as for the interest, I forgiue it you" (l. 1732). When this bargain fails, Gerontus asks, "Pay me the one halfe, if you will not pay me all" (l. 1737); when Shylock's bargain fails, "one half" of his estate is forfeit to Antonio (4.1.348). Moreover, Shylock seems to take up both the rhythm and the language of Gerontus's addresses to the judge: Gerontus's "then learned Iudge" and "most puissant Iudge" (ll. 1698, 1730)—rhythmically quite distinct from Mercadorus's flat "My lord Iudge" (l. 1719)—are reiterated in Shylock's "O wise young judge," "O noble judge!" "Most rightful judge!" and especially "most learnèd judge" (4.1.219, 241, 296, 299); the rhythm of these phrases is distinctive enough to be parodied by Graziano (4.1.307–8, 313). But these echoes of Gerontus in Shylock are not in my view the only reason to consider Three Ladies a probable source for Merchant; I suggest some additional similarities below.

43. L. Kermode's defense of Wilson's dramatic sophistication gives a full account of the contemporary economic and social circumstances reflected in the play ("Playwright's Prophecy"); Kermode has the distinction of being one of very few critics who take the play seriously on its own terms, without comparing it to Marlowe or Shakespeare.

44. In his brief comment on Three Ladies, Ferber adduces Usury's and Lucre's move to London as evidence that England seemed poised to take over the economic position of a declining Venice, along with "all the ills of worldly wealth" ("Ideology," 452).

45. Thomas Wilson, A Discourse vppon vsurye, cited in Mithal, "Three Ladies," xix–xx.

46. Francis Bacon, "Of Usury," cited in Trachtenberg, Devil, 192; see 191–92 for additional evidence that Christian moneylenders were frequently simply called "Jews."

47. The Three Lords and Three Ladies is decidedly pessimistic about the purified England it portrays. Although Usury's comrades all announce their plans to desert England for Spain because "here is no liuing for vs in London, men are growen so full of conscience and religion" (ll. 1427–28), apparently only Simony actually leaves; Fraud and Dissimulation are still present at the end and disquietingly take part in the final wedding masque ostensibly celebrating the restoration of a rehabilitated Love, Conscience, and Lucre in England (ll. 2224–26).

48. "The Jews that London knew, and Shakespeare might have met, were not Shylocks. They were men like Nunez or Leavis or Alvares, contented, prosperous

citizens, who reaped the rewards of compromise and submission to the law" (Sisson, "Colony of Jews," 50).

49. For the topicality of the issue of hospitality, see, e.g., Heal, "Idea of Hospitality," who notes that pamphlets lamenting the decay of hospitality proliferated in England especially between the 1580s and the 1630s (68, 80); and for an account of the cultural contestations embedded both in the cultural practices and in the dramatic representations of hospitality, see Palmer, *Hospitable Performances*. Oddly, Palmer does not include *The Three Ladies of London* in this account, and his later discussion of the play ("Merchants and Miscegenation") focuses on the kinds of cultural miscegenation entailed by emergent mercantile practices rather than on hospitality. Though neither Heal's essay ("Idea of Hospitality") nor her later book (*Hospitality in Early Modern England*) mentions Wilson's play, her work makes it clear that Wilson's Hospitality participates in the contemporary debate at several points, particularly in his insistence that his job is to feed the poor rather than to provide a great man's feast and in his specification that he does not provide hospitality to strangers (see *Three Ladies*, ll. 631–32, 619; and Heal, "Idea of Hospitality," 75–77). Wilson is partly conventional in opposing Hospitality to Usury; Heal notes that early modern writers opposed "hospitality as a frank offering and free benefit to the greed of those who were a part of the cash nexus" (*Hospitality in Early Modern England*, 19). But Wilson aligns this traditional opposition with the xenophobia of his play when he makes Lucre's Venetian servant Usury—rather than a merely generalized greed—the murderer of Hospitality. Hospitality was often depicted as a specifically English virtue (see Heal, "Idea of Hospitality," 71); by attributing its demise specifically to Usury, Wilson links it to the invasion of England by the kinds of proto-capitalist values characteristic of Venice.

50. The contamination of Love and Conscience which is at the center of the play depends on Hospitality's inability to help them once he has been ruined by Usury; and though they can be rehabilitated, his loss is permanent. The description of his funeral, attended by the poor, is one of the great moments in *Three Ladies*, and his death is still being lamented at the end of *Three Lords*, even when other English values have apparently been securely reestablished.

51. In *Il Pecorone*, there is no suggestion that the merchant has rescued the usurer's clients or lent money gratis; the Jew's only motive is that "he wished . . . to be able to say that he had put to death the greatest of the Christian merchants" (cited from Bullough, *Narrative and Dramatic Sources*, 472).

52. Usury's hard heart, as well as his profession and his parentage, makes him into the type of the Jew even before he is explicitly identified as one in *Three Lords*, since hard hearts were traditionally associated with Jews, specifically with their failure to recognize Jesus as the Messiah. But the analogy with Pharaoh (see, e.g., Romans 9.15–18 and the discussion in chap. 2 below) is potentially problematic, since God famously hardened Pharaoh's heart, a theological twist that Conscience introduces when she later prays that God will "mollifie and lesten Useries hard heart" (*Three Ladies*, l. 1304). As I argue below, Foxe wrestles extensively with this problem in his *A Sermon preached at the Christening of a Certaine Iew*.

53. See, e.g., Usury's characterization of Hospitality as a "franke Gentleman" at l. 1025. Especially taken together, the terms "frank" and "free" had long been associated

with liberality (hence the question—"Which was the moost fre?"—that concludes Chaucer's "Franklin's Tale"). The *Oxford English Dictionary* (hereafter *OED*) cites Caxton's 1484 advice that "the knyght must be free and frank" under its definition of "frank" as "liberal, bounteous, generous, lavish." Heal's use of the terms (cited in n. 49) suggests that in the early modern period they may have specifically invoked the values of hospitality as opposed to those of the "cash nexus."

54. Most critics consider the Gerontus scenes in isolation from the rest of the play and cite them as evidence that early modern attitudes toward Jews were more complicated than is usually supposed (see, e.g., Cartelli, "Shakespeare's *Merchant*, Marlowe's *Jew*," 259; Kaplan, *Merchant of Venice: Texts and Contexts*, 154); for Dessen, the scenes serve to bolster Hunter's claim that "Jewishness" is a "spiritual or moral condition" rather than a racial one ("Elizabethan Stage Jew," 233). These views do not account for Gerontus's role in a play that also—and in my view crucially—includes the figure of the crypto-Jew Usury. L. Kermode notes the contrast between the play's two moneylenders but attributes it to Wilson's general ambivalence about aliens and to Gerontus's specific location in Turkey, where Jews were familiarly known as mediators between the English and the Turks ("Playwright's Prophecy," 64, 66); the contrast also serves Nugent's argument that the stigma attached to usury was being transferred to counterfeiting as usury became more respectable during this period ("Usury and Counterfeiting," 201–17).

55. For this sense of "Judaizing," see, e.g., Herbert's "Self-condemnation," cited in n. 25. It is a relatively familiar move to read Gerontus as a commentary on the morally debased English; see, e.g., Dessen, "Elizabethan Stage Jew," 244; L. Kermode, "Playwright's Prophecy," 62, 63.

56. Fraud is later given a fake French accent in *Three Lords*, but that is part of the trick by which he cheats Simplicity by pretending to be a French merchant who needs to unload his wares in a hurry; even though Fraud turns out to be part French in fact, he has no accent elsewhere in either play.

57. Gerontus's early vow "by mightie Mahomet" (l. 1545) temporarily invokes fears of a Turkish-Jewish alliance by conflating Jew with Muslim; for that habitual conflation, see Burton, who adduces Mercadorus to support his thesis that the softening of Elizabethan attitudes toward Turks produced a compensatory hardening of attitudes toward Jews (*Traffic and Turning*, 198–206, 219–21). But *Three Ladies* does not invoke this conflation elsewhere, nor does it use its Turkish judge's presumed status as Muslim to complicate the strict antithesis between Christian and Jew by interjecting a third term; instead, that status functions to make him an apparently authoritative witness to the fixed opposition between the two categories.

58. The implied comparison between Sir Peter and Mercadorus provides an interesting commentary on contemporary English fears about enforced conversion to Islam (for those fears, see, e.g., Vitkus, "Turning Turk in *Othello*," esp. 145–52; and see Palmer, "Merchants and Miscegenation," 42–43, for the case of a merchant's factor who converted in 1583 to save his life and, having spoken the words of his conversion, was told, "now thou shalt die in the faith of a Turk"). However serious those fears were, conversion in *Three Ladies* is not a horror perpetrated by the Turks; it is the consequence of a moral economy in which everyone—the Christian who would turn Turk, the Catholic who

would turn Protestant, and the Protestant who would turn Catholic—is considered functionally Jewish.

59. The Judge specifies that Mercadorus is to "become a Mahomet" (l. 1713), but Mercadorus himself twice proclaims that "me will be a Turke" (ll. 1555, 1720), and he enters the court scene "in Turkish weedes" (l. 1710), apparently to confirm his intention to switch nationality and religion at the same time.

60. *OED* cites this line in support of its definition I.4.b of "indifferent" ("Of a word: Of neutral signification or application, hence, Equivocal, ambiguous; of either gender"). The joke here depends on the fact that although "homo" is grammatically masculine, it is "indifferent" insofar as it is "'unmarked' i.e., it can refer to individuals of either (any) gender" (I am grateful to Ralph Hexter for this formulation). It is perhaps not coincidental that Sir Peter's gender shape-shifting, along with its sodomitical antecedent, emerges in his conversation with the Italianate Simony. The association of sodomy with Italians and Catholics was familiar; see, e.g., Thomas Nashe's reference to "the Sodom of Italy" in *The Unfortunate Traveller* (278) or Foxe's assertion that the requirement that priests remain celibate "tended to 'augment horrible sodomitry'" (*Acts and Monuments*, cited in Epp, "John Foxe and the Circumcised Stage," 294). We might expect this Italianate vice to be a result of contamination by Simony, but here it is strikingly homegrown.

61. L. Kermode notes that Judge Nemo is not the first of the Nemo figures, which he characterizes as "flitting authority figures of emptiness": "We have already met Sir Nicholas Nemo and been told repeatedly that the joke lies in this character's nonexistence. . . . Perhaps there is no judge, no arraignment, and no sentencing" ("Playwright's Prophecy," 78).

62. For an account of the sermon and of the future fate of Foxe's Jew, see Shapiro, *Shakespeare and the Jews*, 70, 141–42; Shapiro usefully elucidates the Elizabethans' "extraordinary interest" in the conversion of the Jews and sets the sermon in the context of the various uses religious controversialists made of Jewish converts (133–46). According to Wooden, the conversion was "a great public spectacle" and Foxe preached to an overflow audience (*John Foxe*, 15). The sermon was subsequently published in expanded form in three editions (one in Latin and two in English) in 1578. The English edition that I cite—*A Sermon preached at the Christening of a Certaine Iew, at London, by Iohn Foxe*—was printed together with "The confession of faith, which Nathanael a Iewe borne, made before the Congregation in the Parish church of Alhallowes" in a small quarto volume of the kind that (according to Anthony Bliss, curator of Rare Books for the University of California's Bancroft Library) would have been have been hawked on street corners for a penny.

63. Though Foxe says in his "Preface to the Christian Reader" that his sermon is "directed to the behoof of the Iewes chiefely," he adds, "yet (I trust) it wil not be altogether vnprofitable to the Christian readers" (C7v); he clearly wanted the testimony of his converted Jew to shore up the beliefs of wavering Christians. For Catholic idolatry as an impediment to Jewish conversion, see, e.g., *Sermon*, M7v–M8v, and "Confession," B3v–B6r. Nathanael specifies that England is "a blessed land" because it is free of the idolatrous practices that have blinded the Jews to the truth of Christianity, and he attributes his coming there to God (B3v–B4r). Nathanael's insistence that the English

version of Christianity entails "no more than our scriptures most truely conteine" (B6v) similarly affirms the Protestant reliance on scripture alone that Foxe repeatedly stresses (see, e.g., his "Preface to the Christian Reader," C5v–C6r). Elsewhere in his sermon, Foxe is perfectly happy to conflate—rather than contrast—Jews with what he characterizes as the "Romish Synagogue," for example, allying Catholic insistence on its direct lineal ancestry from Peter with Jewish pride in literal ancestry, or Catholic idolatry with Jewish adherence to outward performance rather than inward faith; see, e.g., C1v–C2v, B3v–B4r, and L5r. For instances of this conflation in *Acts and Monuments*, see Achinstein's "John Foxe and the Jews," 93–94, 100–103; Achinstein provides a very useful account of the complexities of Foxe's attitudes toward Jews as they are inflected by theology, politics, and racialism.

64. This title comes immediately after Foxe's preface; its emphasis is echoed in both the Latin and the second English edition (*De Oliva Evangelica. Concio, in Baptismo Iudaei habita Londini; De Oliva Evangelica, The True and Gladsome Olive Tree. A Sermon preached at the Christening of a certain Jew, at London*).

65. Romans 11.17, as cited in *Sermon*, A2v–A3r.

66. Paul prophesied that the Jews would be returned to the olive tree "when the fulnes of the Gentiles shall come"; according to Foxe's calculations, 1564 was the year in which that fullness was accomplished (M6v–M7r). The extent to which Foxe himself had millenarian expectations is contested, and Achinstein rightly notes that the sermon itself does not make the link between the conversion of the Jews and the coming of the Last Days explicit ("John Foxe and the Jews," 105); but P. Olsen notes the "millenarian implications" of Foxe's calculation ("Was John Foxe a Millenarian?" 624). Whatever the exact status of Foxe's beliefs, Yehuda's conversion and Foxe's sermon fueled millenarian hopes; see Shapiro, *Shakespeare and the Jews*, 142–45.

67. As Foxe notes, "Under the title of the Roote, [Paul] doeth note Abraham, and other holy Patriarches" (A5r).

68. The broadly Calvinist doctrine of election was central to sixteenth-century English Protestantism, officially enshrined in article 17 of the Thirty-nine Articles of the Church of England (see, e.g., Hunt, *Shakespeare's Religious Allusiveness*, 52) and generally accepted by both centrists and reformers within the church, though with varying degrees of fervor and not without some dissent (see, e.g., Lake, "Calvinism and the English Church," esp. 34–42).

69. The imaginary Jews in Foxe's audience are always stuck at the present moment of the Crucifixion, in effect amalgamated with their ancestors; see, e.g., D1v ("Why doe ye not produce then his buryed carkasse") and L3r ("Why may I not iustly accuse you, as partetakers of the same crime?"). These passages, and others in the *Sermon* (see below), should qualify Achinstein's claim that Foxe had "little interest in figuring the Jews as Christ-killers" ("John Foxe and the Jews," 96); but Achinstein also notes that Foxe's view of the Jews became increasingly negative (89) and substantiates that claim in a compelling analysis of the ways in which the indexes of editions of *Acts and Monuments* increasingly emphasize "the danger Jews posed to Christian society" (111).

70. Luther, "That Jesus Christ Was Born a Jew" (1523), 201. Twenty years later, when he had turned against the Jews because of their disappointing refusal to convert en masse,

Luther too excoriated Jewish pride in ancestry; see "On the Jews and Their Lies" (1543), 140.

71. "Top" is Capell's commonly accepted emendation of Quarto's "tooth'" and Folio's "to'th'" (*Arden Shakespeare: King Lear*, ed. Muir, 24). Its horticultural sense, current at the time, brings Edmund's implied metaphor fully in line with Foxe's. See *OED*, verb 3, "to cut off the top of (a growing tree, a plant, or the like)," "to lop, prune, or shorten back (branches or shoots)."

72. Jesus greets his new convert Nathanael as "in dede an Israelite, in whom is no guile" (John 1.47). Calvin comments, "We know how greatly the Iewes did boast of their father Abraham, how boldlie they boasted of the holinesse of their stocke . . . while ther was scarce one found amongst an hundred, that was not altogether growne out of kinde, & far from the faith of the fathers. Therefore [Christ] defineth briefly a true Israelite. . . . For they that would be accounted the children of Abraham, & the holy people of God, were about to be shortly after the deadly enemies of the gospel. Therefore . . . he warneth & telleth them betimes, that there are few true Israelites, of many that pretende the name of Israelites" (*Commentarie vpon Gospel of Iohn*, 39).

73. Although Foxe's sermon in its original form could hardly have been addressed to unconverted Jews, he apparently had hopes that in its written form his refutation of Jewish claims to special status and his long and sarcastic account of Jewish practices and prophetic texts as merely shadows of the Christian truth to come would serve not only to shore up Christian belief but also to convert actual Jews. Achinstein reports that "Foxe cared so much for this sermon that he sought to have it translated into German, for the benefit of both Christians and Jews in Germany" ("John Foxe and the Jews," 115). The issue of the audience for Nathanael's "Confession" is similarly vexed. Its full title claims that it is "The confession of faith, which Nathanael a Iewe borne, made before the Congregation in the Parish church of Alhallowes in Lombard Streete at London," but the publisher's note at the beginning of the volume containing both sermon and confession specifies that Nathanael's confession was "written first by him selfe in the Spanish tongue, and now translated into English for the more benefite of the godlie Reader" (C1v). If this document in fact records Nathanael's spoken confession, what were the non-Spanish-speaking parishioners at Alhallowes doing while he was addressing them in Spanish? Moreover, despite its ostensible English Protestant audience, the document attributed to Nathanael initially addresses itself to an audience of newly converted Jews: "Men and brethren, to whom God hath reuealed in these later dayes the secrete of his sonne which was hidden from you many ages, it is not vnknowen vnto you how that in the dayes of our forefathers God chose vs to be a precious people vnto himself aboue all the people that are vpon the earth" (B1r). Only one-third of the way through his lengthy confession does the referent of "you" shift to "you the Gentiles" presumably in his audience (B4r).

74. Foxe would have expected his audience to identify themselves with "all other nations." He repeatedly refers to them as "vs Gentiles" (see, e.g., A3v, A4r, A6v), a term that refers to "any or all of the nations other than the Jewish," according to *OED*'s first definition of "Gentile." In theological contexts, "the nations" and "the Gentiles" are in fact interchangeable terms (see *OED*'s definition 2a: "*The nations:* in and after Biblical

use: . . . the Gentiles"). Foxe uses the phrase with notable pride because he himself is speaking on the authority of Paul, apostle to the gentiles (A2v).

75. The identification of England with Israel was commonplace (see, e.g., Collinson, "John Foxe and National Consciousness," 10), but the extent to which Foxe himself thought that England had a unique role to play as the new elect nation is the subject of ongoing controversy. Haller's claim in *Foxe's Book of Martyrs and the Elect Nation* that Foxe played a central role in the ideology identifying England as an "elect nation" has been widely criticized (see, e.g., Bauckham, *Tudor Apocalypse*, 86: "It is clear enough from all Foxe's writings that his feeling for the English nation and church could never override his dominating belief in the church as an international body,' the company of Christ's elect members in all ages and places"). Until recently, the wholehearted rejection of Haller's thesis appeared to have become the new orthodoxy.

But there have been some recent qualifications of that orthodoxy. In *Forms of Nationhood* Helgerson rejects Haller's thesis but nonetheless concedes that Foxe "grants England a quite extraordinary place in the universal scheme" (263). Loades similarly rejects the "elect nation" thesis but agrees that Foxe "had a special destiny in mind for the English" ("Afterword," 283). Collinson distinguishes sharply between "an" and "the" elect nation: "That England, typologically Israel, was 'an' elect nation was a commonplace, in the pulpit and elsewhere, but . . . the claim that England was *the* only elect nation, God's exclusive favorite, was rarer" ("John Foxe and National Consciousness," 10). Collinson wryly notes that "Haller's elect nation thesis ought to have been about the reception of Foxe, a book not so much about Foxe as about his readers" (17). Reception history has in fact become one way to reconcile the divergent views of Foxe; see, e.g., accounts by Lander ("'Foxe's' *Books of Martyrs*") or Nussbaum ("Whitgift's 'Book of Martyrs'") of the various uses to which *Acts and Monuments* could be put. But in the course of charting some nationalistic elements in that reception history, Parry notes both the developments in Foxe's thought and the ambiguities in his texts that made "the language of national election always available in *A & M*" ("Elect Church or Elect Nation?" 180). Despite all Foxe's claims elsewhere in the *Sermon* that God's mercy is not the inheritance of any one nation (see, e.g., K3r or K6v), his reference to "a people that shall glorifie his name" seems to me to constitute one such ambiguity.

For the broader claim that "English Protestants generally remained uncertain whether their basic collective identity as Christians bound them to a national, parochial, or supranational fellowship," see Knapp, *Shakespeare's Tribe*, 15. Knapp's claim that theater, and particularly Shakespeare, had a special role to play in promoting an Erasmian space of good Christian fellowship that was nondoctrinal and strongly internationalist provides an important corrective by underscoring the ambivalences in Shakespeare's—and, more broadly, English Protestantism's—nationalism.

76. Foxe had what Collinson characterizes as a "semi-detached relationship with the national church" ("John Foxe and National Consciousness," 28). For Foxe's increasing skepticism about the progress of "godly reformation" in England, see, e.g., Loades ("Introduction," 3–4) and Betteridge, who analyzes Foxe's shift from prophetic history in the 1563 *Acts and Monuments* to apocalyptic history in the 1570 edition ("From Prophetic to Apocalyptic"). According to Betteridge, "the 1570 text is marked by the fears and failures of the godly after the defeats of the 1560's, with the success of the Reforma-

tion being constructed as far more problematic and therefore needing to be guaranteed by the apocalyptic course of history itself" (213).

77. *A Sermon of Christ Crucified*, cited in Wooden, *John Foxe*, 86. The term "angle" had long been associated with England through geography, settlement by the Angles, and the pseudo-etymology of Gregory's famous conflation of English boys with angels (see, e. g., Howe, "An Angle on This Earth," 2–3). Foxe would have known at least the scurrilous sodomitical version of the Gregory story from Bales's rewriting of Bede (Robinson, "John Foxe and the Anglo-Saxons").

78. Foxe's struggle to define the reprobation of the Jews reiterates issues at stake in sixteenth-century England's broader struggles to define predestination: does God predestine the fates only of the elect (as the Thirty-nine Articles implied) or of both the elect and the reprobate? If the latter (the more strictly Calvinist "double predestination" endorsed by reformers like Foxe as well as by many moderates within the church), then to what extent could the reprobate still be held responsible for their reprobation? Does God choose reprobation for them and then punish them for his choice? For a convenient summary of Foxe's views on election and predestination, see V. Olsen, *John Foxe and the Elizabethan Church*, 102–3; and see Hunt, *Shakespeare's Religious Allusiveness*, 99–102, for a convenient summary of the controversy. Lake gives both a detailed account of the controversy as it played out in the 1590s and some fascinating local instances of the difficulty in reconciling individual responsibility with double predestination (*Moderate Puritans*, esp. 103, 150–55, 201–42). Although Foxe's dilemma in the *Sermon* reiterates this general difficulty, it seems to me that his Jews nonetheless represent a special—and more urgent—case. Foxe needs his Jews to be fundamentally distinct from Christians and fundamentally culpable both because the distinction between Christian and Jew is foundational for Christianity and because the reliance of Christian election on Jewish reprobation would otherwise create intolerable guilt.

79. This pattern is repeated yet again when Foxe excoriates the Jews for not repenting, exhorts them to repent, and then acknowledges that repentance comes only from God (L8v).

80. Foxe here echoes a phrase with which Catholics taunted Calvinists for their belief in double predestination; see, e.g., Lake's account of the response of John Bridges, future bishop of Oxford, to this taunt: "Such a position did not imply, as the papists falsely alleged, that God 'delighteth in their destruction whom he hardeneth or is the author or partaker of their wickedness'" ("Calvinism and the English Church," 36). When Bridges goes on to insist that "God's works to the wicked are just and righteous and that he saveth some it is his mercy. He might have damned all if he had would," he suggests how readily the doctrine led to questions about God's justice (ibid.).

81. Foxe once again answers his own question by repeating that only the overthrow of the Jewish nation could confirm the prophets and pluck out the rule of Law rooted in men's hearts (M3v–M4r). But the repetition suggests the instability of any given answer, and in fact this answer is immediately followed by the passage characterizing the Jews as innocent victims of God's cruelty.

82. Since Foxe is wrestling precisely with the conundrums of innocence and guilt here, I am assuming that "seely" still carries the valence of innocence for him (see *OED*, definition 5, "innocent, harmless. Often as an expression of compassion for persons or

animals suffering undeservedly"). Foxe uses the word in this way elsewhere, e.g., in his description of a Protestant martyr as a "silly lamb" killed by "Catholic executioners" (cited in Helgerson, *Forms of Nationhood*, 254). But given Foxe's delight in pointing out what he considers Jewish foolishness, its more recent sense (*OED*, definition 8, "foolish, simple, silly") probably comes into play as well.

83. Achinstein's observation that the language of this passage evokes "fears about the responsibility of the Jews for the Black Death" strikes me as particularly acute ("John Foxe and the Jews," 106).

84. Insofar as the pure-blood laws were instituted exactly at the point that the difference between Christian and Jew was threatened by mass conversion (see chap. 3), the underlying mechanism is the same as in Foxe's appeal to inheritable disease here. Freinkel similarly understands anti-Semitism as a response to elements in Luther that destabilized the distinction between Christian and Jew (*"The Merchant of Venice:* 'Modern' Anti-Semitism and the Veil of Allegory"); though I doubt that Shakespeare or his audience shared her reading of Luther, her claim that anti-Semitism, like other racializing discourses, "constructs its object . . . precisely starting from the dread that there is *no* objective correlative to the Jewishness of the Jews" (125) seems to me exactly right.

85. Foxe's last phrase associates the killing of Christ with the so-called blood libel, in which Jews were accused of killing Christian children at Easter in order to use their blood to make matzah and for other rituals. Elsewhere in the sermon, Foxe alludes to these murders ("your intolerable Scorpionlike sauagenes, so furiously boyling against the innocent infants of the Christian Gentiles"); the marginal note obligingly adds, "Christen mens children here in Englande crucified by the Iewes Anno. 1139 & anno. 1141 at Norwiche &c." (E3r). The first documented blood libel accusations were in England; for their spread from England to Europe, see, e.g., Hsia, *Ritual Murder*, 2–4.

86. Recent historians and literary critics have succeeded in revising the notion of a perfectly Protestant England and, with it, the notion of a perfectly Protestant English national poet. Among historians, see, e.g., magisterial works by Duffy (*Stripping of the Altars*) and Questier (*Conversion*). Among literary critics, I have found the accounts of Bishop ("Shakespeare and Religion") and Marotti ("Shakespeare and Catholicism") particularly balanced and useful; see also Callaghan's strong warning against business-as-usual in the study of Shakespeare and religion ("Shakespeare and Religion"). Bishop concludes that Shakespeare may have been "outside the strict boundaries of denomina-tional faith . . . in a space of novel possibility opened up by the incomplete character of the English Reformation" (27), a speculation in which he is joined by Greenblatt (*Will in the World*, 113), among many others. Whatever the precise nature of Shakespeare's belief—and most critics would agree with Collinson that it is not recoverable ("Religious Inheritance," 251–52)—the concerns about God's deselection of the Jews reflected in Foxe's sermon would have been familiar to him, and not only because he would have found them in the Geneva Bible (see chap. 2, n. 2, for Shakespeare's use of that Bible). The conundrum of a Jewish deselection that is simultaneously the fault of Jewish blindness and the product of God's will is far older than the Reformation and is as problematic for Paul as it is for Foxe (see Morrison, *Understanding Conversion*, 45–46, 82–83, for some other pre-Reformation instances).

As for Shakespeare's religious beliefs as they might be visible specifically in *Merchant:* many have argued convincingly that some in Shakespeare's audience would have heard a critique of the Puritans in Shakespeare's portrayal of Shylock (see, e.g., Milward, "Religious Implications," 32–38). But a critique of Puritans, which in these accounts tends in any case to be based more on social than on theological grounds (Puritans practice usury, dislike festivity, and are hypocrites who cite the Bible to justify their practices), does not in itself imply Catholic leanings, since many within the Church of England similarly criticized what they saw as Puritan tendencies. In *Merchant* as elsewhere, Shakespeare draws on the rich emotional vocabulary of Catholicism (see, e.g., Klause, "Catholic and Protestant, Jesuit and Jew," 66–67, for that vocabulary, particularly in relation to Portia); but attempts to link the play with specifically Catholic beliefs or with Southwell and the situation of English Catholics (Milward, "Religious Implica-tions," 38–45; Klause, "Catholic and Protestant, Jesuit and Jew," 71–91) seem to me unconvincing. If anything, *Merchant* could serve to heal divisions among Christians and thus serve the purposes of the irenic Shakespeare portrayed, e.g., by Hunt (*Shakespeare's Religious Allusiveness,* xii) or Knapp (*Shakespeare's Tribe,* esp. 49–57, 136–37): in its Jew, the play works to unify divided Christian factions by giving them a figure they could all agree to hate.

CHAPTER TWO

1. For the institution of this prohibition by the Fourth Lateran Council, see, e.g., Edwards, *Jews in Christian Europe,* 16; M. Cohen notes a similar prohibition as early as the fifth century Theodosian Code (*Under Crescent and Cross,* 35). For its importation specifically into England, see, e.g., Maitland, "Deacon and Jewess," 261; and Roth, *History of the Jews in England,* 42. This was still a live issue in 1655, immediately before Jews were given the legal right to live in England; see Roth, *History of the Jews in England,* 163, for an attempt to reinvoke the prohibition. Live or not, the prohibition was hard to enforce, particularly when the line between Christian and Jew was blurred. See chap. 1, n. 21, for Thomas Wilson, a Christian servant in London who testified in court about his converso master's Judaizing; in Sisson's view, "it is difficult not to see in this action some reflection of a sense of insecurity in the mind of this young Londoner serving in a Jewish family" in the aftermath of the Lopez trial ("Colony of Jews," 45).

2. As always unless specified, this citation is to the Geneva Bible. Shakespeare refers to other versions of the Bible (most prominently the Bishops'), but Geneva was the version he used most often; Shaheen accordingly finds it "only natural to assume that he owned a copy" (*Biblical References in Shakespeare's Tragedies,* 34). Stritmatter notes that "an impressive scholarly tradition documents the pervasive use of many Genevan Bible marginal notes in Shakespeare" ("By Providence Divine," 97). In an elegant and plausible essay, Black traces Horatio's comment that Hamlet "must be edified by the margin" (*Hamlet,* 5.2.114.1–2) to the Geneva Bible's description of its marginal notes, included "for the edifying of the brethren" (*Edified by the Margent,* 8).

3. This is the rationale given in Maitland's summary of the reasons for the prohibi-tion's introduction into England in 1222: "Jews are not to have Christian servants, it

being contrary to reason that the sons of the free woman should serve the sons of the bond" ("Deacon and Jewess," 261). This theological justification for the prohibition was widespread; see, e.g., Ruether, *Faith and Fratricide*, 187, 209.

4. Danson reads Lancelot's shift of masters in relation to two other New Testament metaphors of service: it is, first, "a preposterous redaction of Christ's injunction in the Sermon on the Mount, 'No man can serve two masters . . .'" and, second, a reminder of Paul's distinction between the servants of sin and the servants of righteousness in Romans 6.15–18 (*Harmonies*, 72–73). The first of these identifications seems to me implausible, since Lancelot has no desire to serve two masters at once; the second more nearly fits Lancelot's situation. Lancelot's confused ambitions in 2.2 may in fact dramatize the implicit contradiction between the servant-master metaphor in Galatians and the metaphor of two different kinds of servants in Romans: Lancelot wants to be a servant and a master simultaneously.

5. In the course of a complex argument about adequate and inadequate fathers, Rockas notes that "Lancelot goes as the plot goes, abandoning Shylock for Christian mercy," and that Gobbo's doves serve as the central symbol for that mercy ("'Dish of Doves,'" 348). Building on Rockas's work, McLean sees in the doves "both a reminder of God's original covenant with the Jews and a symbol of the transfer of that covenant to the Christians, when the gift intended for Shylock is given to Bassanio instead" ("Prodigal Sons," 50).

6. This hiccup in Lancelot's identity is recuperated not only by Gobbo's subsequent recognition of him but also by the reconfiguration in 2.2 of one of its biblical sources. When Gobbo calls his allegedly dead son "the very staff of my age, my very prop" (2.2.57–58), he is reclaiming the staff—and the phrase—from Tobias's mother, who uses it to refer to her son both when he leaves home and when she later thinks that he is dead; see Tobit 5.23 and 10.4, as cited from the Bishops' Bible by Shaheen (*Biblical References in Shakespeare's Comedies*, 116).

7. Danson notes this "oddly *Lear*-like moment" (*Harmonies*, 74). In fact, the anticipation of Edgar's deception of Gloucester is startlingly exact: both scenes turn on the son's deception of his blind father; and both locate that deception in proximity to concerns about the father's sexual misdeeds and (as I shall argue) to a story about competing brothers. In both instances, the conjunction seems partly to stand in for broader anxieties about legitimacy and paternal legacy.

8. In *Radical Jew*, Boyarin argues that Paul's theology was a response to the tension between "narrow ethnocentrism and universal monotheism" within Judaism, particularly as the latter was inflected by Hellenism. In Boyarin's brilliant account, Paul's allegorizing hermeneutic allows him precisely to displace the particularistic claim and to embrace oneness while retaining the centrality of "Israel" (see esp. chap. 1, "Circumcision, Allegory, and Universal 'Man,'" and 52–53); Boyarin is throughout concerned with the political consequences of this hermeneutic, which allowed Paul to read Jews "as the literal . . . of which Christians are the allegorical signified" (156). The extent to which Paul in fact intended to cast off his fleshly fathers along with their fleshly law has been the subject of intense controversy, particularly as scholars attempt to reclaim him from the Reformation reading of his relation to Judaism, in which Judaism figures as sterile and legalistic devotion to works; see Boyarin's powerful account of these controversies

and of Paul's problematic attempt to include "genealogical" Jews in his spiritual universalism (esp. chap. 2, "What Was Wrong with Judaism? The Cultural Politics of Pauline Scholarship," and chap. 6, "Was Paul an 'Anti-Semite'?"). The Paul to whom I refer here and elsewhere in this book is generally Paul as Foxe would have understood him, though much in that understanding was the common property of Christianity.

9. As though enacting a version of the Freudian family romance, Nathanael seems eager to cast off his disappointing fleshly forefathers in order to gain access to a spiritualized father Abraham, but his confession nonetheless shows signs of continued, if ambivalent, pride in his Jewish heritage. He marks his conversion from his fleshly lineage by a name change, but he disavows his Hebrew name only after invoking it with pride and recalling the covenant that brought him into the Jewish people: he forsakes the name "which was giuen me at my circumcision (being Iehuda) though in it selfe it be honourable" ("Confession," B7v). And though he takes a new name—"desiring that as I haue receiued a new gift from the Lord, so in token thereof I may be called Nathanael" (B7v)— that new name memorializes his Jewish origin: its meaning—"gift from the Lord"— would be clear only to those who knew Hebrew. Moreover, the "man Jesus" that he now embraces is consistently "Meshiach," not Messiah; like the God to whom he is returned—"the God of Abraham, Isaac and Iacob"—this spelling insists on the Jewish lineage of the religion he is about to embrace. See Morrison, *Understanding Conversion*, 53–54, for an account of ambivalence similarly registered by a twelfth-century convert from Judaism.

10. This lineage is firmly established in the dominant Christian traditions, though it is contested by both Mark and John; see Fredriksen's account of the ways in which the varying valuations of Jewish lineage—and of Judaism—in the four evangelists were intertwined with their historical circumstances and their theological agendas (*From Jesus to Christ*, esp. 20–52, 180–204, 206–12).

11. Augustine, *Citie of God*, 16.42 (616), 16.37 (611).

12. Ishmael was known as a mocker of Isaac (see Noble's citation of the Bishops' Bible gloss to Genesis 21.9, "Ismael mocked Gods promise made to Isahac," in *Biblical Knowledge*, 267)—hence "that fool of Hagar's son."

13. The extent to which Foxe feels called upon to challenge the Jewish claim to Abraham in his *Sermon preached at the Christening of a Certaine Iew* suggests that this claim was still a live issue in early modern England (see chap. 1), as do the length and strenuousness of his attempts to refute the Jewish understanding of its own founding text (see, e.g., C5r–C6r, D5r–E2v, E6r–G4r, G7v, I4r). Few critics note Shylock's destabilizing of Christian hermeneutics here (for exceptions, see, e.g., Lampert, *Gender*, 149; Holmer, *Merchant of Venice*, 91–92), but several comment more generally on the hermeneutic contest over possession of the patriarchs and of the Hebrew Bible in *Merchant*. Coolidge, for example, thinks that the Christians win hands down; in his reading, *Merchant* is an exercise in the corrective Christian reading not only of scripture but also of Jessica's flight, Portia's ring, and many other elements traditional to comedy ("Law and Love"). For more skeptical treatments of this contest, see, e.g., Rosenheim, "Allegorical Commentary," esp. 184–86; Marx, *Shakespeare and the Bible*, 120–24; and Lampert, *Gender*, 140–41, 146–49, all of whom think that *Merchant* at least partially qualifies the Christian hermeneutic triumph assumed by Coolidge.

14. Shell calls attention to Folio's version of 1.3.70 ("I, he was the third") to suggest that Shylock confuses himself with Jacob ("Wether," 52); that confusion would in any case have been audible in the pun on "ay" that Folio makes visible. But several commentators have suggested that the story that Shylock goes on to tell at least partly destabilizes this identification. Shylock would like to base his claim to "use" on the precedent of Jacob's clever management of Laban's sheep, but when the play enacts the story of Rachel's flight from her father Laban's house, it puts Shylock in the position of Laban, not of Jacob; see, e.g., Coolidge, "Law and Love," 247; or Engle, "'Thrift,'" 32.

15. References to the so-called Bishops' Bible are to *The holie Bible* (1572).

16. Calvin, *Commentarie vpon Genesis*, 356–57.

17. When Brown cites *Jew of Malta*, 1.1.103–4, as a gloss to Shylock's allusion to Abram, for example, he silently transforms Barabas's "Abram" into "Abraham" as though the name change made no difference (*Arden Shakespeare: Merchant of Venice*, 25). Shaheen in fact insists that it makes no difference; in his view, Shakespeare's choice of "Abram" for "Abraham" reflects merely metrical concerns ("Shylock's 'Abram'"). But elsewhere Shakespeare managed to fit "Abraham" into iambic pentameter (see n. 20), and even a name initially chosen for metrical reasons—if "Abram" was—can accrue meaning beyond the metrical, particularly in a play so insistently concerned with issues of scriptural interpretation. Rosenheim is one of the few who takes the name seriously; she reads it as a sign of the limitations of a Judaism that would restrict Abraham's promise to his biological heirs ("Allegorical Commentary," 191–92). Lupton's reading is closer to mine; for her, Shylock's use of "Abram" dramatizes "a specifically Jewish hermeneutics" ("Exegesis," 124).

18. Augustine, *Citie of God*, 16.28 (604).

19. Ainsworth explains, "*Abram* signifieth *A high father*: and the first letter of *Hamon* (that is, *a Multitude*) being put unto it, maketh *Abraham*, as if it were *Abraha-mon*, that is, *A high father of a multitude* of nations" (*Annotations*, N3r). In Clapham's simplified version, "For printing this Couenant more deepe in the brests of *Abram* and *Sarah*, the Lord calleth *Abram* (in English, High-father) ABRAHAM (in English, *The Father of a great Multitude*)" (*Briefe of the Bible*, 31–32).

20. See, e.g., *Richard II*, 4.1.95, and *Richard III*, 4.3.38; that both of these passages are in verse vitiates Shaheen's claim (see n. 17).

21. Coolidge, e.g., reads Antonio's contrast between outer and inner as a comment on the "specious plausibility of the Jew's interpretation of the text" in contrast to the plain outside and beautiful inside of proper Christian scriptural interpretation, epitomized by the lead casket ("Law and Love," 251). Lampert would agree that Antonio is referring to the internal corruption of a faulty Jewish hermeneutics (*Gender*, 146), but she understands this moment not as the triumph of Christian hermeneutics but as part of the play's persistent disruption of an idealized Christian exegesis that claims to be able to read reliably from outer to inner. And for Whigham, Antonio's "series of complacent sententiae" indicate not his superior hermeneutics but "the rigidity of his conceptual vocabulary" ("Ideology and Class Conduct," 104–5).

22. For this uneasiness, see, e.g., Nuttall, who reads Antonio's speech as "the words of a man who is holding fast to a conviction that his opponent must be wrong, but cannot quite see how" (*New Mimesis*, 128).

23. Shakespeare's only "good" younger son—Orlando—triumphs over his elder brother, not Jacob-like, through deception, but by waiting on events, as the biblical commentators say Jacob should have done (see below).

24. See, e.g., the Norton edition's gloss to these lines; according to the Arden edition's gloss, Lancelot's line is "proverbial, but usually transposed."

25. For a brilliant reading of the echoes of Jacob and Esau in the brothers of *The Comedy of Errors* as an allusion to the promised reconciliation of Christian and Jew in Christ, see Parker, *Literary Fat Ladies*, 77–81; *Merchant* seems to me to encode a much darker view of that promised reconciliation and a much more anxious version of the Jacob and Esau story. The echo of Isaac's blessing of Jacob in 2.2 has often been observed (see, e.g., Hockey, "The Patch Is Kind Enough"), but usually in the service of an argument in support of the supersessionist narrative that is assumed to govern the play. Danson, for example, reads the reference to Jacob and Isaac in 2.2 as "a comic allusion to the Christian scheme of salvation-history" (*Harmonies*, 76); for Colley, Lancelot acts out "a symbolic version of Jacob's ambiguous (yet divinely inspired) theft," and Shylock is the "elder brother who has been cheated, rightfully, out of his birthright" ("Launcelot, Jacob, and Esau," 188, 189). Even those who question the legitimacy of that supersessionist narrative tend to read the echo of Jacob and Esau in 2.2 as evidence of its triumph; see, e.g., Engle, for whom it—like Shylock's later resemblance to Laban—registers Shylock's loss of control of the Jacob story ("'Thrift,'" 32), and Lupton, for whom it serves as a corrective to Shylock's Jewish hermeneutics ("Exegesis," 125–26).

But for Fortin, the Jacob-Isaac analogy counters the easy move from the old to the new dispensation—and thus the supersessionist narrative—by reminding us of the bond of filial piety that should obtain between Christian and Jew ("Launcelot and the Uses of Allegory"); in his reading of 2.2 as an "oblique commentary on the tensions between the Judaic and the Christian traditions" (262), his argument anticipates aspects of mine. Rosenheim extends Fortin's reading in a complex analysis in which the biblical identities of Lancelot and Gobbo are refracted onto Antonio and Shylock, each of whom is guilty of failing to recognize his familial relation to the other; in her view, the transformation of the Jacob-Isaac story into the prodigal son story in 2.2 serves as a model for a reciprocal father-son relationship between Judaism and Christianity that neither Shylock nor Antonio is capable of enacting ("Allegorical Commentary," esp. 160–69, 180–83, 201). (Poliakov's *History of Anti-Semitism* would complicate the potentially sentimental reading of the father-son relationship implicit in Fortin and Rosenheim: in his reading—or at least in the reading that he attributes to a hypothetical psychoanalyst and then endorses—the older brother in this triumph of younger son over older "is present only to screen the father . . . in reality we are concerned with a direct and successful aggression against the father. Thus Judaism would be the supplanted father, inspiring extraordinarily violent and mixed feelings: hatred, fear, remorse"; 160.) Marx is at the furthest extreme from those critics who see in 2.2 simply the reinforcement of the supersessionist narrative: in his reading, the allusion to Jacob's trickery serves partly as an analogy for Paul's own trickery in taking possession of the Hebrew Bible (*Shakespeare and the Bible*, 121–23). Zachary Cannon first opened up these issues for me in 1995, in an evocative undergraduate paper in which he identified Lancelot not with Jacob but with the Esau who gives up his paternal inheritance and is—like the Christians who reject their father Judaism—left empty.

26. Coolidge notes that "the moral and theological implications of Jacob's career were felt to be a problem almost from the beginning of the biblical tradition" and cites as evidence the Bible's own revision of the story of Laban's sheep in Genesis 31.11, where the merely human tricksy plot of 30.31–43 is said to have been revealed by God in a dream ("Law and Love," 247). Danson adds that "the most pious exegete may be permitted to see potential moral difficulties, and therefore perhaps the possibility for comedy" in the Jacob-Isaac episode (*Harmonies*, 75).

27. Calvin, *Commentarie vpon Genesis*, 567, 575.

28. Ibid., 575.

29. Augustine, *Citie of God*, 16.42 (616).

30. Ibid., 16.37 (611).

31. Babington, *Certain Plaine, Briefe and Comfortable Notes*, 104r, 104v.

32. Ainsworth, *Annotations*, V3r.

33. See Williams, *Common Expositor*, 169–73, both for a summary of commentaries—all troubled—on the Jacob-Esau story and for its relation to the doctrine of election.

34. Calvin, *Thirteene Sermons*, 17v.

35. The interlude frames the story of Jacob and Esau with the doctrine of election both in its prologue and in its epilogue by "the Poete," and it scatters references to the doctrine in the play proper; see *Iacob and Esau*, ll. 8–19, 891–92, 1471–91, 1801–21.

36. Calvin, *Commentarie vpon Genesis*, 577.

37. Calvin, *Thirteene Sermons*, 160r, 168r–v.

38. For the debate on Calvinist double predestination, see chap. 1, n. 78.

39. See chap. 1.

40. Calvin, *Commentarie vpon Romanes*, 122v.

41. Calvin, *Thirteene Sermons*, 161r–v.

42. See, e.g., versions of the proverb cited in the Norton, Arden, Penguin, and Harper-Collins editions. When Lancelot refers to Fortune as "a good wench for this gear" a few lines later (2.2.149–50), the word "gear" seems to be an escapee from the proverb Lancelot has just rewritten.

43. The marginal gloss erroneously cites Genesis 49.15 instead of 48.15, but 48.15 is clearly what is intended; Genesis 48.15 in fact directs readers forward to this passage in Hebrews.

44. "I know my son well" is also audible in Jacob's words; is this formulation perhaps in part responsible for Lancelot's "It is a wise father that knows his own child" (2.2.66)?

45. Hebrews 11.21 conflates two moments: the blessing of Joseph's children in Genesis 48.15 and the scene immediately preceding that blessing, when Jacob extracted a vow from Joseph to bury him with his fathers and then "worshipped toward the beds head" (47.31); the Geneva gloss to Hebrews 11.21 refers readers to both passages. The reading of "staff" for "bed" in Genesis 47.31 apparently derives from the Septuagint (see Plaut's *Torah*, 302) and is reproduced in Hebrews 11.21, despite the fact that the Geneva Bible's version of Genesis 47.31 makes no mention of a staff.

46. Shaheen follows Noble (*Biblical Knowledge*, 269) in considering Shylock's reference to Jacob's staff "primarily a reference to Genesis [rather than Hebrews], since

throughout the play Shylock refers extensively to the Genesis account about Jacob" (*Biblical References in Shakespeare's Comedies*, 118).

47. Babington, *Certain Plaine, Briefe and Comfortable Notes*, 129v.

48. Engle, e.g., reads it this way ("'Thrift,'" 32).

49. Babington, *Certain Plaine, Briefe and Comfortable Notes*, 133r.

50. Calvin, *Commentarie vpon Genesis*, 681, 683.

51. Ibid., 685.

52. Portia's wealth has frequently been read as spiritual riches; see, e.g., Danson, *Harmonies*, 9–10. For supersessionist critics, the wealth that comes to the Christians from Shylock unproblematically stands in for the transfer of spiritual wealth from Jew to Christian. This allegorical reading is particularly useful in mitigating Jessica's otherwise-embarrassing theft from her father: see, e.g., Lewalksi, "Biblical Allusion," 333; Milward, "Religious Implications," 31. For Holmer, even Jessica's exchange of her mother's ring for a monkey is saved because the exchange represents her rejection of her father's idolatry (*Merchant of Venice*, 127). Years ago Auden pointed out the problem with spiritualized readings of Portia's wealth: "Without the Venetian scenes, Belmont would be an Arcadia without any relation to actual times and places, and where, therefore, money and sexual love have no reality of their own, but are symbolic signs for a community in a state of grace. But Belmont is related to Venice. . . . Because of Shylock and Antonio, Portia's inherited fortune becomes real money which must have been made in this world, as all fortunes are made, by toil, anxiety, the enduring and inflicting of suffering" ("Brothers & Others," 234). And Engle implicitly critiques these spiritualizing readings of wealth when he notes wryly that "the theological terms in which many economic issues . . . appear are also shown in the play to define a system of exchange or conversion which works to the advantage of the 'blessed': those who, by religion and social situation, are placed to take advantage of exchange patterns" ("'Thrift,'" 21).

53. For the spoiling of manna when more than is needed is gathered, see Exodus 16.20; for the displacement of manna by the "true bread from heauen," see John 6.27–35. Unsurprisingly, Danson reads Lorenzo's reference to manna in the light of his harmonious-supersessionist understanding of the play: "Lorenzo's reply appropriately accepts the good news of a New Dispensation with imagery that encompasses the Old" (*Harmonies*, 180). But for others, the reference functions (for a moment at least) to undercut the Christian exclusion of Shylock. See, e.g., Tanner, for whom it serves as a reminder of "the long archaic biblical past stretching back behind Shylock" ("'Which Is the Merchant Here?'" 58); for Shell, it is a reminder that Shylock and his money stand behind Portia's dispensation and that Belmont is thus subject to the same commensurability of men and money as Venice ("Wether," 79).

54. Critics of *Merchant* have commented extensively both on the long-standing incompatibility between wealth and Christian values and on the Protestant reshaping of that incompatibility. See especially Moisan, who finds the play simultaneously ratifying and questioning the new ideology that associates wealth with God's favor; in his reading, tensions within that ideology necessitated the excoriating of the usurer, who can then absorb blame for economic ills construed as excesses of the new capitalism rather than as elements inherent within it ("'Which Is the Merchant Here?'" esp. 196–97).

55. Calvin, *Commentarie vpon Genesis*, 582, 579.

56. See chap. 1.

57. Of Shakespeare's twenty-eight references to "prodigal" and its derivatives, five are in *Merchant;* even *Timon of Athens,* which is explicitly about prodigality, has only three. Critics usually argue that the presence of the parable in *Merchant* valorizes forgiveness, spiritual generosity, and risk-taking over pharisaical righteousness and therefore Christian grace over Jewish works (see, e.g., Tippens, "Prodigal Son Tradition," 64, 70; McLean, "Prodigal Sons," 48, 60; Milward, "Religious Implications," 31). In addition to Bassanio and Antonio, Jessica often figures as a prodigal daughter in these arguments both because of her prodigal spending and because Graziano's speech about the prodigal (2.6.14–19) occurs just as she is about to run away from her father (see, e.g., Tippens, "Prodigal Son Tradition," 62; McLean, "Prodigal Sons," 51–52; Rosenheim, "Allegorical Commentary," 177); Lampert argues that Jessica's prodigal actions literalize the parable's supersessionist allegory insofar as Shylock's wealth and bloodline are transferred to the Christians through her (*Gender,* 148).

But the doubleness of prodigality in the play—its status as the term of choice both for wastrel spending and for Christian liberality—undercuts a simple supersessionist reading; see, e.g., Moisan, for whom that doubleness registers anxieties about the status of wealth, Christian or otherwise ("'Which Is the Merchant Here?'" 198). In fact, the presence of the parable in *Merchant* is sometimes taken as a critique of the play's Christian characters: for Pastoor, for instance, Antonio is allegorically a successful father-God to Bassanio's prodigal, but tropologically a failure because he never imitates that father's mercy to his eldest son in Shylock ("Subversion," 8–9, 12, 18); for Rosenheim, Antonio is the prodigal son who cruelly mistreats his father Shylock ("Allegorical Commentary," esp. 167–69, 176–78).

Both McLean ("Prodigal Sons," 50) and Rosenheim ("Allegorical Commentary," esp. 166–67, 175, 196) argue for the importance of the prodigal son parable specifically in 2.2. Though I do not always agree with Rosenheim's conclusions, she is especially noteworthy as the only critic who attempts to think strenuously through the consequences of the simultaneous presence of both the Jacob-Isaac story and the prodigal son parable in that scene (see n. 25).

58. For the prodigal son as a trope for conversion, see, e.g., Morrison, *Understanding Conversion,* 38, 202n16.

59. Shylock is usually identified with the Pharisees by critics who see traces of the prodigal son parable in *Merchant:* see, e.g., Milward, "Religious Implications," 31; Tippens, "Prodigal Son Tradition," 72; or McLean, "Prodigal Sons," 52. Although Lewalski does not refer to the prodigal son parable, her identification of Shylock with the Pharisee of Luke 18 is clearly the prototype for these readings, as for other supersessionist readings of *Merchant* ("Biblical Allusion," 331–32).

60. The classic account of Portia's demonstration of the Pauline inadequacy of the Law is Lewalski's "Biblical Allusion," 340. Danson extends her account by stressing the distinction between abrogating and fulfilling the Law; in his view, Portia succeeds in fulfilling the Law (and hence in harmonizing justice and mercy) by revealing "the spirit of the law latent in its letter, yielding mercy through rigor" (*Harmonies,* 57, 63). For more on Pauline Law, see chap. 4 (esp. at nn. 31 and 35).

61. Robbins considers the parable the basis for all conversion narratives in part

because the relation between its two brothers "figures the figural relationship between the two testaments"; the elder brother is thus inscribed within the parable "*as* its outside, as a trace of the rejected alternative [that] makes the spiritual understanding of the parable possible" (*Prodigal Son/Elder Brother*, 11, 21–22, 41). According to Wailes, Jerome's and Augustine's "historical allegory," in which the elder brother stands in for the superseded Jews, "dominates medieval understanding" (*Jesus' Parables*, 242). Calvin grudgingly admits the continued validity of this allegory ("They that thinke that the people of the Iewes are described vnder the figure of the elder sonne, though they do it not without some reason, yet they seeme to me not sufficiently to marke the whole course of the texte"; *A Harmonie vpon the Three Euangelists*, 495), and it is reflected in the Geneva gloss to Luke 15.31, which identifies the elder brother as a Jew (see n. 62). Unsurprisingly, Shylock is usually identified as the prototypical elder brother in this scenario (see, e.g., Milward, "Religious Implications," 31; Tippens, "Prodigal Son Tradition," 72; McLean, "Prodigal Sons," 52). But for Rosenheim, he serves simultaneously as the blind father Isaac who doesn't recognize his Christian son and as the wronged father in the prodigal son parable ("Allegorical Commentary," 162–68).

62. The Geneva gloss to Luke 15.31 partly implies this inclusiveness, but of course only at the cost of the Jew's conversion ("Thy parte, which art a Iewe, is nothing diminished by that the Christ was also killed for the Gentiles: for he accepteth not the persone, but feedeth indifferently all them that beleue in him, with his bodie and blood to life euerlasting"). Others find this cost too high. Parsons argues forcefully against the traditional supersessionist reading of the parable; in his view, the parable "subverts the rejected elder son theme that demands one be chosen and the other rejected. Both are chosen" ("Prodigal's Elder Brother," 171). Both Pastoor and Rosenheim concur in aspects of this reading: for Pastoor, the parable should teach Christians mercy to the Jews ("Subversion," 12, 16, 18); for Rosenheim, the parable stands for the possibility of mutual recognition and familial love between Christian and Jew ("Allegorical Commentary," 182–83). Achieving this mutual recognition is the point of Ruether's *Faith and Fratricide*; see especially her powerful and moving attempt to develop a Christian theology that does not depend on the exclusivity of Christian revelation and thus does not mandate either a supersessionist narrative or the conversion of the Jews (226–61).

63. For accounts of the tendency to eliminate or severely marginalize the elder brother, see Parsons, "Prodigal's Elder Brother," 149, 153, 154, 161–64, 169; Robbins, *Prodigal Son/Elder Brother*, 41. Parson's report of the horror Ruskin provoked when he interjected a question about the older brother into an evangelical séance suggests what is at stake in his absence ("Prodigal's Elder Brother," 162). The figure of the older brother apparently haunted the parable from the time of its earliest interpreters. Wailes identifies the problem in his account of Jerome—"Jerome has now arrived at that problem in the parable which he identified early in his letter, the apparent justice of the elder brother. If this figure represented the Jews [as it does in Jerome], its claim and the seeming agreement of the Father cannot be taken at face value" (*Jesus' Parables*, 240)—and gives evidence of the attempts of Jerome and Augustine to evade it. Augustine, e.g., concludes that the "Father's words 'all that is mine is thine' must be understood as the result of implicit conditions, for *if* the pious Jews will enter into the Father's house peacefully and joyously, *then* they will share in God's fullness" (242).

64. The traditional association of Jews with blindness is evident in passages from Foxe's *Sermon* cited in chap. 1; see also Nathanael's "Confession" (B3v) or the Geneva Bible's introductory summary of Romans 11 ("God hathe blinded the Iewes"). The trope was so familiar that Clement VIII called his 1593 bull expelling most Jews from the papal territories *Caeca et Obdurata* (Edwards, *Jews in Christian Europe*, 74). Both Rosenheim ("Allegorical Commentary," 163–64) and Lampert (*Gender*, 147) read Gobbo/Isaac's blindness as a trope for his "Jewishness"; Gobbo is redeemed from this association for Lampert when he gives those doves to his son's new Christian master, and for Rosenheim when he is transformed into the father who recognizes and welcomes his prodigal Christian son.

65. Calvin's commentary on Isaac's blindness associates him with a kind of "Jewish" preference for flesh over spirit: "with a foolish and rash affection of the flesh" Isaac "is blindly carried with the loue of his first borne sonne, to preferre him before the other: and thus he striueth with the oracle of God. . . . The peeuish loue of his sonne, was a certeine kinde of blindnesse, which hindered him more, then the externall dimnesse of his eyes" (*Commentarie vpon Genesis*, 568–69). For Isaac as a figure for Christ, see, e.g., the Geneva Bible's introductory summary of Genesis 22, which states simply, "Izhak is a figure of Christ."

CHAPTER THREE

1. See chap. 2, n. 52, for critics who regard the "transfer" of Shylock's wealth to the Christians—including the new Christian Jessica—as a reference to the passing of spiritual riches from Jew to Christian. Insofar as Jessica's theft recalls Rachel's theft from her father, Laban, and therefore puts Shylock in the position of Laban (see chap. 2, n. 14), it similarly allies her with Jacob in another version of that supersessionist narrative.

2. Calvin, e.g., notes that Isaac was "deceiued with the craft and subtiltie of a woman," though he ultimately tends to excuse her on the grounds of her faith and zeal (*Commentarie vpon Genesis*, 569). The interlude *Iacob and Esau* twice plays uncomfortably on the sense that Jacob is a mama's boy. Early in the interlude, when Esau's servant asks whether or not Jacob will come hunting with them, Esau replies, "Nay, he must tarrie and sucke mothers dugge at home: / Iacob must keepe home I trow, vnder mothers wing" (ll. 99–100); and very near the end, Esau complains to his mother that Jacob is her "deinty dearlyng" (l. 1723) and imagines him infantilized ("I would he were rocked or dandled in your lappe: / Or I would with this fauchon I might geue him pap"; ll. 1727–28).

3. Gollancz (*Allegory and Mysticism*, 25), Lewalski ("Biblical Allusion," 333), and Brown (*Arden Shakespeare: Merchant of Venice*, 3) think that the name derives from "Iscah" or "Jesca" (Genesis 11.29), which means "she that looks out" in Hebrew; Lewalski adds that Shakespeare plays on that name in 2.5 when Shylock warns Jessica not to look out the window and Lancelot advises her to "look out at window for all this" (2.5.39). But Holmer argues plausibly for a derivation from "Ishai" (Jesse) rather than the exceedingly rare "Iscah" because "Jesse" "is a very familiar name with associations that are meaningful for the Judaeo-Christian lineage of the Church of God" (*Merchant of Venice*, 86, 90); though we disagree about how that lineage functions in Jessica's name and in *Merchant*, I am very much indebted to her for this suggestion. Orgel entertains the

possibility of this latter derivation, though ultimately he traces "Jessica" to a Scottish diminutive of Jessie as part of his broader project of "Englishing" Shylock ("Shylock's Tribe," 44).

4. "Confession," B8r; for more on this rabbinic principle, see n. 6 below.

5. The Geneva Bible's gloss on Paul's "separated me from my mothers wombe" tries to undo its oddness by transforming it into his "appointing from the mothers wombe," that is, into his election while still in the womb; but that gloss itself indicates that Paul's phrase was seen as something in need of explanation. And despite this gloss, "separated" became standard; it is reproduced, e.g., in the King James Bible.

6. It is unlikely that Shakespeare or his audience knew that Judaism was transmitted matrilineally; see S. Cohen, *Beginnings of Jewishness*, esp. chaps. 9–10, for the development of this rabbinic principle, which was in place by the second century CE. But whether or not they did, the hermeneutic that understands Judaism as merely fleshly maps easily onto the Aristotelian association of flesh with the female inheritance. For the equation of Jew with flesh, see, e.g., Boyarin, *Radical Jew*, 31; for the equation of flesh with woman, see, e.g., my *Suffocating Mothers*, 6; and for a complex argument about the ways in which the fleshliness of Jew and woman positions them similarly as embodiments of the letter in Christian hermeneutics, see Lampert, *Gender*, 21–57.

7. In the course of a very different argument, Normand similarly reads Graziano's words as a parodic incarnation ("Reading the Body," 56–57); he usefully notes that Lancelot's characterization of Shylock as "the very devil incarnation" (2.2.21) helps to secure this reading.

8. See, e.g., Shapiro, *Shakespeare and the Jews*, 120; Metzger, "'Now by My Hood,'" 59; Loomba, "'Delicious Traffick,'" 215; Lampert, *Gender*, 144, 164.

9. "Nation" is derived from Latin *nasci*, "to be born"; "country" carries a punning reference to the female genitals (see, e.g., Hamlet's taunting "country matters"; 3.2.105).

10. Supersessionist critics generally seem to agree with Jessica that her conversion-by-marriage will be unproblematic, presumably because it is in accord with Paul's dictum that "the unbeleeving wife is sanctified by the husband" (1 Corinthians 7.14, cited in Lewalski, "Biblical Allusion," 333). But matters were not so simple. Jessica apparently has no plans to convert before her marriage, and a long history of laws from the Fourth Lateran Council on forbade the marriage of Christian and Jew; see, e.g., Trachtenberg, *Devil*, 187, 251n33, for the general prohibition, and Kaplan, *Merchant of Venice: Texts and Contexts*, 303–4, for specifically English law on the subject.

11. "Get" is a familiar short form of "beget," used nearly as often by Shakespeare as the long form; Spevack's *Harvard Concordance* lists twenty-two instances of "beget" and fifteen instances of "get" in the sense of "beget." An audience's readiness to hear "beget" in this line might have been prompted not only by Shakespeare's habitual use of the short form but also by the unfamiliarity of "get thee" in the sense of "possess thee" in Shakespearean usage. Although "get thee" occurs in Shakespeare's works seventy-one times according to the *Harvard Concordance*, it is used in the sense of "possess thee" in only one other instance. In sixty of the instances, "get thee" is followed by an indication of place (as in "get thee gone"). Of the eleven instances in which it is followed by a direct object and clearly means "get possession of," "thee" is the indirect object (as in "get thee

a wife") nine times. Only here and in Henry V's rough wooing (*Henry V*, 5.2.192) does the phrase occur with "thee" as the direct object to be possessed.

12. Quarto 1, Quarto 2, and the First Folio all have "do"; as Brown notes, "If F2's 'did' is accepted, *get* is used for beget, as in III.v.9" (*Arden Shakespeare: Merchant of Venice*, 46). Furness's 1888 *Variorum* has "doe" but summarizes the editorial preference for "did" among those editors who wish to protect Jessica from the taint of her father's Jewishness; Furness himself rather charmingly confesses to preferring "did," but on the grounds of protecting her father from the pain she has caused him ("In thus supposing Jessica to be no child of Shylock, I confess the wish to be, for Shylock's sake, the father to the thought"; 81). Rockas takes F2's variant as evidence that Jessica "may be part Christian" but concludes that the "irregularities" associated both with her birth and with her marriage are "merely pleasant rebukes of intermarriage" ("Dish of Doves," 349); "Pleasant for whom?" I am tempted to ask. At least one Nazi production took them deadly seriously: Lothar Müthel's 1943 production in Vienna in effect literalized the F2 reading, adapting the text "so that Jessica became the result of an adulterous affair between Shylock's wife and a gentile, making her acceptable under the Nuremberg laws" (Edelman, introduction to *Merchant of Venice*, 53). See J. Gross, *Shylock*, 295–97, for more details about participants in this production and for a corrective to Edelman's view; Gross notes that "the real-life child of such parents would still have been classified as a mongrel—'a *Mischling* first class,' subject to persecution and marked down for eventual extermination" (295).

13. I owe my reading of "marry" here to my colleague and friend Steven Goldsmith, who pointed out the pun to me.

14. John 3.3. Nicodemus's literalist response—"How can a man be borne which is olde? can he enter into his mothers wombe againe, and be borne?" (John 3.4)—emphasizes the peculiarity of the image and illustrates the literalist imagination behind Lancelot's insistence.

15. The Norton edition appears to be alone in substituting "gentile" for "gentle," a substitution that does not have the authority of Folio or Q1, Norton's usual authority, though it does appear in Q2. Brown notes that "the words were not completely distinguished in spelling at this time" (*Arden Shakespeare: Merchant of Venice*, 49); his note to 2.4.34 calls "gentle" "a pun on Gentile" and directs the reader to Graziano's use of "gentle" here. In proximity to "Jew," "gentle" nearly always carries the residue of "gentile"; although Norton's substitution of F2's "gentile" for the more familiar "gentle" does not have much textual authority on its side, that proximity would have encouraged Shakespeare's audience to hear "a gentile" here (see also 1.3.173 and 4.1.33). Normative usage would also incline the audience in that direction, since "gentile" can function more readily than "gentle" as a substantive in the singular (see *OED*, "gentle" B1, which calls its use as a substantive in the singular—"*a* gentle"—rare); "gentle" is not used as a substantive in the singular elsewhere in Shakespeare.

16. *OED*'s first meaning for "stranger" is "one who belongs to another country, a foreigner; chiefly (now exclusively), one who resides in or comes to a country to which he is a foreigner; an alien." The second meaning similarly emphasizes non-nativeness over lack of familiarity; the sixth is "a person not of one's kin; more fully, *stranger in blood.*" (The latter sense gives added richness to Lear's proclaiming Cordelia "strangered with our

oath," "a stranger to my heart and me" [1.1.205, 1.1.115]; he is proclaiming her not only banished and unrecognizable but also not of his blood.)

17. See chap. 1 for the use of this term to refer to the conversos.

18. The claim that racism as we know it could not exist until the development of the full intellectual apparatus that supported it in the eighteenth and nineteenth centuries has often been made; see, e.g., Hannaford's *Race: The History of an Idea in the West.* Though this claim would seem to be axiomatically true, the trouble with such claims is that they implicitly function to make certain kinds of questions unaskable and certain kinds of figures invisible; see, e.g., Boose's wonderful set of questions about what exactly would have constituted "racial" difference in early modern England ("'Getting of a Lawful Race'") or Hall's strong reinstatement of the figure of the black woman that Hannaford's formulation would occlude ("Reading What Isn't There"). Hannaford himself suggests that the idea of race "was cobbled together as a pre-idea from a wide variety of vestigial sources during the thirteenth to sixteenth centuries" (8); see esp. his chap. 6, "New Methods, New Worlds, and the Search for Origins," which deals in part with the sixteenth-century "pre-ideas"—several of them clustered in the decades immediately before and after *Merchant*—on which later concepts of race drew. Hannaford's insistence that "race" in this period generally referred to the "good, noble, and pure" lineage of kings and bishops (147) and especially his claim that "race" in Foxe has this meaning (155) are contradicted by evidence cited in chap. 1, as well as by the quotation that opens this chapter. For the fluidity of the term in early modern English usage, see, e.g., Loomba, "Racial Question," 36–40; and for more on early signs of racialization specifically of Jews, see chap. 1, n. 18.

19. In proximity to "Jew," "gentile" functions not only to distinguish Christian from Jew but also to distinguish non-Jewish "nations" from the nation of the Jews; see chap. 1, n. 74.

20. The two categories are of course mutually exclusive only insofar as the possibility that a gentile/Christian might convert to Judaism is not admissible to thought.

21. This speculation may seem altogether improbable, but in 1584, for example, the Inquisition inquired into the activities of two Jews who allegedly implied the existence of two separate gods while performing an exorcism on a Christian child: they conjured the spirits "by the God of the Christians and by the God of the Jews" (Pullan, *Jews of Europe,* 77).

22. Shakespeare appears to have associated the failure of at least one of these doomed relationships with sexual satiety; see my *Suffocating Mothers* (38–63) for a reading of *Troilus and Cressida* in those terms.

23. Older criticism tended to celebrate Jessica's ease and playfulness in Belmont as part of the play's harmonious resolution. The classic statement of this view is Barber's: "Lorenzo is showing Jessica the graciousness of the Christian world into which he has brought her; and it is as richly golden as it is musical! Jessica is already at ease in it, to the point of being able to recall the pains of famous lovers with equanimity, rally her lover on his vows and turn the whole thing off with 'I would out-night you'" (*Festive Comedy,* 188). Most recent critics are less willing to white out the signs of Jessica's uneasiness; see, e.g., Tanner, "'Which Is the Merchant Here?'" 48–49; Metzger, "'Now by My Hood,'" 60; Lampert, *Gender,* 165. The stakes of the earlier reading are high, since

readings that emphasize signs of Jessica's discomfort threaten to undercut Lorenzo's famous proclamation of cosmic harmony (for more on that harmony, see below). Though Berley overliteralizes these signs, he usefully reminds us that Lorenzo does not necessarily speak for Jessica or the play ("Jessica's Belmont Blues").

24. *Acts and Monuments*, as cited by Loomba, "Racial Question," 36.

25. See, e.g., Yerushalmi's compelling use of the Iberian example to contest the claim that racial anti-Semitism could not exist before the modern period (*Assimilation and Racial Anti-Semitism*, esp. 19). Insofar as Jews constituted both a lineage and a people, perhaps they were ideally situated to mediate between the older and the newer senses of "race" and hence to be early victims of "racism." Jewish racial difference is not prominent in much early work on race by early modern literary critics, who understandably tended to focus on the black-white divide. But for some important exceptions, see Boose, "'Getting of a Lawful Race,'" 39–40; Callaghan, "Re-reading *Miriam*"; and Stolcke, "Invaded Women"; the last of these is especially notable for tracing the afterlife of the Iberian model in the colonies. The intersection of race and religion has recently been more generally acknowledged; see, e.g., Loomba's exemplary treatment of the intersection of race, religion, and skin color in both Jews and Moors in the period ("'Delicious Traffick'"). Among works that address this topic specifically in *Merchant*, the two most useful for my purposes have been those by Shapiro (*Shakespeare and the Jews*) and Metzger ("'Now by My Hood'"). Although Shapiro's book was published before Metzger's essay, I saw Metzger's essay in an early form before Shapiro's book was published, while we were both working on some of the same materials; I am especially indebted to it for several generative formulations and many bibliographical references. For an entirely different understanding of skin color and race in *Merchant*, see essays by Spiller ("From Imagination to Miscegenation") and Japtok and Schleiner ("Genetics and 'Race'"), both of which read the episode of Laban's sheep via a set of early modern discourses that attribute skin color to maternal imagination; see also Hall, who noted this possibility in 1992 ("Guess Who's Coming to Dinner?" 108n16). Though this model is persuasive in relation to Laban's sheep, I would find it more compelling for *Merchant* as a whole if the play were less obsessed by blood and if there were other signs that maternal imagination was an issue in it.

26. Cited in Wolf, "Jews in Elizabethan England," 22.

27. Cited in Katz, *Jews in the History of England*, 58.

28. Wolf, "Jews in Elizabethan England," 7; see also chap. 1.

29. Supersessionist critics, for whom Shylock's conversion must allude to the final convertibility of the Jews, cannot afford to hear the racializing strain in Antonio's lines; for Lewalski, e.g., "'Kind' in this context implies both 'natural' (in foregoing unnatural interest) and 'charitable'; thus Antonio suggests that voluntary adoption of these fundamental Christian principles would lead to the conversion of the Jew" ("Biblical Allusion," 334). F. Kermode in fact comes dangerously close to reproducing that racializing strain in his approving comment on Antonio's lines: "'Gentleness' in this play means civility in its old full sense, nature improved; but it also means 'Gentile,' in the sense of Christian, which amounts, in a way, to the same thing" ("Mature Comedies," 221). Hall's reading of "kind" is more congruent with my own: "The pun on 'kind' . . . reminds us that the courtesy and 'kindness' shown in the play's world is only extended to

those who are alike and judged of human 'kin' by Christians" ("Guess Who's Coming to Dinner?" 100).

30. For the *foetor judaicus*, see, e.g., Trachtenberg, *Devil*, 48–50. Shapiro characterizes belief in this hereditary smell as "unusually persistent" in England (*Shakespeare and the Jews*, 36). According to Katz, "It was a universally accepted fact that Jews had a peculiar smell, an odour which was not dissipated by baptism, but was instead a racial characteristic" (*Jews in the History of England*, 108). Not quite universally accepted perhaps: in his comparatively philo-Semitic phase, Luther mocked those who thought that Jews who didn't stink must have Christian blood ("That Jesus Christ Was Born a Jew," 229), and Sir Thomas Browne notably wrestled with this issue (see, e.g., Callaghan, "Re-reading *Miriam*," 169, 333n31; Shapiro, *Shakespeare and the Jews*, 37, 172); Trachtenberg in fact gives several stories about the disappearance of the *foetor judaicus* at baptism (*Devil*, 48–50). For the imposition of distinctive clothing, see, e.g., Trachtenberg, *Devil*, 44–46; or Poliakov, *History of Anti-Semitism*, 64–67. According to Roth, the regulations mandated by the Fourth Lateran Council, including the wearing of the badge, were enforced more rigorously in England than elsewhere (*History of the Jews in England*, 76, 95).

31. Maitland, "Deacon and Jewess," 261–62. It is a commonplace that the badges were necessary because, despite the physical stereotypes, Jews were not readily distinguishable without them; see, e.g., Edwards, *Jews in Christian Europe*, 23; Poliakov, *History of Anti-Semitism*, 93; Roth, *History of the Jews in England*, 95. Here, e.g., is a contemporary description of William Añes, a member of the London Sephardic community: "he is a young fellow of twenty, well built, with a fair and handsome face and a small fair beard" (cited in Wolf, "Jews in Elizabethan England," 16). Since this description was written by a Spaniard for a Spaniard, its standard for light skin and hair may have been different from an English standard; nonetheless, it strongly suggests that, despite traditional stereotyping, Jews were not always physically distinct from their English hosts.

32. See n. 30.

33. Friedman, "Jewish Conversion," 26. Friedman's thesis is anticipated by Yerushalmi's elegant essay on the emergence of racial anti-Semitism in early modern Spain and modern Germany, both of them societies characterized by the rapid assimilation of Jews (*Assimilation and Racial Anti-Semitism*, esp. 17–18); and it is supported by Netanyahu's massive work on the racialist motivations of the Spanish Inquisition, which emphasizes that "it was the very life of the conversos as Christians, and the difficulty of finding fault with their Christianity," that forced the move toward vilifying the conversos racially as Jews (*Origins of the Inquisition*, 1052). Netanyahu's larger claims about the spread of racialist thinking across Spain are in part contested by Kamen, especially in his 1998 revision (*The Spanish Inquisition: A Historical Revision*) of his earlier *Inquisition and Society in Spain in the Sixteenth and Seventeenth Centuries*; in his 1998 chapter entitled "Racialism and Its Critics," Kamen emphasizes both the unevenness of the development and enforcement of the *"limpieza de sangre"* statutes and the considerable resistance to them, while nonetheless conceding their racialist basis (230–54). See Shell for an account of the role of the pure-blood laws in transforming the Christian doctrine that "all men are brothers" into the doctrine that "only my brothers are men" ("Marranos," esp. 307–16). Ruether notes that "such laws remained on the books in Catholic religious orders, such

as the Jesuits, until the twentieth century" and considers them "the ancestor of the Nazi Nuremberg laws" (*Faith and Fratricide*, 203).

34. Friedman, "Jewish Conversion," 3, 16–18 passim (emphasis in the original).

35. Although such variables as diet, climate, age, and gender could affect humoral balance and thus the color, weight, and heat of blood, there was proverbially "no difference of bloods in a basin." See Paster's extraordinary chapter on blood in *Body Embarrassed* (64–112) and especially her comment on this passage from *All's Well:* "Like Shylock, the king seeks to validate the lack of essential difference in blood beyond any question by reference to medical discourse, proverbial utterance, and the familiar surgical practice of bloodletting" (86).

36. Particularly in combination with "seed," which refers to semen as well as offspring, the genealogical thrust of "derived" is clear; Shakespeare uses "derived" in this genealogical sense, for example, in *Two Gentlemen of Verona* (5.2.23), *Midsummer Night's Dream* (1.1.99), and *Henry V* (1.1.90). Norton obscures the concern with blood lineage here by glossing "derived" as "gained"; the Arden gloss, which adds "also inherited" and notes that "seed" is "a quibble on the (biblical) sense of offspring, progeny," more accurately reflects Aragon's concern with lineage.

37. The quotations are from *A Comparison of the English and Spanish Nation* (19, 20), Antonio Perez's *A Treatise Paraenetical* (22), and William of Orange, *The Apologie or Defence, of the Most Noble Prince William* (O2r). In *The Coppie of the Anti-Spaniard*, the Spanish are "Marranos" and their king is "this demie Moore, demie Iew, yea demie Saracine" (17, 9); in Florio's 1598 dictionary, "Marrano" is defined as "a Jew, an infidel, a renegado, a nickname for a Spaniard" (cited in Shapiro, *Shakespeare and the Jews*, 18).

38. Metzger similarly argues that Shakespeare "struggled with competing notions of Jewishness circulating in early modern England" and resolved them "by creating not one Jew but two": Jessica to sustain the universal promise of conversion to Christianity and Shylock "as the other against which English identity could be inscribed as white and Christian" ("'Now by My Hood,'" 53, 59). I have earlier registered my debt to Metzger's fine essay in a general way, but let me add here that this is one of the formulations that I found most generative, although ultimately I am more skeptical about Jessica's escape from a racializing discourse than Metzger is.

39. Critics interested in race frequently note that outsider women are often constructed as fairer and therefore less racialized and more convertible than outsider men; see, e.g., Callaghan, "Re-reading *Miriam*," 170; Boose, "'Getting of a Lawful Race,'" 41; and Loomba "'Delicious Traffick,'" 215. The classic statement of this principle specifically in relation to Jessica is Metzger's: Lorenzo's praise of her whiteness "creates a color difference between father and daughter that justifies her removal," and his later reference to Lancelot's Moor shows "how her whiteness and femaleness make possible her reproduction as a Christian in the eyes of the 'commonwealth'" ("'Now by My Hood,'" 57). Kaplan specifies Metzger's argument by adducing both gender ideologies that would have kept the Jewish woman reassuringly inferior even after her conversion and Aristotelian beliefs about conception that would have discounted her role in the transmission of race ("Jessica's Mother," esp. 16–25); my own view is that the mother's contribution of matter to the infant only exacerbates concerns about the transmission of race. Lampert's account is closer to mine; she reads Jessica's fairness less as a sign of her

de-racializing than as a challenge to the Christian hermeneutic that would unproblematically read through outer to inner: her "beautiful exterior may belie an intractable Jewish
essence, which she, through her marriage to Lorenzo, threatens to spread into the
commonwealth" (*Gender*, 143).

40. Despite the wide variation both in contemporary usage of the term "Moor" and
in the skin color of actual and literary Moors, Shakespeare nearly always associates
Moors with blackness (see Loomba, "Outsiders," 157). Shakespeare in fact uses the terms
"Moor" and "Negro" interchangeably in referring to Lancelot's own Moor (3.5.32–33).

41. Fray Prudencio de Sandoval, cited in Yerushalmi, *Assimilation and Racial Anti-
Semitism*, 16; see also Friedman, "Jewish Conversion," 16–17. This striking quotation
has become canonical in essays on Shakespeare and race: see, e.g., Metzger, "'Now by My
Hood,'" 55; Shapiro, *Shakespeare and the Jews*, 36; Lampert, *Gender*, 155–56; Loomba,
"Racial Question," 50; Loomba, "'Delicious Traffick,'" 208. Metzger's work first led
me—and I suspect many others—to Friedman and thence to Fray Prudencio, but I here
cite him from Yerushalmi, who begins the passage one sentence earlier than Friedman,
with Fray Prudencio's worries about the eradication of difference in the oneness of God,
and thus allows us to see his determination to make Jewishness indelible in response to
that eradication. Yerushalmi, moreover, specifies that the Spanish for "one family-line
alone" is "*sola una raza*"; about the vexed term "*raza*," he notes that one famous
contemporary dictionary defines it as indicative of pure breeding in horses but in human
lineages it "is understood in a bad sense, such as having within oneself some of the
lineage of Moors or Jews" (*Assimilation and Racial Anti-Semitism*, 15). Kaplan rightly
notes that critics interested in race in *Merchant* tend to use the Inquisition's pure-blood
laws as an explanatory framework instead of drawing on indigenous English medieval
racializations of the Jews ("Jessica's Mother," 1–2), but I think that she underestimates
the extent to which a quasi-Inquisitorial concern with blood taint plays out in both
Jessica and Shylock, despite the English distaste for the Inquisition.

42. See Genesis 10.6. Folio's "Chus" is followed by most editors; Norton's "Cush"
does not appear to have textual warrant. But the spellings appear to have been interchangeable: Calvin's commentary on Genesis 10, for example, has "Cush" in the text
quoted from the Bible and "Chus" in the commentary (*Commentarie vpon Genesis*, 249).
See Shaheen, *Biblical References in Shakespeare's Comedies*, 108, for a full discussion of
both versions of the name in the Bibles available to Shakespeare, along with variants in
the name of Chus's countryman Tubal. Commentators followed Josephus in making
Chus ancestor of the Ethiopians (*Antiquities of the Jews*, 37); see, e.g., the Geneva Bible's
gloss on Genesis 10.6 ("of Cush & Mizraim came the Ethiopians & Egyptians") or
Gibbons's *Questions and Disputations*, 410. Although Calvin is dubious about some
attempts to derive national lineages from the Bible, he is sure about Chus: "It is certeine
that this Chus was the Prince of the Aethiopians" (*Commentarie vpon Genesis*, 240).
And this was not obscure knowledge: Williams notes that "Cush, Mizraim, and Caanan
among the sons of Ham are quite well known as names of the Ethiopians, the Egyptians,
and the Caananites [sic]" (*Common Expositor*, 160). Critics interested in race frequently
note Shylock's surprising countryman, usually by way of positing an association between
blackness and Jewishness: see, e.g., Hall, "Guess Who's Coming to Dinner?" 100–101;
Shapiro, *Shakespeare and the Jews*, 172; Metzger, "'Now by My Hood,'" 55; Kaplan,

Merchant of Venice: Texts and Contexts, 129, 176–77; Loomba, "Racial Question," 51. Rockas's early formulation—"Morocco and Launcelot's Moor can only be in the play to darken Shylock's presence in Christian society" ("Dish of Doves," 349)—anticipates these later critics. Though this association has only recently become a critical common-place, Gilman asserts that it is "as old as Christian tradition" (*Difference and Pathology,* 31); see Kaplan, "Jessica's Mother," 4–10, for some particularly striking examples. Othello himself may draw on it when he compares himself to a "base Iudean" in the Folio version of *Othello.* And it is persistent: see Boyarin, *Unheroic Conduct,* 299, for a striking nineteenth-century instance.

43. Morocco himself may be arguing for his superior vigor—and hence for the superior redness of his blood—as much as for its universality (see, e.g., Normand, "Reading the Body," 55; Spiller, "From Imagination to Miscegenation," 151); but Shylock's use of the same metaphor to argue for "a physiology of insistent commonality" in his famous appeal to blood (Paster, *Body Embarrassed,* 85) seems to me to put the emphasis as much on blood likeness as on difference. And for an audience accustomed to thinking that all blood was alike in a basin (see n. 35), the hypothetical difference between kinds of blood would (I suspect) register less vividly than the triangulated difference between fair, black, and red: compared to the sharp contrast between fair and black, all blood is equally red. This is in fact how most critics read Morocco's offer to incise himself: see, e.g., Hall, *Things of Darkness,* 165; Rosen, "Rhetoric of Exclusion," 75; Tanner, "'Which Is the Merchant Here?'" 59; Ungerer, "Portia and the Prince of Morocco," 114.

44. Danson would like us to assume, "in charity to her," that by "complexion" Portia means Morocco's temperament rather than his skin color (*Harmonies,* 101), but Morocco himself has already used the term to refer to his skin color (2.1.1), and Portia's earlier use of it to contrast Morocco's "complexion of a devil" with his inward "condition of a saint" (1.2.109–10) tilts the balance decisively toward skin color, since devils were notoriously black. (Japtok and Schleiner point nicely toward the function of this association in blackening Shylock when they link Portia's comment at 1.2.109–10 with the play's many references to Shylock as a devil; see "Genetics and 'Race,'" 166.) The term "complexion" itself seems to have been shifting in the direction of Morocco's—and Portia's—use of it, perhaps partly in response to a new racializing of skin color; *OED* gives 1568 as the first use of "complexion" to mean skin color rather than temperament.

45. Ever since Hall insisted on the absent presence of Lancelot's "unheard, unnamed, and unseen" Moor as "a silent symbol for the economic and racial politics" of the play ("Guess Who's Coming to Dinner?" 89), she has become a familiar trope among critics who consider race in *Merchant:* see Hall's witty account of earlier attempts to write her out of the text ("Reading What Isn't There," 28–29); and for her recent canonization as a trope for concerns about miscegenation, see, e.g., Metzger, "'Now by My Hood,'" 57–58; Shapiro, *Shakespeare and the Jews,* 173; Lampert, *Gender,* 142–43, 163; Loomba, "'Delicious Traffick,'" 216. Many critics follow Hall ("Guess Who's Coming to Dinner?" 102, 105) in considering her a contrast to—rather than an analogue for—Jessica, but see Shapiro and Lampert for readings closer to my own. To those who consider her unequivo-cally a contrast to Jessica, I would point out that she can function as a contrast only

insofar as the possibility of similarity is first acknowledged, so that the positions of the two always threaten to collapse into one another.

46. The figural relationship I propose here may have been literal in Shakespeare's England, where at least some of the Moors appear to have arrived as servants to the conversos. See Wolf's description of the household of Hector Nuñez, which consisted, in 1582, of "his wife, three clerks, a butler, and two negresses" ("Jews in Elizabethan England," 9). These or other "blackmores" were apparently still there in the 1590s, when Thomas Wilson relied on what "their blackmores which they kept told me" in his testimony to the Court of Chancery about secret Jewish practices in that household (Sisson, "Colony of Jews," 45). Sisson reports that in 1594 another converso household (that of Ferdinand Alvares, one of the merchants in the Court of Chancery case) included "his wife Philippa, a widow Anne Alvarez, Alvares de Lima and his wife, his servant Thomas Wilson, two other servants, Lewis Alvarez and Grace Anegro, and several blackamoors" (45). Does Grace Anegro's name contain the hint that racial mixing of the kind Lancelot engages in had already occurred in this household?

47. Quoted from Strack, *The Jew and Human Sacrifice*, 175; Newall ("Jew as Witch Figure," 114) erroneously attributes the quotation to Augustine. The error is understandable: the passage occurs in Strack as part of a quotation from the thirteenth-century monk Thomas Cantipratanus (Thomas of Cantimpré), who attributes it to Augustine and uses it as part of his evidence for the blood libel, specifically for the belief that Jews need Christian blood to cure the disease they brought down upon themselves and their posterity when they cried out, "His blood be upon us, and on our children." The passage Thomas attributes to Augustine turns out to be from a pseudo-Augustinian sermon (see Johnson, "Between Christian and Jew," 88n44). I am grateful to Thomas Cattoi, faculty member of the Jesuit School of Theology at Berkeley, for answering the email plea of a total stranger and helping me to sort out the misattribution of this passage.

48. For a strong reading of the ways in which this transmission of race threatens the gender ideology underwriting patriarchal authority, see Boose, "'Getting of a Lawful Race,'" 45–54; in her view, this threat accounts for the "unrepresentability" of black women in early modern literature.

49. Desdemona's desire for loves and comforts that "increase / Even as our days do grow" (2.1.191–92) gestures toward the biblical injunction to increase and multiply—an outcome prevented by her death. The centrality of miscegenation in *Othello* was first brought home to me by Neill's compelling essay "'Unproper Beds': Race, Adultery, and the Hideous in *Othello*," which appeared in its original form in 1989 in *Shakespeare Quarterly* and is reprinted in his *Putting History to the Question*; I am indebted to this essay for my reading of the centrality of miscegenation in *Merchant*.

50. Warner, *Albions England*, A4r, B1r. Though the borders are sometimes fuzzy, this tripartite division was a commonplace; Ainsworth (*Annotations*, 11r) and Gibbons (*Questions and Disputations*, 407) both follow this division, though both give portions of Asia as well as Europe to Japheth's sons. The tripartite division was under some pressure from the discovery of new lands; see, e.g., *Holinshed's Chronicles*, 1:2–4, for an attempt to update it in the light of these discoveries.

51. Foxe's Nathanael thus laments that "wee that come of the stocke of Abraham

after the fleshe . . . are strangers out of the land of Israel our owne countrie" ("Confession,"
B2r).

52. Half a century ago, Williams called attention to the importance of the lineages in
Genesis 10: "To an age which saw in Genesis the only authentic account of nearly the
first two thousand years of human history, the identification of the Japhetic line was of
immense importance. In nearly all the works on English history and antiquities, one finds
fairly extensive treatment of this matter. Ralegh, Drayton, Warner, Purchas, and Heylyn
all devote greater or lesser space to ascertaining which of the Gentile peoples sprang from
which of the descendants of Japheth" (*Common Expositor*, 155). Haller similarly notes
that the works of the sixteenth-century English chroniclers "were all designed to keep
the Elizabethan public supplied with what appeared to be precise information consisting
of names, dates and factual details which would enable readers to perceive the continuity
of the present moment in their own and the nation's existence with the whole sequence
of providentially directed events since the first day of creation. . . . Thus any reader could
work out for himself how the English people came down from Adam and Noah by way of
Japhet" (*Foxe's Book of Martyrs*, 145). See Kidd's extensive analysis of "the Mosaic
foundations of early modern European identity" as based on Genesis 10 (*British Identities*, esp. 9–72). Edward Gibbon's wonderfully dismissive comment—"On a narrow basis
of acknowledged truth, an immense but rude superstructure of fable has been erected; and
the wild Irishman, as well as the wild Tartar, could point out the individual son of Japhet
from whose loins his ancestors were lineally descended" (cited in Kidd, *British Identities*,
9–10)—illustrates both the diffusion and the persistence of the Noachic lineages.

53. Both Noble (*Biblical Knowledge*, 104–5) and Shaheen (*Biblical References in
Shakespeare's Comedies*, 109) note this incongruity; Noble considers it evidence of
Shakespeare's defective knowledge of the Bible. But the names seem to be carefully
chosen to represent all three of the Noachic lines; surely their incongruity is the point.
Holmer would agree that "Shakespeare appropriates these names . . . primarily because
they are *not* in the Judaeo-Christian line of direct descent," but she understands this
(mis)appropriation largely in triumphalist terms as a statement of the potential unity of
all in the knowledge of Christ (*Merchant of Venice*, 73, 77). Perhaps; but this reading does
not account either for the play's manifest interest in diverse nations or for the inherent
weirdness of putting Shylock at the center of this potential unity, especially given his
unregenerate Jewishness and his claim to a separate nationhood.

54. Josephus has the figure he calls Thobel founding "the Thobelites, who are now
called Iberes" (*Antiquities of the Jews*, 36). Williams reports that the misidentification of
"Iberes" with Spain caused most later commentators to consider Tubal the progenitor of
the Spanish, although some considered him the progenitor of the Italians (*Common
Expositor*, 157–58); the Geneva Bible's gloss to "Tubal" at Isaiah 66.19 identifies him with
Italy, but the gloss at Ezekiel 32.26 identifies him with the "Italians, or Spanyardes, as
Iosephus writeth." The Spanish themselves proudly claimed Tubal as their ancestor and
rested their claim to antiquity and pure blood on him (Shell, "Marranos," 311). But at
least one anti-Spanish propagandist considered this ancestry no cause for pride: "It is
certaine that *Spaine* is of great antiquitie, bearing that name vnder the first Monarchie;
but when we shall consider the significations of her and of her first inhabitant, we shall

find her age no ornament . . . but a great deformitie considering her incommodities, and peruerse qualities of that people: all naturall defects being made more imperfect by continuance or alteration of times. [Spain] was not long after the diuision of tongues, first inhabited by the third sonne of *Iaphet* named *Iobel* or *Tubal*, signifying worldly, or of the world, confusion and ignomie" (Daunce, *Briefe Discourse of the Spanish State*, A8v–B1r). In fact Daunce organizes his entire condemnation of Spain according to the various wicked characteristics associated etymologically with Tubal.

55. Babington, *Certain Plaine, Briefe and Comfortable Notes*, 40r. Kidd stresses the "one-blood" interpretation as part of his general claim that neither racialist nor national-ist thinking were prominent in the period: "It is important to stress that the Mosaic paradigm emphasized affiliation and relationships within the Noachic family tree rather than the notions of difference and otherness which we associate with modern national-ism"; "Beneath the superficial variety of mankind early modern literati sought a hypothesised and Biblically authorised unity" (*British Identities*, 30, 289). But both Spain's manifest unwillingness to consider the descendants of Shem and Ham "one blood" with the descendants of Japheth/Tubal and *Merchant*'s demonstrable interest in national divisions seem to me to qualify that claim.

56. This time warp seems worth noticing. Like Foxe's Jews, who are always caught irremediably in their ancestral past (see chap. 1), Shylock and his countrymen are simultaneously Noachic progenitors and descendants, as though the archaic past were always present in the Jew.

57. Calvin, *Commentarie vpon Genesis*, 239; Geneva Bible's marginal gloss to Genesis 10.1.

58. For the status of England as an elect nation in Foxe, see chap. 1, n. 75.

59. As with the concept of race, the full development of the concept of the nation came well after the early modern period; but (again, as with race) the early modern period is for many the crucible out of which a proto-nationalism was formed. Hobsbawm, e.g., thinks that the characteristically modern nation-state was "in many ways antici-pated by the evolving European principalities of the sixteenth–seventeenth centuries" and finds in Shakespeare's history plays "something close to modern patriotism" (*Nations and Nationalism*, 80, 75). Some claim that England was in fact the first modern nation; see the useful summary of this position in D. Baker, *Between Nations*, 2–3. OED notes in its first definition of "nation" that "In early examples, the racial idea is usually stronger than the political"; the first citation in which the political sense appears to be decisively present is from 1538. For the increasing consolidation of "nations" as political entities within land boundaries, see Helgerson's magisterial account of the transition from "universal Christendom, to dynastic state, to land-centered nation" as it is reflected in the work of early modern cartographers and chorographers (*Forms of Nationhood*, 107–47; the phrase quoted is on 120).

60. For an extensive consideration of the complications of this national project as they are reflected in *Henry V*, see especially D. Baker, *Between Nations*, 17–65. Baker's reading of MacMorris's outburst focuses largely on the difficulties of folding four nations or quasi-nations with ambiguously "national" populations into the notional unity of an Anglocentric "Britain" (31–44), but he also calls attention to the ways in which tensions

between different kinds of nationhood—including Henry V's "retrograde" claim to a nationhood based in lineage and patrimony—serve to catch "a sense of nationalism . . . just as it is coalescing . . . around an imagined trans-island locus. The place of *Henry V*, therefore, is *both* a royal demesne, stretched loosely across the British Isles, *and* the spatially distinct and regulated domain that we have now come to think of as a nation" (62–63). Shylock's invocation of the blood basis for sacred nationhood seems to me both to anticipate and to complicate these concerns in *Henry V*.

61. For Foxe's anxieties about Jewish ancestry, see chap. 1; for Shylock's claim to that ancestry, see chap. 2.

62. This was still one of the dominant associations of the word "tribe." *OED* notes that it enters English through this biblical usage and retains this association for some time; its first definition ("a group of persons forming a community and claiming descent from a common ancestor; *spec.* each of the twelve divisions of the people of Israel, claiming descent from the twelve sons of Jacob") is followed by many medieval and Renaissance examples.

63. For "nation," see, e.g., Foxe, *Sermon*, B3v, B5r, C2v, L3v; in each of these instances, Foxe uses "nation" in close proximity to "race" and seems to regard them (pace Hannaford) as equivalent terms.

64. See chap. 1, n. 74, for Foxe's uses of "us Gentiles" and the equivalence of "the Gentiles" with "the nations."

65. "Confession," B1v–B3v. This reading of Jewish dispersal is entirely conventional: see, e.g., Alexander Silvayn's "The Orator" ("Is it not for their iniquitie that God hath dispersed them, without leaving them one onlie foot of ground?" quoted from Bullough, *Narrative and Dramatic Sources*, 486). For a seventeenth-century Jewish rebuttal to this argument on the grounds that the diaspora antedates the birth of Christ, see Yerushalmi, *Spanish Court*, 381–84. The terms of this debate were familiar; it is anticipated, e.g., in Calvin's *Ad quaestiones et obiecta Judaei cuiusdam Responsio* (see Baron, "John Calvin and the Jews," 158).

66. See Williams, *Common Expositor*, 155, for the claim that "Gentile" had become synonymous with "European." The Geneva Bible shows some anxiety about the potentially troublesome word "yles"; its marginal gloss is "The Iewes so call all contreis which are separated from them by sea, as Grecia, Italie, &c. which were giuen to the children of Iapheth, of whome came the Gentiles."

67. The precise moment when the various legends concerning wandering coalesced into the story of the Wandering Jew is hard to determine, but there seems to be some agreement that the story either took its definitive form or got a new lease on life in the early seventeenth century. Poliakov dates its spread through Europe from 1602, when *The Brief Account and Description of a Jew Named Ahasuerus* first appeared "and enjoyed tremendous popularity"; "within the year [it] went through eight editions in German [and] was quickly translated into every European language" (*History of Anti-Semitism*, 183, 242). Anderson's extensive study cites a variety of early forms of the legend, not all of them associated with Jews, and concludes that the Reformation and fears of the Antichrist gave the legend a new impetus after 1550; he cites a 1620 English version of the legend in manuscript which refers to a number of early-seventeenth-century sightings of the legendary figure and reports that "all the cuntrie was full of Ballads, expressinge the

same" (*Legend of the Wandering Jew*, 63–65). Newall locates the beginnings of the legend in the thirteenth century, during the period of mass expulsions of the Jews from western Europe, but she too reports on renewed interest in the early modern period, noting that "during the sixteenth century there were reports of visits by the Wandering Jew from the leading cities of Europe," including "local variants . . . collected in Britain" ("Jew as Witch Figure," 98, 100). Whenever it began, the legend does not appear to have been wide-spread in the Middle Ages, despite the old association of Jews with the wandering Cain, who was the "typological ancestor" of the Wandering Jew (Ruether, *Faith and Fratricide*, 134); for that association, see, e.g., the papal bull of 1208 cited in Poliakov: "God made Cain into a vagabond and a fugitive upon the earth, but marked him . . . lest he be killed. Thus the Jews, against whom the blood of Jesus Christ calls out, although they are not to be killed . . . must remain vagabonds upon the earth, until their faces be covered with shame and they seek the name of Jesus Christ the Lord" (*History of Anti-Semitism*, 242). Perhaps it took not only the Reformation and fears of the Antichrist but also a national identity attached to land for the legend to reach its full force in the popular imagination. Shapiro similarly speculates on the resurgence of the legend in the context of the puzzling national status of the Jews (*Shakespeare and the Jews*, esp. 176–77).

68. Cited in Haller, *Foxe's Book of Martyrs*, 245; see chap. 1, n. 75, for the identification of England as the new Israel. In a brilliant comment on this passage in an earlier version of this essay, Catherine Gallagher noted that "there is a hint that Israel serves as the precursor-figure for the lost national purity and identity that is becoming merely metaphorical. When Elizabeth says she's the nursing mother of Israel, she is both wishing for the confluence of territory, genealogy, and religion, and yet . . . admitting the newness of her creation, registering its break with the past."

69. For the famous "openness" of Venice, see Pullan, *Jews of Europe*, esp. 3–4, 22, 51. For English attitudes toward that openness, see Pullan, *Jews of Europe*, 51; Gillies, *Shakespeare and the Geography of Difference*, 123–25; and chap. 1, n. 41. Gillies reads the conflict between Antonio and Shylock as a playing out of the contradiction between Venice as the new Babelesque commercial city and as heir to the closed ancient city-state, with Antonio seeking "to recover the sacred core of the city from the twin abominations of 'interest' and intrusion" (129).

70. Hall ("Guess Who's Coming to Dinner?" 99) reads this passage in terms very similar to my own; though our emphases are different and we often disagree about details, my debt to her work should by now be obvious.

71. For the Ditchley portrait, see, e.g., Helgerson, *Forms of Nationhood*, 115. The queen overwhelms the map so entirely that her body takes the place of her country; as Helgerson notes in a different context, "by putting the queen *on* the map, the Ditchley artist had hidden . . . a representation of the land itself" (112). For the anatomical resonance of Belmont, see, e.g., the "stately Mount" of Venus in *The Faerie Queene*, 3.6.43.

72. The classic paean to this possibility is Coghill's: after its demonstration of mercy, the play returns to Belmont "to find Lorenzo and Jessica, Jew and Christian, Old Law and New, united in love; and their talk is of music, Shakespeare's recurrent symbol of harmony" (cited in Brown, *Arden Shakespeare: Merchant of Venice*, li). But in Lorenzo's speech, this is specifically a harmony that cannot be heard. For skeptical responses more

in line with my own, see, e.g., Burckhardt, who warns that "mere lyrical splendor is, in the world the play defines, a kind of sentimentality, a parasitical self-indulgence, possible only because, and insofar as, others bear the brunt of the law" (*Shakespearean Meanings*, 226), or Moody, for whom the effect of the speech "is not to praise but to place [the Christians], to show how far from the ideal they are" (*Shakespeare*, 87). Rabkin treats this speech, and more broadly the relation of Lorenzo and Jessica, as evidence of the wrong-mindedness of thematic readings that cancel out the divergent responses provoked by the play (*Shakespeare and the Problem of Meaning*, 17–18). Did Milton hear the potential ambiguity of Lorenzo's gesture toward the golden floor of heaven? Even in heaven, his Mammon admired "more / The riches of Heav'n's pavement, trodden gold, / Than aught divine or holy" (*Paradise Lost*, 1.681–83).

73. Spenser, *View of the Present State of Ireland*, 92.

74. Gibbons, *Questions and Disputations*, 408.

75. Spenser, *View of the Present State of Ireland*, 91.

76. The association of cross-racial or cross-religious marriages with adultery and therefore of their offspring with bastardy was implicit in the understanding of adultery as improper mixture; see Neill's discussion of forbidden mixture and blood pollution (*Putting History to the Question*, 133–35) and particularly his account of the way in which Iago activates this association for Othello and his audience (254, 263–68, 470–71n54). As Neill notes, Volpone's brood consists of misshapen bastards because they are the product of his adulterous unions with "Gypsies, Jews, and black-moors" (142). Shakespeare's Sonnet 127 draws on the same association in the not-quite-covert imagery of its opening lines ("In the old age black was not counted fair, / Or if it were, it bore not beauty's name; / But now is black beauty's successive heir, / And beauty slandered with a bastard shame"): just visible beneath the conundrum of a "fair" black beauty is the image of an illegitimate "heir" whose blackness proclaims it a bastard and who shames its parent "beauty" by wrongly bearing its name. This association had legal, as well as social, consequences: Trachtenberg notes that in medieval church law, intermarriage with a Jew was punishable as adultery (*Devil*, 187).

77. This fantasy of a pure-blood nation is of course already compromised, not only by the realities of invasion and migration but also by England's own myths about its origins. *Holinshed's Chronicles*, for example, traces the "originall beginner" of England to a son of Japhet just as we would expect, but then recounts the violent displacement of that line by Albion, a descendant of Cham: "and thus was this Iland bereft at on time both of hir ancient name, and also of hir lawfull succession of princes descended of the line of Japhet" (1:6, 9). If Albion is the son of Cham, he is Chus's near relative—and therefore (in the logic of this play) a near relative of Jessica, Morocco, and the pregnant Moor.

CHAPTER FOUR

1. In a set of powerful essays, Lupton has argued that the Christian universalism derived from Paul is "universalism minus the circumcised" and that circumcision is therefore a more significant marker of difference than race in the early modern period (see "*Othello* Circumcised," 74–78, 84; "Ethnos and Circumcision," 206); Boose anticipates this argument in "Getting of a Lawful Race," 40. But both *Merchant*'s insistence on

proto-racial categorization in the case of Jessica (who is perforce uncircumcised) and Foxe's phrase here suggest that a newly developing concept of race could be called upon to shore up exactly the religious differences signaled by circumcision—an intersection that Lupton seems to me to underplay in her reading of *Othello*.

2. Calvin, *Commentarie vpon Genesis*, 363r.

3. Shakespeare is unusually precise about the timing of her public appearance and therefore about the gratuitousness of the disguise. Act 2, scene 6, ends with Jessica's and Lorenzo's exit and Antonio's exhortation to Graziano to hurry onto Bassanio's ship, which is about to sail; 2.8 begins with Salerio's statement that the Duke arrived too late to search the ship but "there"—at the port, and presumably shortly after the ship sailed— "was given to understand / That in a gondola were seen together / Lorenzo and his amorous Jessica" (2.8.7–9). Apparently, she sheds her disguise sometime between leaving the house and entering the gondola.

4. *OED* cites this line from *Merchant* to support its definition 2 of "garnish" as "outfit, dress," noting that this usage is obsolete and rare; Norton chastely glosses "garnish" as "dress." But "garnish" frequently carries the sense specifically of something added to ornament or beautify; see *OED*, definition 3b, for "garnish" (noun), and definitions I.3 and I.4 for "garnish" (verb). Shakespeare uses "garnish" in this latter sense in *Love's Labors Lost*, 2.1.78, and *King John*, 4.2.15. Given *Merchant*'s concern with male appendages, Lorenzo's use of the word in response to Jessica's disguise as a boy seems to me to call attention to the pleasure of the add-on, shading over into *OED*'s definition 3 ("An ornament, ornamental appendage"), although *OED* gives 1615 as its first occurrence.

5. "Gild" and "geld" are related not only through the similarity of sound but also through the proximity of each to "gelt," which functions as a kind of shifter between them: "gelt" is both the past participle of "geld" and a noun meaning "money" (*OED* adds "perhaps a pseudo-archaism for gold"), thus appropriate to the ducats Jessica gilds herself with. Spenser uses "gelt" in this double sense in "Prosopopoia: or Mother Hubberds Tale," l.520. Shell notes the series of puns in Jessica's "gild" but applies it to Shylock, who loses his "*Geld*" and is gelded when Jessica is gilded; like the pun on "stones" as testicles—now familiar enough that it is canonized in most recent editions— the "gild" puns serve his argument about the commensurability of men and money ("Wether," 62–63, 72).

6. Taylor castigates Freud for confusing castration with circumcision and thinks that early moderns would not have made the same mistake because they knew that castration involved removal of the testicles and did not necessarily involve the penis (*Castration*, 16, 52, 135–36), but he is discounting the powerful work of fantasy. This "confusion" is not the invention of Freud, though he doubtless popularized it; it is at least as old as Paul, who "expresses the wish that the [circumciser's] knife may slip and finish the job of 'mutilation' (Phil. 3:2; Gal. 5:12)," as cited by Ruether, *Faith and Fratricide*, 100. For late medieval and early modern instances, see, e.g., the form of interrogation used in early ritual-murder accusations ("How was the foreskin on the penis cut off and which Jews cut off the penis and what was done with it?"; Hsia, *Ritual Murder*, 74) or the seventeenth-century French verse that recommends that "there be removed from them entirely / That member which in them is already imperfect" (cited in Poliakov, *History of Anti-*

Semitism, 194); and see Shapiro, *Shakespeare and the Jews*, 114, for additional instances. Foxe himself sometimes elided the difference between the two; see Epp, "John Foxe and the Circumcised Stage," 294, for letters in which he first characterized entering the priesthood as a circumcision and then as a castration. Given this elision, it's not surprising that the Jew in Alexandre Sylvain's "The Orator"—reprinted by Bullough as an analogue to *Merchant* but considered a probable source by Brown (*Arden Shakespeare: Merchant of Venice*, xxxi) and Shapiro (*Shakespeare and the Jews*, 122, 126)—asks, "What a matter were it then, if I should cut of his privie members, supposing that the same would altogether weigh a just pound?" (Bullough, *Narrative and Dramatic Sources*, I:484).

7. Graziano's joke works for an audience only insofar as they recognize that the "man" who has the ring is the already-gelded Nerissa; as Belsey says, "The clerk *is* 'gelt,' of course, to the extent that in the Renaissance . . . women are incomplete men" ("Love in Venice," 47). The fantasy that a woman's "lack" makes her equivalent to a gelded man is persistent in Shakespeare; as the transvestized Viola punningly tells us, it's her "little thing" that "would make me tell them how much I lack of a man" (*Twelfth Night*, 3.4.268–69).

8. Jews were often characterized as womanish, and not only because of the conflation of circumcision with castration and castration with femaleness. In addition to the references to Jewish male menstruation in n. 92 below, see Boyarin's *Radical Jew*, 17, 22, 181, 230; "Masada or Yavneh?" 306–7; and *Unheroic Conduct*, esp. 8–11, 210–11. In the first of these works, Boyarin is concerned to demonstrate the hermeneutic that constructs both Jew and woman as flesh and therefore as difference; in the latter two, he turns the stereotype of the womanish Jew around by demonstrating the ways in which one strain within Judaism deliberately poses itself in opposition to hegemonic masculinity, in effect valorizing the sissy. Garber's evidence for Jewish feminization is mainly from the nineteenth and twentieth centuries, but in her view that later feminization drew on material already implicit in *Merchant*: "we might . . . suspect that representations of Shylock over the years would have touched on this slippage between 'Jew' and 'woman,' from the [skirtlike] 'Jewish gaberdine' to the constant taint of questionable manhood (Shylock 'gelded' of his daughter and his ducats)" (*Vested Interests*, 229).

9. Jessica's intense shame at her disguise—a shame miles away from the jaunty self-assurance with which Portia assumes her male disguise—seems out of proportion to its occasion. Hinely accordingly associates it with her "deeper unease about the course she has taken" ("Bond Priorities," 221); Berley thinks that she "cloak[s] the 'heinous sin' of being ashamed to be who she is under the shame of her cross-dressing" ("Jessica's Belmont Blues," 197); and Garber justifies it by noting that similarly provocative transvestite disguises were worn by Venetian courtesans (*Vested Interests*, 87–88).

10. See *Troilus and Cressida*, 1.2.264–69, 2.2.60–71.

11. See chap. 3, n. 3.

12. The resemblance between the Dinah story and the Jessica subplot was noted in 1965 by Bracher ("Lorenzo-Jessica Subplot and *Genesis* XXXIV"), who treats the allusion to Dinah mainly as an instance of dramatic irony that predicts Shylock's loss of Jessica; he suggests that Jessica's monkey may have come from the monkey in the ornamental D (for Dinah) that opens Genesis 34 in the Bishops' Bible. Holmer also notes the resemblance but considers it an "interesting contrast" to Jessica's story, since "honorable

marriage, not rape, is her blessing" (*Merchant of Venice*, 83). Neither Bracher nor Holmer considers the drastic outcome of the story for the Shechemites, but Boose anticipates my argument by suggesting in a brief note that it might have been an "ur-location" for the circumcision/castration anxieties of both *Merchant* and *Othello* ("Getting of a Lawful Race," 306n11).

13. In addition to its proximity to the Jacob material that Shakespeare drew on, Genesis 34 was a Proper First Lesson, that is, an Old Testament chapter substituted for the Old Testament lesson that ordinarily would have been read on a particular day. Shaheen cautions Shakespeare scholars that "particular attention should be paid to these Proper First Lessons, since these were the passages from the Old Testament that he heard when he attended church" ("Shakespeare's Knowledge of the Bible," 210–11). The story—and the fear of circumcision that it encoded—remained familiar enough that it could be used to serve the purposes of anti-Jewish propaganda in the naturalization controversy; see Felsenstein for a report of a 1753 *London Evening-Post* parable in which the Jews, "not satisfied with having deflowered the maidens of England, proceed to circumcise their menfolk and 'whilst their Private Parts were sore . . . took up their Swords, and slew every Male of the Britons,'" an allusion that would presumably work its full horror only if its readers recognized its biblical source in Genesis 34 (*Anti-Semitic Stereotypes*, 119).

14. Dinah is literally raped ("Whome when Shechem the sonne of Hamor the Hiuite lord of that countrie sawe, he toke her, and lay with her, & defiled her"; Genesis 34.2), but the repeated references to theft in the Lorenzo-Jessica union (2.6.23, 3.1.78–79, 4.1.380, 5.1.19) underscore the element of *raptus* in that union as well; from the point of view of the fathers, both would count as seizures of the father's property.

15. For Babington, see his *Certain Plaine, Briefe and Comfortable Notes*, 134v; for Ainsworth, see his *Annotations*, Aa4r. These commentators all follow Calvin: Dinah "ought to haue tarried quietly at home. . . . Therefore, fathers are taught to keepe their daughters vnder streight discipline" (*Commentarie vpon Genesis*, 693–94).

16. Calvin, *Commentarie vpon Genesis*, 700; see Epp, "John Foxe and the Circumcised Stage," 310–11, for the *Glossa Ordinaria*.

17. Ainsworth, *Annotations*, Aa4v.

18. Calvin, *Commentarie vpon Genesis*, 697–98, 701.

19. Donne, "Sermon," 192. The Shechemites have a kind of shadowy presence in this sermon. Donne doesn't refer to the story of their disastrous intermarriage, but he does use their slaying to testify to the "sorenesse and incommodity" attendant upon adult circumcision as part of his praise of Abraham's unquestioning obedience of God's injunction to be circumcised (191).

20. See Maitland, "Deacon and Jewess," 260–76, for a full account of this case. The case appears in *Holinshed's Chronicles* (see n. 30 below) and in sixteenth-century law books, where it served as the precedent for burning heretics. Maitland stresses its renewed importance in the sixteenth century: "Once more Parliament was dealing with the matter [of punishment for heresy]. . . . The old law-books were being put into print. Every one could read . . . how Langton burnt a deacon who turned Jew for love" (276). When Tovey states in 1738 that the deacon "was desperately in love" with a Jewish woman but "cou'd obtain from her Parents no other condition than Circumcision"

(*Anglia Judaica*, cited in Israel Abrahams's prefatory note to Maitland's essay, 257), he inadvertently testifies to the association between these two circumcision stories, since that condition—central to Genesis 34—does not appear in any of his sources.

21. Maitland, "Deacon and Jewess," 262. Though the Fourth Lateran Council had already instituted the wearing of the badge in 1215, this is the local instance that gave that regulation its force in England in 1222.

22. You can try this experiment at home: ask students who have read *Merchant* cursorily to identify this speech. If they are like my students, most of them will tell you that it is a description of what happens to Antonio's ships. Though they are wrong at the level of plot, they are nonetheless responding to something real—and peculiar—in the text.

23. Shell, citing Stanley Cavell, notes the forfeit/foreskin pun ("Wether," 73), and many others have followed suit. But Cavell's reading of this pun and therefore of Shylock's revenge is much more interesting than the usual citation of him would suggest: it's not only that Shylock would "carve Antonio into a Jew"; in that revenge, which Cavell thinks works according to the principle of analogy set up in the "Hath not a Jew eyes?" speech, "he will be doing what has been done him. So he is telling us that he perceives Antonio's refusal of acknowledgment as mutilation—the denial, the destruction of his intactness"—and telling us, moreover, that "there is no proof for you that I am a man, that I am flesh, until you know that you are flesh" (*Claim of Reason*, 480). Fienberg gives convincing evidence that the "hood" in Graziano's "Now by my hood, a gentle and no Jew" also refers to the foreskin ("Circumcision"); it would thus underscore circumcision as the marker of difference between Jew and gentile even in this address to a Jewish woman. The thesis of Shapiro's chapter on circumcision—"The Pound of Flesh"— is that "an occluded threat of circumcision informs Shylock's desire to cut a pound of Antonio's flesh" (*Shakespeare and the Jews*, 114); he notes not only the signs that contemporary English were in a variety of ways obsessed by circumcision but also that Shylock's use of the word "flesh"—often a sixteenth-century euphemism for the penis— would tend to localize the initially unspecified wound there (121–22).

24. For a good account of the dispersal of the ritual-murder accusation in England, see Shapiro, *Shakespeare and the Jews*, 100–111. Holinshed refers to it (see n. 45 below), and the marginal glosses to Foxe's *Sermon* make sure that his readers don't forget it (see chap. 1, n. 85). Circumcision was so familiar an attribute of ritual murder that a murderer who wished to provide compelling evidence that the Jews were the murderers circumcised the corpse (Hsia, *Ritual Murder*, 126, 158); see also the protocols for interrogation cited above in n. 6. Hsia advises us to "note the prominence of circumcision as an iconographic motif" in the widely reproduced woodcut of the martyrdom of Simon of Trent (*Trent 1475*, 57); see Shapiro, *Shakespeare and the Jews*, 103, for the introduction of this woodcut into England. According to Shapiro, the English were unusually prone to believing that Jews circumcised their victims during these murders (see, e.g., 89, 111, 113). For a local instance at Norwich in 1235, see Trachtenberg, *Devil*, 131; and see Felsenstein, "Jews and Devils," 25, for a mid-seventeenth-century reference to circumcision in this 1235 case. Fascinated horror at circumcision was apparently so great in England that the hostile crowd of Venetian Jews who declined to be converted by Thomas Coryate is transformed into a rabbi pursuing him with a knife on one title-page illustra-

tion of *Coryats Crudities* and then into "Jews [who would] circumcise thee" in a dedicatory poem to the same volume (see Shapiro, *Shakespeare and the Jews*, 115 and illustration 9).

25. If so, he would be departing from his prototype. Jacob himself disapproved of his sons' actions, though partly (again) for self-serving reasons; in Genesis 34.30 he worries that he will now "stinke among the inhabitants of the land," who will gather together to destroy him. Ainsworth notes that "for this fact of theirs, Iakob deprived these his two sons of the birthright, which ells they might have injoyed" (*Annotations*, Aa4v, referring to Genesis 49.6–7). Ainsworth works hard to turn this disturbing story into a story about disobedient sons. When Levi and Simeon talk back to Jacob in his version of Genesis 34.31 ("And they sayd: Should he deal with our sister, as with an Harlot"), he rather charmingly speculates about that capitalized Harlot: "In the Hebrue Zonab, the first letter is extraordinarily great, for some hidden meaning. What if it be, to signify the stout & big words of these yong men to their father?" (*Annotations*, Aa4v). At least one recent commentator is less certain that the Bible registers disapproval of the sons' actions; Sternberg ("Delicate Balance in the Rape of Dinah") argues that the biblical narrative is carefully shaped to promote sympathy toward the sons' actions and disapproval of Jacob's silence and inaction.

26. In Shell's elegant formulation, Shylock's revenge is a species of *lex talionis*: "For the loss of his daughter—his own flesh and blood—he will take the flesh and blood of Antonio" ("Wether," 61). Tennenhouse is more specific: after demonstrating that Jessica's loss is "felt as castration by Shylock," he adds, "For the loss of his daughter, his ducats, his two bags, his two stones, Shylock determines that the literal terms of the contract be fulfilled and the flesh cut *off* from Antonio's body" ("Counterfeit Order of *Merchant of Venice*," 58, 59).

27. Shakespeare seems to have been particularly sensitive to the brokenness in "bankrupt" around the time *Merchant* was written: see *Richard II* ("bankrupt like a broken man"; 2.1.258), *Romeo and Juliet* ("break, my heart, poor bankrupt, break at once!" 3.2.57), and *As You Like It* ("broken bankrupt"; 2.1.57). As for the leanness of the ship: Antonio calls himself "so bated" that he "shall hardly spare a pound of flesh" (3.3.32–33).

28. *OED*'s first definition for "wether"—"a male sheep, a ram; esp. a castrated ram"—has recently been canonized (see, e.g., Bevington's and the Norton's gloss to this line). See Paster, *Body Embarrassed*, 92–93, for a rich account of its relevance to Antonio.

29. See Maitland, "Deacon and Jewess," 266–71, for a very careful account of the various accretions to the story in its many versions. Both the women and the self-crucifying youth are added early on and remain familiar accompaniments to the self-circumcising deacon (266–67). In the thirteenth-century chronicler Matthew Paris's *Historia Minor*, the youth has become not an accompaniment to but a victim of the deacon, who "had taken open part in a sacrifice which the Jews made of a crucified boy"; but in his *Chronica Maiora*, the self-crucifying youth has returned, along with the deacon, for the first time accompanied by a hermaphrodite (cited in Maitland, "Deacon and Jewess," 269–70).

30. *Holinshed's Chronicles*, 2:351–52. Holinshed's fake Christs have also become religious radicals: they "preached manie things against such abuses as the cleargie in those daies vsed" (351).

31. Paul's opposition between the universality of spirit and Jewish genealogical particularity makes circumcision the perfect master-trope for the merely fleshly and particularistic Law (see Boyarin, *Radical Jew*, esp. 15, 36–37, 53–56, 68–69, 230–31). But unlike the Geneva Bible's Paul, Boyarin's Paul would not have comprehended the whole Law under this sacrament, since for him the whole Law perforce included its Christological interpretation (see, e.g., 132–35, 139–41). Paul's views about the law of circumcision are often described as "confused" (see, e.g., Ruether, *Faith and Fratricide*, 100; Shapiro, *Shakespeare and the Jews*, 117). In Boyarin's account, the confusion about the status of Law in Paul lies with his interpreters, who fail to observe that he "fulfills the alleged allegorical sense, while abrogating the literal" (*Radical Jew*, 120).

32. Donne, "Sermon," 186.

33. Calvin, *Commentarie vpon Romanes*, 51v. This comment on Romans 4.11 comes in response to a "doubt . . . whether wee also after the example of Abraham are not to confirme the same righteousnesse by the seale of circumcision"—a doubt that suggests that anxiety about the abrogation of circumcision may still have had some currency even in the sixteenth century.

34. See chap. 1, n. 5, for critics who read 4.1 as a playing out of the supersession of the Law.

35. See, e.g., Ruether's summary of Paul's position ("To take on circumcision is to make oneself responsible for the whole Law. But man under the power of the old Adam must necessarily fail to fulfill the whole Law. Yet the Law says that those who do not obey all its ordinances are cursed"; *Faith and Fratricide*, 100); and see Lewalski, "Biblical Allusion," 340, for the relevance of Galations 3.10 to *Merchant*. Though reliance on the Law was superseded, Calvin gives a moving account of its psychic costs, as though it still presented a problem for contemporary Christians: "who so is truely touched and moued with the feare of God: dare neuer lift vp his eyes to heauen, for the more hee shall striue vnto true righteousnesse, the better hee shall see howe farre he is from it"; "And what should come to passe if the saluation of man were grounded vpon the keeping of the lawe? the consciences shoulde haue no certaynetie, but beeing vexed with a perpetuall vnquietnesse at length shal fall to desperation" (*Commentarie vpon Romanes*, 29r, 53r–v). Recent scholars of Paul tend to characterize the allegedly "Pauline" view that the whole Law must be obeyed as a Lutheran construction serving the purposes of anti-Catholic polemic (see chap. 2, n. 8); see also Boyarin, who refutes that allegedly "Pauline" view partly on the grounds that Paul—who would have known the Jewish position on keeping the whole Law perfectly well—could not possibly have intended to characterize it in this way (*Radical Jew*, esp. 41–43, 116–17, 136–41).

36. An audience would hear "bond" and its derivatives ("bind," "bonds," and "bound") fifty times, twenty-four of them from Shylock; his repetitions of the term— "Let him look to his bond" three times in four lines (3.1.39–42), "bond" six times in 3.3.4–17—inescapably associate the term with him.

37. See chap. 2 for an account of the hermeneutical struggle over the positions of Ishmael and Isaac and for Lancelot's enactment of the trope of bondage and freedom in 2.2.

38. The full gloss is "The false apostles gloried in their circumcision, whereunto S. Paul here alludeth, calling them concision, which is cutting of and tearing asundre of the Church." The Geneva Bible's "false apostles" here are understood to be the same as those

proponents of circumcision against whom Paul warned in Galatians (see the Geneva
Bible's introductory summary of Galatians).

39. In Genesis 22.9 Abraham "bound Izhak his sonne & laied him on the altar vpon
the wood"; in 22.10, "Abraham stretching forthe his hand, toke the knife to kil his
sonne"; the ram appears in 22.13. The word "bound" appears to have been associated
with the sacrifice of Isaac in English as it is in Hebrew, where "the akedah" (the binding)
has become the name for the entire episode. In the depiction of this episode in the
Chester plays, the word occurs twice in the text and three times in the stage directions.
Abraham "byndeth" Isaac before laying him on the altar and then says, "Come heither,
my childe, thou arte soe sweete, / Thou muste be bounde both hande and feete" ("The
Sacrifice of Isaac," ll. 357–58). Isaac asks his father to "bynde" a "carschaffe" around his
head before slaying him (l. 386), and the stage direction that follows reiterates that "Here
Abraham . . . byndes a charschaffe aboute his head." At the moment of sacrifice (between
ll. 420 and 421), the stage directions specify "Here let Abraham take and bynde his sonne
Isaake upon the alter"; the unheard "bind" in that stage direction is perhaps reinforced by
the implicit rhyme with "kinde," the last word of l. 420. I owe the suggestion that
Antonio's "wether" may derive from the ram that substitutes for Isaac—a ram that is in
fact called a "wether" in the Chester play (l. 441)—to Ralph Hexter; given how large my
general debt to him is, it is a pleasure to acknowledge this particular instance.

40. The Geneva Bible's gloss to Genesis 22.12 is "by thy true obedience thou hast
declared thy liuelie faith." Paul takes great pains in Romans 4.9–17 to establish that
Abraham had faith even before he was circumcised so that he could be "the father of
circumcision, not vnto them onely which are of the circumcision, but vnto them also
that walke in the steppes of the faith of our father Abraham, which he had when he was
vncircumcised" (Romans 4.12).

41. The Geneva heading to Genesis 22 calls Isaac "a figure of Christ," and the
Expositor in the Chester "Sacrifice of Isaac" considers him a figure for Christ specifically
in his willingness to be sacrificed ("By Isaake understande I maie / Jesu, that was obedient
aye, / His fathers will to worke alwaie, / And death for to confounde"; ll. 473–76).
Felsenstein cites the Chester play as evidence for his claim that the Abraham and Isaac
story "became in the medieval mind a telling antecedent to the fatal sacrifice of Christ by
the Jews" (*Anti-Semitic Stereotypes*, 32). The play contains no such evidence; in fact, the
Expositor makes Abraham into a type of God ("By Abraham I maie understande / The
father of heaven, that can fand / With his sonnes bloode to breake that bande, / That the
devill had brought us to"; ll. 469–72). But images of patriarchal Jewish figures with knives
(see n. 24 above) nonetheless seem to me to draw their power partly from Genesis's
double insistence on the knife in Abraham's hand (22.6 and 10). Fiedler calls this "an
image which has haunted Europe for nearly two millennia" and identifies Shylock with
this "archetypal Abraham" (*Stranger in Shakespeare*, 118, 125).

42. This was the cry that allegedly called "the curse" down on the Jews, though
Shylock denies having felt it before the loss of Jessica ("The curse never fell upon our
nation till now—I never felt it till now"; 3.1.72–73); allusion to it was a convenient
formula for invoking the blood-guilt of the Jews. Foxe uses it in this way to invoke not
only the Crucifixion but also "your intolerable Scorpionlike sauagenes, so furiously
boyling against the innocent infants of the Christian Gentiles: and the rest of your

haynous abominations, insatiable butcheries, treasons, frensies, and madnes" (*Sermon*, E3r–v); and Nathanael repeats it to signal his new understanding of the curse on the Jews ("Confession," B2r). Its presence behind Shylock's words would have been unmistakable for many in Shakespeare's audience and is acknowledged in most recent editions of the play. The formula was in fact familiar enough to recall the curse on the Jews even in a very different context; Babington, e.g., glosses Rebecca's "Vpon me be thy curse" in Genesis 27.13 by warning that her knowledge that God would bless Jacob may make the phrase lawful in her case, but it "can no wise authorise vs . . . to vse like phrase in an euill matter, as those wicked Iewes did that cryed, his bloud be vpon vs, and vpon our children" (*Certain Plaine, Briefe and Comfortable Notes*, 109v).

43. The side wound of the Crucifixion traditionally "gave access to [Christ's] heart": when St. Bernard meditates on the Crucifixion, he imagines Christ's "pierced side exposing his heart of boundless love," and a fifteenth-century tag to a drawing of "the wounded Christ displaying his heart" ends with the words "Lo! here my hert" (see Duffy, *Stripping of the Altars*, 244–46, 314, and pl. 99, for this and other instances). Stevens notes that, although the liturgy of the Sacred Heart did not emerge until the seventeenth century, "the art of Western Christianity is replete with images of the exposed heart of Christ" ("Sacred Heart and Secular Brain," 263–64); see also Franssen, "'With All My Heart,'" 93n6, for evidence of early devotion to the heart of Christ.

44. See Shapiro, *Shakespeare and the Jews*, 121, for a similar observation about "cut off." Aside from the uses of "cut off" in *Merchant*, the most famous "cut off" in early English literature is probably the Host's "lat kutte hem of" at the end of "The Pardoner's Tale." The Jew in "The Orator" uses "cut off" in ways that similarly suggest that it applies most naturally to flesh that protrudes: "if I should cut of his privie members . . . Or els his head, should I be suffered to cut it off . . . or els if I would cut off his nose, his lips, his eares" (Bullough, *Narrative and Dramatic Sources*, I:484).

45. For this condensation, see, e.g., the famous woodcut of Simon of Trent (n. 24 above) or Samuel Purchas's 1626 claim that one "Jewish crime . . . usual amongst them every year toward Easter [was] to steal a young boy, circumcise him, and after a solemn judgment, making one of their own nation a Pilate, to crucify him" (quoted in Shapiro, *Shakespeare and the Jews*, 89). Purchas is apparently drawing on Matthew Paris, who reported that the Jews circumcised a boy in Norwich in 1235 "with the intention of crucifying him in celebration of Easter" (cited in Trachtenberg, *Devil*, 131). Paris's chronicle was published in England in 1571, with this story intact (see his *Monarchi Albanensis, Angli, Historia Maior*, 549), and it apparently continued to be of contemporary interest; an anonymous pamphlet from 1656 repeats the story, giving Paris as its source (Felsenstein, *Anti-Semitic Stereotypes*, 148). The claim that Jews crucified their victims was familiar enough that Marlowe could draw on it to add a comic *frisson* to the list of Barabas's hypothetical misdeeds: when Friar Barnardine tells Friar Jacomo that Barabas has done "a thing that makes me tremble to unfold," Friar Jacomo asks, "What, has he crucified a child?" (*Jew of Malta*, 3.6.47–48). Holinshed, for example, reports that "they vsed yearelie (if they could come by their preie) to crucifie one christian child or other" (*Holinshed's Chronicles*, 2:437), and the marginal note to Foxe's list of Jewish atrocities (see n. 42 above) directs the reader to "Christen mens children here in Englande crucified by the Iewes" (*Sermon*, E3r). See Shapiro, *Shakespeare and the Jews*, 102–8, for

other examples. Jews were sometimes accused of extracting the hearts of their victims for good measure: see, e.g., Poliakov, *History of Anti-Semitism*, 62; Trachtenberg, *Devil*, 134, 138, 145; Kamen, *Inquisition and Society*, 15–16.

46. See chap. 1.

47. "Englut" anticipates the many references in *Merchant* to Shylock's eating of Antonio's flesh (e.g., 1.3.42, 55, 162–64; 3.1.46). Cannibalism is a familiar theme in the blood libel, often now understood as an act of projection that wards off the cannibalism implicit in the Eucharist (see, e.g., Freccero, "Cannibalism, Homophobia, Women," 74; Lincke, *Blood and Nation*, 148); for this argument specifically in *Merchant*, see Shapiro, who relates it to England's Catholic past (*Shakespeare and the Jews*, 110–11).

48. This anti-Semitic effect is undeniable for critics—perhaps unsurprisingly, mainly Jewish critics—who sense the ritual-murder enactment shaping Shylock's bond. For J. Gross, Shylock "belongs, inescapably, to the history of anti-Semitism" in part because he attempts "to commit ritual murder at one remove" (*Shylock*, 17, 322); for Lampert, the analogy draws the play into "a centuries-old vortex of anti-Semitic accusation" (*Gender*, 150). D. Cohen, who considers the play "profoundly and crudely anti-Semitic," draws attention particularly to Shylock's conjunction of synagogue and bond in 3.1.105–8, in his view "the most deeply anti-Semitic remark in the play" insofar as it constructs the synagogue as "a mysterious place where strange and terrible rituals were enacted," thereby bringing "bloodletting and religious worship . . . into a very ugly and insidious conjunction" ("The Jew and Shylock," 53, 56–57). And as many critics have pointed out, "humanizing" Shylock does not necessarily help: "humanizing [the stereotype] only made it seem more plausible. Israel Zangwill used to tell a story about a Victorian matron who explained, speaking for her social class, that 'of course Shylock is the only Jew most of us know personally'" (J. Gross, *Shylock*, 287). For the same reasons Fiedler considers Shylock "unmatched even by [Marlowe's Barabas], who seems too bad to be true" (*Stranger*, 121).

49. Critics have long identified Antonio as an unproblematic Christ-figure: see, e.g., Gollancz, *Allegory and Mysticism*, 32; F. Kermode, "Mature Comedies," 224; Bryant, *Hippolyta's View*, 38–39; Lewalski, "Biblical Allusion," 334, 336, 339; Lampert, *Gender*, 150. Both Gollancz (*Allegory and Mysticism*, 32) and J. Gross (*Shylock*, 79) secure this identification by citing a 1613 poem by Joseph Fletcher that seems to use Antonio to describe Christ ("The cross his stage was, and he played the part / Of one that for his friend did pawn his heart"). Lewalski calls 4.1 "a typical killing of Christ by the Jew" ("Biblical Allusion," 339), and although Jones does not consider *Merchant* in his compelling account of the ways in which the mystery cycles influenced Shakespeare's dramaturgy (*Origins of Shakespeare*, 31–84), traces of the pattern he isolates in the Passion plays—the strong role given to the "enemy" and the relative silence of the victim, a stress on the legalistic process through which the victim was ensnared, and the increasing isolation of the victim from his friends, who are unable to help him (48–54)—do indeed seem to shape the dramaturgy of 4.1.

But the analogy of Antonio to Christ cuts both ways. Holmer notes that it "weighs heavily on Antonio's shoulders" because it mandates forgiveness of his enemies (*Merchant of Venice*, 206; see also Danson, *Harmonies*, 31), and several critics have called attention to the presumption, self-pity, and desire for a return on his investment that characterize Antonio's imitation of Christ: see, e.g., Shell, "Wether," 78; J. Gross, *Shylock*, 79; Franssen, "'With All My Heart,'" 93–94. Rosenshield argues that the merchant deliberately constructs himself as Christ in order to differentiate himself from "Jewish" economic practices too close to his own ("Deconstructing the Christian Merchant," 37, 43–45).

50. Leviticus twice specifies that only "a male without blemish" can be sacrificed (1.3, 10). According to Deuteronomy 23.1, Antonio could not even enter into the temple ("No one that is hurt by bursting, or that hathe his priuie membre cut of, shal entre into the Congregacion of the Lord"); since the usury prohibitions come only eighteen verses later (23.19–20), it is likely that Shakespeare was familiar with this prohibition.

51. Donne, "Sermon," 193.

52. Shapiro's reading of Shylock's incision—with "the literalism that informs all his actions in the play . . . Shylock will cut his Christian adversary in that part of the body where the Christians believe themselves to be truly circumcised: the heart" (*Shakespeare and the Jews*, 127)—is very close to my reading here, although mine preserves some ambiguity about the location of the wound. Shell sees a shift from literal to spiritual circumcision when Antonio mandates Shylock's conversion: "Just as Shylock once intended to circumcise the bodily part of Antonio (and hence turn him into a Jewish brother), so Antonio now intends to circumcise the spiritual part of Shylock (and hence turn him into a Christian man)" ("Wether," 73). I see no indication that Antonio's forced conversion of Shylock addresses issues of the inner spirit; Shapiro's formulation—that Antonio's "consummate revenge" is to "metaphorically uncircumcise" Shylock (130)—seems to me closer to the mark.

53. See n. 43 above for this Christ; and see Franssen's discussion of Antonio's confused participation in the emblematic tradition of disembodied hearts as a signifier of both profane and divine love ("'With All My Heart,'" 91–93).

54. Critics sometimes use the trope of the circumcision of the heart to invoke the negative idea of the "Jew within" without registering either how problematical it is or how far their meaning is from Paul's; Danson, for example, cites it to make the argument that Antonio's malice toward Shylock makes him "spiritually 'a Jew'" but that "Antonio and the audience will have an opportunity to render another kind of judgment, one which rejects the flesh desired by the inner 'Jew' and accepts instead the spiritual circumcision of the heart" (*Harmonies*, 32).

55. Morocco would incise his skin to show his inner quality (2.1.6–7) but doesn't apply the distinction between inner and outer to the caskets and so discovers that "Gilded tombs do worms infold" (2.7.69); Aragon prides himself on his capacity to pry to the interior (2.9.27) but misjudges his own desert; and Bassanio talks his way toward the right casket by citing many instances of the thesis that "the outward shows [may] be least themselves" (3.2.73–101).

56. The Arden gloss to this line notes that "searched" is "a term of surgery"; see *OED*, "search," definition I8, "to probe (a wound)."

57. Like the slow, heavy vowels of the opening line, the three-beat silence mimics the affect—or at least one of the affects—of melancholy. The first line, with its triple I-sound (I-why-I), its negatives (know/no not), and its forbidding of knowledge (Ay, know not why), beautifully evokes not only this affect but also the combined self-display and

denial of access associated with melancholy. Daniel's 2006 University of California dissertation on melancholy provides the most brilliant reading of this aspect of melancholy—and of its complex realization in Antonio's later turn toward masochism— that I know of. In his view, both "Antonio's melancholic self-absorption and his masochistic self-sacrifice . . . transform suffering into the raw material for particular kinds of pleasurable exposure which are realized socially, in collaboration with others" ("'I Know Not Why I Am So Sad,'" 131).

58. Erasmus, *Praise of Folly*, 39.

59. The phrase occurs in the course of Fiedler's discussion of the Antonio of *Twelfth Night* as a revivification of *Merchant*'s Antonio in his forlorn love (*Stranger*, 92). Fiedler himself thinks that Portia's dream rather than Antonio's "motivates the plot" of *Merchant* (134), apparently because she gets everything she wants; but measured by that criterion, Antonio can't be the dreamer of *Twelfth Night*.

60. Psychoanalytic critics have long suspected the intensity of Antonio's feelings for Bassanio; see Holland, *Psychoanalysis and Shakespeare*, 99, 138–39, for a summary of their views. Essays by Midgley in 1960 ("*Merchant of Venice*") and Auden in 1963 ("Brothers & Others") introduced the homosexual hypothesis into mainstream criticism, and Hyman gave a good reading of the competition between Antonio and Portia for Bassanio's love in 1970 ("Rival Lovers"). But Brown had cautiously canonized this hypothesis as early as 1955 in the Arden edition. Although Brown considers the relationship between Antonio and Bassanio an instance of "the nobility of friendship" in his introduction (xlv–xlvi), his gloss to "fie, fie" suggests something well beyond friendship: "the hesitation suggested by the incomplete decasyllabic and the ambiguous nature of Antonio's answer (it is an exclamation of reproach rather than a clear negative) might indicate that Solanio has got close to the real cause of the melancholy" (7). More recent work by Bray suggests that Antonio himself might not have had to choose between noble friendship and sexual love as descriptors of his relationship with Bassanio; see Bray's "Homosexuality and the Signs of Male Friendship" for the ways in which the tropes of friendship could serve to express homoerotic feelings—and perhaps even homosexual acts—while deflecting them away from the dreaded specter of sodomy. But as Bray says, "this distinction was neither as sharp nor as clearly marked as the Elizabethans would have us believe" (47); and Antonio's strong sense of himself as tainted seems to me to argue that, at least in his case, this deflection is incomplete.

61. See Britomart's "Huge sea of sorrow, and tempestuous griefe, / Wherein my feeble barke is tossed long," itself a reworking of Petrarch's *Rime sparse* 189, perhaps with a nod toward Wyatt's "My Galley" (*Faerie Queene*, 3.4.8); and while we're on *The Faerie Queene*, see Amoret for a heart cut open and bleeding for love (3.12.20–21). In a brilliant and undercited (if overly gnomic) essay on metonymy by way of Coleridge's comparison of Gray and Shakespeare, Christensen reads Antonio's ruined ships both as a figure of his desire for Bassanio—their loss appropriately provoking punishment by Shylock as a manifestation of the "loss of self in reckless and unacknowledged desire"—and as a symptom of Antonio's (and Shakespeare's) "inability to distinguish between things and persons" ("Mind at Ocean," 124, 127). I saw this essay only after I had come to my own conclusions about those ships.

62. Brown's gloss to Graziano's line in the Arden edition is "Sighs and groans were

thought to drain blood from the heart; Clarendon compared *MND.*, III.ii.96–7: 'pale of cheer, / With signs of love, that costs the fresh blood dear.'" See also *Much Ado about Nothing*, 1.1.204, where Benedick denies that he will ever lose any blood from love. Graziano's next line refers by contrast to "blood . . . warm within"; perhaps the pallor of the blood loss associated with love's sighs helped to generate the image of the alabaster funeral monument that follows, since alabaster was notably pale as well as silent (see *Othello*, 5.2.4–5).

63. For "bosom" as "the repository of secret thoughts and counsels: hence used for 'inward thought'" and as "the seat of emotions, desires, etc.: hence used for 'desire,'" see *OED*, definitions 6a and 6b; both definitions are illustrated with citations from Shakespeare. Portia uses the word in this way when she calls Antonio "the bosom lover" of her lord Bassanio (3.4.17); that earlier usage helps to mobilize its double meaning in 4.1.

64. Barber (*Festive Comedy*, 171–72) notes this transfer and associates the merchant-marring rocks with Shylock, Antonio's "stony adversary" (4.1.3).

65. Perhaps Salerio owes his odd use of the word "stream" to this association. "Stream" commonly referred to rivers and other narrow bodies of water rather than the "ocean" (1.1.8) that Salerio imagines Antonio's ships on; "sea" would be the more natural word and would maintain both the alliteration and the rhythm of the line. But "stream" as both noun and verb is often associated with the flow of blood in Shakespeare (see *Lucrece*, l. 1774; *1 Henry VI*, 3.7.55; *Richard III*, 5.8.37; and *Julius Caesar*, 3.1.202); and it had recently been heard on stage most spectacularly in Faust's cry, "Christ's blood streams in the firmament" (*Dr. Faustus*, 5.2.143)—perhaps an appropriate subtext, given *Merchant*'s association of Antonio with Christ.

66. See *OED*, definition I.1, for "touch": "The action or an act of touching (with the hand, finger, or other part of the body); exercise of the faculty of feeling upon a material object." *OED*, definition I.1.b, notes that "touch" can be a euphemism for sexual contact; Shakespeare uses it in this way in *Measure* (3.1.279, 5.1.140), *Othello* (4.2.87), and *The Winter's Tale* (1.2.416).

67. Shell considers Antonio's equation of purse and person largely as a trope for the commensurability between property and persons ("Wether," 60–69). For an equation of purse and person with an explicitly sexual valence, see the Lord Chief Justice's accusation that Falstaff has used the hostess "both in purse and person" (*2 Henry IV*, 2.1.106); Antonio's use of "lie"—a word often sexualized in Shakespeare (see, e.g., Sonnet 138; *Othello*, 4.1.33–35; and, in *Merchant* itself, 5.1.261 and 284)—may underscore that valence here. Like many others, Hammond thinks that Antonio's offer here is "at once financial and sexual"; he also notes that Granville's 1701 adaptation of *Merchant* substitutes "Are all my Friend's" for the more volatile "lie all unlocked" as part of his program of purging the homoerotic potential from male friendship in the play (*Figuring Sex between Men*, 91, 105–6). In an essay that beautifully combines emotional with economic issues, Engle notes not only the "wistful homoerotic suggestion" of these lines but also—in a reading that anticipates mine—the way in which Antonio here "seems to be imagining, even desiring, an 'occasion' for self-sacrifice" ("'Thrift,'" 24).

68. But in one sense Bassanio responds to this deeply coded invitation fittingly, by producing an extended image of shafts shot in boyhood (1.1.140–44), as though following

out the logic of Antonio's offer to open himself up; Smith notes in a different context that "the bow and arrow is one of the oldest anatomical puns in English" (*Homosexual Desire*, 101). In a graduate course on Shakespeare, David Robinson long ago pointed out to me the lack of decorum in this implied relationship, in which the older man imagines opening himself up to the younger; as though in response to this impropriety, Bassanio invites Antonio to shoot the next set of arrows (1.1.147–49), metaphorically righting the decorum of their relationship while maintaining the premise that wealth is their medium of sexual exchange.

69. This phrase inadequately registers my debt to Cavell's work, and especially to "The Avoidance of Love," his seminal essay on *King Lear*, in *Claim of Reason*.

70. In Daniel's beautiful account of the relationship between melancholy and masochism, "It is this ambition to be known through a violation of interiority that the melancholic solicits, and that the extraction of the pound of flesh threatens to realize so gruesomely" ("'I Know Not Why I Am So Sad,'" 122). As often happens with the best students, it is no longer possible for me to tell exactly which components of this idea originated with him and which with me, though I suspect that my focus on knowledge here has partly been framed by his work as well as by Cavell's and Winnicott's; in any case, I am happy to register the pleasure it has given me to work with him.

71. Portia tells him to "prepare your bosom for his knife" at 4.1.240, and he has "prepared" himself by l. 259, at the start of what he imagines as his farewell speech; at least in my ideal production, he would not begin to reclothe himself until after l. 331, when it becomes clear that Portia's strategy will save him.

72. Nashe, *Unfortunate Traveller*, 262.

73. Circumcision had long been known as a curb to unruly desire. The *Glossa Ordinaria* read it as "a remedy to lust" (cited in Epp, "John Foxe and the Circumcised Stage," 310); Calvin thinks that it was "set in the partes of shame . . . to shewe that what soeuer is begotten by man, is corrupt and sinnefull" (*Commentarie vpon Genesis*, 363); and Donne imagines Abraham asking, "why does God command me so base and uncleane a thing, so scornfull and mis-interpretable a thing, as Circumcision, and Circumcision in that part?" and answering his own question by reasoning that it is set there because "*that* part of the body is the most rebellious part" ("Sermon," 190, 191). See Shapiro, *Shakespeare and the Jews*, 119, for additional evidence of this understanding of circumcision.

74. Bray (*Homosexuality in Renaissance England*) and others have argued that before the development of the molly houses in the eighteenth century, male-male desire was less likely to be coded as effeminate than male-female desire (see, e.g., *Romeo and Juliet*, 3.1.108–10, or *Antony and Cleopatra*, 4.15.22–23; and see Sinfield, *Cultural Politics—Queer Reading*, 12–18, for a particularly good account of this issue). But Epp argues that an earlier "linkage of sodomy and effeminacy is hardly uncommon" and gives several examples ("Vicious Guise," 304). Excessive desire of any sort can be read as effeminizing through the old association of passion with women; as Sinfield says, "manly same-gender devotion may betray an excess that hints at both effeminacy and dissident sexuality" (*Shakespeare, Authority, Sexuality*, 91). And insofar as Antonio desires inappropriately to be "unlocked" to Bassanio, his desire would put him in the passive position, which was often coded as effeminate (see, e.g., Smith, *Homosexual Desire*, 186, 211). Moreover,

Antonio's incapacity to act on his desire can be understood as his unmanning; the play in fact worries the status of his masculinity on that basis early on, when Graziano associates his silence both with impotence and with the unfulfilled desire of an unmarriageable woman (silence is "only commendable / In a neat's tongue dried and a maid not vendible"; 1.1.111–12; Arden's gloss directs us to the "bawdy allusion" in "neat's tongue").

75. I am using "closet" in the older sense of *OED*, definition 1 ("a room for privacy, . . . an inner chamber"). *OED*'s 1586 example specifies that "we doe call the most secret place in the house appropriate unto our owne private studies . . . a Closet." When the poet of Spenser's *Amoretti* tells us that his beloved's worth is written "Deepe in the closet of my parts entyre" (Sonnet 85), he suggests how easily this architectural term can be applied to the privacy of the self. "Subjectivity" is of course a vexed term for this period, and specifically homosexual subjectivity even more vexed; whatever the terms in which same-sex desires and acts were imagined—and Smith's *Homosexual Desire* suggests that there were many different options—the consensus is that "the gender of one's sexual partners was not the starting point for anyone's self-identity in 1600" (Smith, "What! You, Will?" 46). But Maus forcefully rebuts those who would claim that a sense of inwardness is anachronistic for the period (*Inwardness and Theater*, esp. 3–12, 27–28); and Smith argues for the "beginnings of a specifically homosexual subjectivity" in Shakespeare's sonnets and locates that subjectivity in the context of developing notions of privacy and inwardness, especially figured as locked interior spaces (*Homosexual Desire*, esp. 23, 232–38, 254–55). Bray's argument that Renaissance codes of friendship and of hierarchical male relationships permitted the relatively free expression of homosexual desire and that those who committed homosexual acts simply did not identify them as "sodomy" ("Homosexuality and the Signs of Male Friendship"; *Homosexuality in Renaissance England*, 67) would seem to preclude the need for a closet, but Bray may underestimate the effort that went into that particular form of not-knowing. Certainly, Antonio's love for Bassanio is entirely out in the open and is publicly construed as a form of friendship, however extreme; but his insistence both on his opacity to himself and on an unspecified inner taint may register the cost of that public presentation and hence the conditions under which something like a closeted subjectivity of the sort that Smith sees in the sonnets might develop.

Sinfield, who thinks that postmodern scholars who proclaim the absence of subjectivity "catch not the absence of the modern subject, but its emergence," speculates that "the development of the modern subject [may be] in some ways dependent on the development of the gay subject" (*Cultural Politics—Queer Reading*, 14). Shakespeare is often credited with developing the concept of subjectivity that we have inherited; in addition to whatever the sonnets allow us to surmise about his sexual desires, his derivation from a Catholic family would have given him particularly strong motives for conceptualizing the self as hidden. Maus, e.g., posits that "the awareness of a secret interior space [is] an almost inevitable result" of the religious upheavals of the period (*Inwardness and Theater*, 16).

76. I am quoting from Winnicott's wonderful essay, awkwardly entitled "Communicating and Not Communicating Leading to a Study of Certain Opposites" (185, 186). Much in Shakespearean tragedy seems to me illuminated by Winnicott's formulation of

this dilemma, from Hamlet's game of revelation and concealment to Othello's "I must be found" and Lear's rush toward self-exposure on the heath.

77. It has long been recognized that Antonio's situation resembles the situation Shakespeare portrays in the sonnets (see, e.g., Brown's citation of E. K. Chambers's 1925 comment to that effect in the Arden edition, xlvi); Fiedler calls Antonio "that projection of the author's private distress" (*Stranger*, 97). Antonio may also be affiliated with Shakespeare insofar as he figures himself as an actor (1.1.77–79): see Skura's brilliant analysis of the ways in which Antonio as imperfect Christ in 4.1 is the model of the humiliated and self-sacrificing actor who performs for the benefit of his audience (*Shakespeare the Actor*, 211–14). But in an extraordinary and unsettling act of imaginative rereading, K. Gross sees Shakespeare's embrace of the actor's shame—along with his rage and his desire to have the heart of his audience—as evidence for Shakespeare's likeness to Shylock rather than to Antonio (*Shylock Is Shakespeare*, 17, 82–84).

78. Wilton not only imagines the knife; he imagines "what a kind of death it might be to be let blood till a man die" (Nashe, *Unfortunate Traveller*, 263). The ease with which the figure of the anatomy could recur any time a body was opened up is suggested, e.g., by Gascoigne's "The Spoyle of Antwerpe": he reports that there were men with their heads and shoulders burnt off "so that you might looke down into the bulk & brest and there take an Anatomy of the secrets of nature" (596).

79. See Hillman's suggestive essay on anatomy as a proposed solution to the skeptical problem of other minds in Shakespeare ("Visceral Knowledge," esp. 81–85); Hillman does not cite this particular instance. In my reading of *Merchant*, the anatomist's fantasy of exposure works, as it were, from the inside out; if, in Hillman's terms, some characters in Shakespeare "seem to imagine that penetrating the other's body would somehow solve the riddle of knowing the other" (82), Antonio seems to me to imagine this penetration as the solution to the problem of being known.

80. Despite the English use of the same technique, the association of the Spanish Inquisition with torture was commonplace (see, e.g., *Faerie Queene*, 5.11.19), and the rack is often specified as their instrument of choice; see, e.g., the first page of "The Translatour to the Reader" in Montanus's *Discouery* for "the monstruous racking of men" (A2r; additional references are sprinkled liberally throughout the text, e.g., at B4r, 3r, 21v, 22v, 23r, 23v, 26r, and 29v). Foxe gives an account of the Inquisitors' "whippings, and scourgings, irons, tortures, and racks" (*Acts and Monuments*, 4:452), and Warner writes that "From those *Inquisitors* escape but verie fewe or none. / Euen so by racking out the ioynts, or chopping off the heade, / *Procustes* fitted all his Guests vnto his iron beade" (*Albions England*, 230).

81. Bacon, *Works*, 8:178. Bacon contrasts the tyrannous practices of Rome with Elizabeth's unwillingness to make such windows into men's souls "except the abundance of them did overflow into overt and express acts and affirmations."

82. Warner, *Albions England*, 230; Montanus, *Discouery*, 7v.

83. Foxe, *Acts and Monuments*, 4:453. Foxe calls this exposure "a spectacle of rebuke and infamy" (452); and Montanus repeatedly emphasizes the element of shame, including the Inquisitors' propensity for stripping their victims "starke naked" (*Discouery*, 23r).

84. Montanus, *Discouery*, 23r.

85. Ibid., 84r.

86. See chap. 1 at n. 34.

87. For Catholics as Judaizers, see chap. 1, nn. 40 and 63; for the Spanish as mongrel Jews, see chap. 3 at n. 37. "Popish Sinagoge" is the phrase of Montanus's English translator (*Discouery*, A2r); Foxe similarly refers to "the synagogue of the inquisitors" (*Acts and Monuments*, 4:453). Inquisitors are familiarly compared with Christ-killing Jews: in Montanus, Inquisitors mock their victims as the Jews mocked Christ and go about "of purpose to destroy the kingdome of Christ, as did the wicked Iewes" (*Discouery*, 25r, 49v); in William of Orange's *Apologie*, the Spanish "keepe this vertue of their Auncestors, who solde for readie money downe tolde, the life of our Sauiour" (O2r). William of Orange in fact thinks that the Inquisition was "deuised and inuented in Spaine by certaine Iewes and Renegados" who were working against the interests of the king, or at least he claims to think so in order to persuade Philip to abandon it (*Supplication*, B3v).

88. Warner, *Albions England*, 242. For Warner, Spanish, Jesuits, and Jews tellingly blur in the figure of Judas: the pro-Catholic traitors in England are "their Iesuistes, (our Iudasses)" (242).

89. See, e.g., Montanus, *Discouery*, A4r, 34r, 54r; in the 1569 edition's Epistle Dedicatory to the Archbishop of Canterbury, the Inquisitors are once again—like Shylock—"most cruell and rauenyng Wolues" (A3v).

90. These quotations are from Montanus's *Discouery* (B3v), the Epistle Dedicatory to the 1569 *Discouery* (A3r), and *A Fig for the Spaniard* (B4v). Barber notes that Shylock's pound-of-flesh bond "involved taking literally the proverbial metaphors about money-lenders" (*Festive Comedy*, 169); apparently, they were the proverbial metaphors about Inquisitors as well. Foxe's complaint about the "cruel ravening of those catholic inquisitors of Spain, who, under the pretensed visor of religion, do nothing but seek their own private gain" (*Acts and Monuments*, 8:513), was commonplace: see n. 89 for their wolvish "rauenyng" in *Discovery*, and see complaints about their avarice in Daunce, *Briefe Discourse of the Spanish State*, C1v; William of Orange, *Supplication*, C2v; *Present State of Spaine*, D2r.

91. Montanus, *Discouery*, 7r; Warner, *Albions England*, 230.

92. According to Trachtenberg, menstruation was the most commonly mentioned ailment of the Jews in the medieval period, with hemorrhoids a close second (*Devil*, 50); for a qualification of that claim, see Johnson, who argues that male blood flux was not conflated with menstruation and thereby gendered until the early modern period ("Between Christian and Jew," 92). But Resnick gives two apparent instances of this conflation from thirteenth-century texts and traces the combination of medical, theological, and popular traditions—among them, the belief that both menstruation in women and blood flux in Jews were the consequence of divine curses—that made the conviction that male Jews menstruate "quite explicit" by the early fourteenth century ("Medieval Roots," 258–59, 260). For instances of Jewish male menstruation from 1494 and 1531, see Poliakov, *History of Anti-Semitism*, 143, and Hsia, *Ritual Murder*, 130; and see Shapiro, *Shakespeare and the Jews*, 37–38, for specifically English instances. According to Yerushalmi, the belief was current enough in sixteenth- and seventeenth-century Spain and Portugal that it was one of the ten slanders against the Jews that Cardoso addressed at length (*Spanish Court*, 123, 126–30, 360). Yerushalmi reports on a

comic episode in which Cardoso was able to turn the tables on Don Juan de Quiñones, who had written a treatise attributing hemorrhoids and tails (along with menstruation) to the Jews and who came to him for treatment for the same condition (123); he also reports that Quiñones cites a version of the pound-of-flesh tale to support his general claim about Jewish bloodthirstiness (131).

93. I am of course alluding to Paster's wonderfully useful—and widely used—formulation of gender in the humoral body ("woman is naturally grotesque—which is to say, open, permeable, effluent, leaky. Man is naturally whole, closed, opaque, self-contained"), a formulation central to her reading of both Portia and Antonio in 4.1 (*Body Embarrassed*, 92–93).

94. *Problemes of Aristotle*, D1r. For the popularity of this pseudo-Aristotelian compendium, see Lawn, *Salernitan Questions*, 99–101; Lawn counts at least fifty-six Latin editions between 1483 and 1686, including one in London in 1583. *Problemes* was first published in English in 1595, with additional editions in 1597 and 1607; versions of it continued to be reprinted in chapbook form up until the twentieth century. In its catalog, *Problemes* omits one potential cause of hemorrhoids with possible—though distant—resonance for *Merchant*: see Smith, *Homosexual Desire* (159, 162), for the disease's association with the "female" position of the catamite.

95. *Problemes*, D1r.

96. Ibid., D1r–D1v.

97. For these diseases and their link to the blood curse, see, e.g., Trachtenberg, *Devil*, 50–51, 148; Poliakov, *History of Anti-Semitism*, 143; Yerushalmi, *Spanish Court*, 129–30; Hsia, *Ritual Murder*, 127; Resnick, "Medieval Roots," 248–52, 260–61. The passage that Thomas of Cantimpré erroneously attributes to Augustine provides the conceptual link between blood taint and curse that is literalized in these diseases (see chap. 3 at n. 47 and Resnick, "Medieval Roots," 249).

98. According to Hsia, "the legend [of ritual murder] consisted of the belief that Jews required Christian blood for their ritual and magic" (*Ritual Murder*, 2; see also 29–30, 121); see Trachtenberg, *Devil*, 132–38, for additional evidence. Controversialists on both sides of the Catholic-Protestant divide held the Jewish ritual use of Christian blood as an article of faith (for Zasius, see Hsia, *Ritual Murder*, 116; for Eck, 127; and for Luther, 133). Those who wrote or spoke against the blood libel similarly testify to the centrality of this belief: for Pfefferkorn, see Hsia, *Ritual Murder*, 121; for Osiander, 138; and for Abraham zum Bock, accused of ritual murder in Worms in 1563, 167. Hsia gives evidence of the continuation of this belief well after it was condemned by official sources (see, e.g., *Ritual Murder*, 197–223, 228–29); it was revived by the Nazis, and formulations like Zasius's—"the Jews thirst after Christian blood, which these bloodthirsty bloodsuckers seek day and night" (Hsia, *Ritual Murder*, 116)—partly formed the basis for the Nazi portrayal of Jews as bloodsuckers on the German nation (Lincke, *Blood and Nation*, 152–53). For the use of Christian blood specifically to cure Jewish blood diseases, see Trachtenberg, *Devil*, 50–51, 148–52; Poliakov, *History of Anti-Semitism*, 142–43; Yerushalmi, *Spanish Court*, 130–31; Hsia, *Ritual Murder*, 30, 127, 130, 138; Resnick, "Medieval Roots," 261–62; Shapiro, *Shakespeare and the Jews*, 37–38.

99. Hsia, *Ritual Murder*, 74; these guidelines were drawn up for the interrogators in the Regensburg case, and in Hsia's view were probably modeled on the guidelines for the

trial in Trent. Hsia gives numerous examples of cases in which Jews were tortured until they produced this "correct" motive for the alleged murders (20, 21, 29, 88, 101, 106, 199) or in which witnesses against the Jews or occasionally the murderers themselves made themselves more credible by testifying to the Jews' need for specifically Christian blood (92, 94, 95–96, 99).

100. Bullough, *Narrative and Dramatic Sources*, 1:484.

101. I do not want to argue that Antonio is literally a converso, but that (to my mind implausible) argument is made with a kind of brilliant logic by Michaels in the course of a discussion of the "mutual contempt between what are called 'universalist' Jews and Jewish Jews" in "My Yiddish," one of the last essays he wrote before his death: "During the centuries of the Spanish Inquisition, Jews turned on Jews. In Shakespeare's *The Merchant of Venice*—assuming the merchant Antonio is a gay *converso*, or new Christian, and Shylock is an Old Testament moralistic Jewish Jew—the pound of flesh, a grotesquely exaggerated circumcision, is to remind Antonio (who says, 'I know not why I am so sad') of his origins" (6).

102. "Sodomy" is a notoriously unstable term, liable to be applied to any "enemy" group; see, e.g., Goldberg, *Sodometries*, 1–26, both for a good summary of its early modern uses and for a startling modern instance of the uses to which that instability can be put. Nonetheless, there is some evidence that Jews were particularly liable to be associated with sodomites. Boswell gives a twelfth-century illustration comparing Jews to hyenas, which were known for their "alleged homosexuality"; he comments that "although Jews and gay people were often tacitly linked in later medieval law and literature . . . such explicit comparisons were relatively rare" (*Christianity, Social Tolerance, and Homosexuality*, illustration 9; see 272 and 292 for evidence of that tacit linkage). But usury was associated with sodomy by Dante, as Auden notes in the course of an argument linking Antonio with Shylock ("Brothers & Others," 231); and as Jews became more firmly identified with usury, the link between Jews and sodomy may have become more explicit (see, e.g., Lipton, *Images of Intolerance*, 45–46, 102–6, for the identification of "Sodomites" as Jews in the *Bible moralisée* on the grounds both of usury and of heresy). In what Kamen calls the most significant of the "street level" anti-Jewish polemics in fifteenth-century Spain, Jews are not only usurers and murderers but also homosexuals (*Spanish Inquisition*, 33–34); see also Felsenstein, "Jews and Devils," 23. It may be telling that *The Unfortunate Traveller* (269) gives the anatomist's fellow Jew— who is never explicitly linked with sodomy—the same sodomist's punishment as Holinshed's or Marlowe's Edward II (see Smith, *Homosexual Desire*, 220, for Holinshed); and when Dekker has his Whore of Babylon complain that "our Babylonian Sinagogues" are now "counted Stewes, where Fornications / And all vncleannesse Sodomiticall . . . are now daily acted" (*Whore of Babylon*, 1.1.32–35), he apparently draws on the association of Jews with sodomy to target Catholics. Kleinberg argues that Antonio himself draws on this association, projecting his self-hatred as a sodomite onto the Jew and thus translating "sexual guilt . . . into ethnic hatred" (*"Merchant of Venice*," 120–21, 124).

103. At least since Fiedler (*Strangers*, 102), some critics have sensed a witchy undertone in Bassanio's golden girl. Fiedler himself associates her with the witch Medea (112–15), Sundelson with the engulfing mother signified by the spider (*Shakespeare's Restorations of the Father*, 83–86), Boose with emasculation ("Comic Contract," 247–50),

and Kofman (following Freud) with death ("Conversions," 148). Gillies notes that most Renaissance uses of the Jason-Medea myth celebrate merchant adventuring, but that Shakespeare is "haunted" by the "disregarded ancient dimension" of it; in his view, this dimension concerns anxieties about "trade, intermixture and miscegenation" that are provoked by Portia but then displaced onto Jessica (*Shakespeare and the Geography of Difference*, 135–37; and see de Sousa, *Shakespeare's Cross-Cultural Encounters*, 71–83, for an extension of his account). If Gillies is right, then we might understand Jessica's theft of her father's stones in part as a displacement of Portia/Medea's castrating potential.

104. For fortune as "strumpet," see, e.g., *King John*, 2.2.61, and *Hamlet*, 2.2.231, 473; in *King Lear*, she is an "arrant whore" (2.4.50).

105. Skura observes that Antonio himself seems to confuse Portia with fortune at 4.1.267–69, where he "moves directly from saying how glad he is that Fortune 'cut me off' from misery to commending himself to Bassanio's unnamed wife, both referred to by the general pronoun" (*Shakespeare the Actor*, 309n37). This confusion about who cut him off—scarcely a neutral term, under the circumstances—seems telling.

106. Poliakov noted the late medieval construction of Jews simultaneously as "hypervirile" and as women in 1965 (*History of Anti-Semitism*, 142–43). Biberman has recently attempted to historicize this duality, arguing that whereas initially the Jew-Devil served as a "ceiling" against hypermasculine behavior in a culture that valorized the masculine Christian knight, Jew-Sissy begins to supersede Jew-Devil in the early modern period as a "floor" beneath which men should not go, in part in response to new concerns about the masculinity of the Christian merchant—a shift that he sees registered in the transformation of Shylock from Jew-Devil to Jew-Sissy (*Masculinity, Anti-Semitism and Early Modern English Literature*, 3, 4, 32–33). Insofar as he sees the construction of the effeminized Jew as defensive, his argument anticipates aspects of mine. For a powerful psychoanalytic reading of Shylock's outraged masculinity—rather than his effeminization—as a defense, see Wheeler, who argues that Shylock's masculinization is a displacement of desires for masculine autonomy that are incompatible both with Antonio's particular desire for self-sacrifice and more broadly with male sexual desire and desire for a nurturing presence ("'And My Loud Crying Still,'" esp. 196–201).

107. Arden notes that "Balthazar . . . appears in some Bibles for Belshazzar, the Babylonian name given to Daniel," and erroneously directs readers to Daniel 5.1; the reference to Daniel as Belshazzar (or Belteshazzar, in the Geneva Bible) is in Daniel 5.12. Holmer makes a strong case for the relevance of this reference to *Merchant* in addition to the more generally cited Daniel of Susannah and the Elders, partly on the basis of its prophetic resonance for the supersession of Judaism and partly because the writing on the wall tells King Belshazzar that he—like Shylock, who carries his own balance into court—is "wayed in the balance, and . . . founde too light" (Holmer, *Merchant of Venice*, 193–95). See Luxton, "Second Daniel," for extensive Protestant commentary on Daniel and for the argument that Shylock reveals that he is not a "true"—i.e., converted—Jew when he mistakes Portia's prophetic Daniel for the Daniel of Susannah and the Elders.

108. See Kahn, "Cuckoo's Note," for a particularly good early account of this doubleness, in which "images of her as male and as female are superimposed" (108).

WORKS CITED

Achinstein, Sharon. "John Foxe and the Jews." *Renaissance Quarterly* 54 (2001): 86–120.

Adelman, Janet. "Male Bonding in Shakespeare's Comedies." In *Shakespeare's "Rough Magic": Renaissance Essays in Honor of C. L. Barber*, ed. Peter Erickson and Coppélia Kahn, 73–103. Newark, NJ: University of Delaware Press; London: Associated University Presses, 1985.

———. *Suffocating Mothers: Fantasies of Maternal Origin in Shakespeare's Plays, "Hamlet" to "The Tempest."* New York: Routledge, 1992.

Ainsworth, Henry. *Annotations Upon the first book of Moses, called Genesis. Wherin the Hebrew words and sentences, are compared with, & explayned by the ancient Greek and Chaldee versions.* London, 1616. No. 210, reel 608, in A. W. Pollard and G. R. Redgrave, *A Short-Title Catalogue of Books Printed in England, Scotland, and Ireland and of English Books Printed Abroad, 1475–1640* (hereafter STC).

Alter, Robert. "Who Is Shylock?" *Commentary* 96 (1993): 29–34.

Anderson, George K. *The Legend of the Wandering Jew.* Providence, RI: Brown University Press, 1965.

Auden, W. H. "Brothers & Others." In *The Dyer's Hand and Other Essays*, 218–37. London: Faber and Faber, 1963.

Augustine. *Of the Citie of God. Englished by I. H.* London: George Eld, 1610. STC 916. Early English Books Online (hereafter EEBO).

Babington, Gervase. *Certain Plaine, Briefe and Comfortable Notes upon Euerie Chapter of Genesis.* London, 1592. STC 1086, reel 195.

Bacon, Francis. *The Works of Francis Bacon.* Ed. James Spedding, Robert Leslie Ellis, and Douglas Denn Heath. 14 vols. London: Longmans, 1857–74.

Baker, David J. *Between Nations: Shakespeare, Spenser, Marvell, and the Question of Britain.* Stanford, CA: Stanford University Press, 1997.

Baker, Elliott. *Bardolatry.* London: Holofernes, 1992.

Barber, C. L. *Shakespeare's Festive Comedy: A Study of Dramatic Form and Its Relation to Social Custom.* Princeton, NJ: Princeton University Press, 1959.

Baron, Salo W. "John Calvin and the Jews." In *Harry Austryn Wolfson Jubilee Volume*, ed.

Saul Lieberman, English Section, 1:141–63. Jerusalem: American Academy for Jewish
    Research, 1965.

Barroll, Leeds. "Looking for Patrons." In *Aemilia Lanyer: Gender, Genre, and the Canon,*
    ed. Marshall Grossman, 29–48. Lexington: University Press of Kentucky, 1998.

Bauckham, Richard. *Tudor Apocalypse: Sixteenth Century Apocalypticism, Millennari-
    anism and the English Reformation; from John Bale to John Foxe and Thomas
    Brightman.* Courtenay Library of Reformation Classics, vol. 8. Oxford: Sutton
    Courtenay Press, 1978.

Belsey, Catherine. "Love in Venice." *Shakespeare Survey* 44 (1992): 41–53.

Berley, Marc. "Jessica's Belmont Blues: Music and Merriment in *The Merchant of
    Venice.*" In *Opening the Borders: Inclusivity in Early Modern Studies; Essays in
    Honor of James V. Mirollo,* ed. Peter C. Herman, 185–205. Newark, NJ: University of
    Delaware Press; London: Associated University Presses, 1999.

Betteridge, Tom. "From Prophetic to Apocalyptic: John Foxe and the Writing of History."
    In *John Foxe and the English Reformation,* ed. David Loades, 210–32. Aldershot, UK:
    Scolar Press, 1997.

Bevington, David. "A. L. Rowse's Dark Lady." In *Aemilia Lanyer: Gender, Genre, and the
    Canon,* ed. Marshall Grossman, 10–28. Lexington: University Press of Kentucky, 1998.

Biberman, Matthew. *Masculinity, Anti-Semitism and Early Modern English Literature:
    From the Satanic to the Effeminate Jew.* Aldershot, UK: Ashgate, 2004.

Bishop, Tom. "Shakespeare and Religion." In *The Shakespearean International Yearbook
    3: Where Are We Now in Shakespearean Studies?* ed. Graham Bradshaw, John M.
    Mucciolo, Angus Fletcher, and Tom Bishop, 11–33. Aldershot, UK: Ashgate, 2003.

Black, James. *Edified by the Margent: Shakespeare and the Bible.* Calgary: University of
    Calgary, Faculty of Humanities, 1979.

Boose, Lynda E. "The Comic Contract and Portia's Golden Ring." *Shakespeare Studies* 20
    (1987): 241–54.

———. "'The Getting of a Lawful Race': Racial Discourse in Early Modern England and
    the Unrepresentable Black Woman." In *Women, "Race," and Writing in the Early
    Modern Period,* ed. Margo Hendricks and Patricia Parker, 35–54. New York:
    Routledge, 1994.

Boswell, John. *Christianity, Social Tolerance, and Homosexuality.* Chicago: University of
    Chicago Press, 1980.

Boyarin, Daniel. "Masada or Yavneh? Gender and the Arts of Jewish Resistance." In *Jews
    and Other Differences: The New Jewish Cultural Studies,* ed. Jonathan Boyarin and
    Daniel Boyarin, 306–29. Minneapolis: University of Minnesota Press, 1997.

———. *A Radical Jew: Paul and the Politics of Identity.* Berkeley and Los Angeles:
    University of California Press, 1994.

———. *Unheroic Conduct: The Rise of Heterosexuality and the Invention of the Jewish
    Man.* Berkeley and Los Angeles: University of California Press, 1997.

Bracher, James T. "The Lorenzo-Jessica Subplot and *Genesis XXXIV.*" In *Shakespeare
    1964,* ed. Jim Corder, 33–42. Fort Worth: Texas Christian University Press, 1965.

Bray, Alan. "Homosexuality and the Signs of Male Friendship in Elizabethan England." In
    Queering the Renaissance, ed. Jonathan Goldberg, 40–61. Durham, NC: Duke
    University Press, 1994.

———. *Homosexuality in Renaissance England*. London: Gay Men's Press, 1982.

Brown, John Russell, ed. *The Arden Shakespeare: The Merchant of Venice*. London: Methuen, 1955.

Bryant, J. A. *Hippolyta's View: Some Christian Aspects of Shakespeare's Plays*. Lexington: University of Kentucky Press, 1961.

Bullough, Geoffrey. *Narrative and Dramatic Sources of Shakespeare*. Vol. 1. London: Routledge and Kegan Paul, 1957.

Burckhardt, Sigurd. *Shakespearean Meanings*. Princeton, NJ: Princeton University Press, 1968.

Burton, Jonathan. *Traffic and Turning: Islam and English Drama, 1579–1624*. Newark, NJ: University of Delaware Press, 2005.

Callaghan, Dympna. "Re-reading Elizabeth Cary's *The Tragedie of Miriam, Faire Queene of Jewry*." In *Women, "Race," and Writing in the Early Modern Period*, ed. Margo Hendricks and Patricia Parker, 163–77. New York: Routledge, 1994.

———. "Shakespeare and Religion." *Textual Practice* 15 (2001): 1–4.

Calvin, John. *The Commentarie of M. Io. Caluine vpon the Gospel of Iohn. Faithfullie translated out of Latine into English, by E. P.* Printed with *A Harmonie vpon the Three Euangelists*. London: George Bishop, 1584. STC 2962, reel 1370.

———. *A Commentarie of Iohn Caluine, vpon the first booke of Moses called Genesis: Translated out of Latine into English, by Thomas Tymme, Minister.* London: John Harison and George Bishop, 1578. STC 4393, reel 488.

———. *A Commentarie vpon the Epistle of Saint Paul to the Romanes, written in Latine by M. Iohn Caluin, and newely translated into Englishe by Christopher Rosdell.* London: John Harison and George Bishop, 1583. STC 4399, reel 414.

———. *A Harmonie vpon the Three Euangelists, Matthew, Mark and Luke, with the Commentarie of M. Iohn Caluine: Faithfullie translated out of Latine into English, by E. P.* London: George Bishop, 1584. STC 2962, reel 1370.

———. *Thirteene Sermons of Maister Iohn Caluine, Entreating of the Free Election of God in Iacob, and of reprobation in Esau. A treatise wherin euery Christian may see the excellent benefites of God towardes his children, and his maruelous iudgements towards the reprobate, firste published in the French toung, & now Translated into Englishe by Iohn Fielde, for the comfort of all Christians.* London: Thomas Man and Tobie Cooke, 1579. STC 4457, reel 416.

Cartelli, Thomas. "Shakespeare's *Merchant*, Marlowe's *Jew:* The Problem of Cultural Difference." *Shakespeare Studies* 20 (1988): 255–60.

Cavell, Stanley. *The Claim of Reason*. Oxford: Oxford University Press, 1979.

———. *Must We Mean What We Say?* Cambridge: Cambridge University Press, 1969.

Christensen, Jerome. "The Mind at Ocean." In *Modern Critical Interpretations: William Shakespeare's "The Merchant of Venice,"* ed. Harold Bloom, 121–28. New York: Chelsea House Publishers, 1986.

Clapham, Henoch. *A Briefe of the Bible*. Edinburgh: Robert Walde-graue, 1596. STC 5332, reel 317.

Cohen, D. M. "The Jew and Shylock." *Shakespeare Quarterly* 31 (1980): 53–63.

Cohen, Mark R. *Under Crescent and Cross: The Jews in the Middle Ages*. Princeton, NJ: Princeton University Press, 1994.

Cohen, Shaye J. D. *The Beginnings of Jewishness: Boundaries, Varieties, Uncertainties.* Berkeley and Los Angeles: University of California Press, 1999.

Cohen, Walter. "*The Merchant of Venice* and the Possibilities of Historical Criticism." *English Literary History* 49 (1982): 765–89.

Colley, John Scott. "Launcelot, Jacob, and Esau: Old and New Law in *The Merchant of Venice.*" In *Literature and Its Audience*, ed. G. K. Hunter and C. J. Rawson, 1:181–89. Yearbook of English Studies, vol. 10. Cambridge: Modern Humanities Research Association, 1980.

Collinson, Patrick. "Biblical Rhetoric: The English Nation and National Sentiment in the Prophetic Mode." In *Religion and Culture in Renaissance England*, ed. Claire McEachern and Debora Shuger, 15–45. Cambridge: Cambridge University Press, 1997.

———. "John Foxe and National Consciousness." In *John Foxe and His World*, ed. Christopher Highley and John N. King, 10–34. Aldershot, UK: Ashgate, 2002.

———. "William Shakespeare's Religious Inheritance and Environment." In *Elizabethan Essays*, 219–52. London and Rio Grande, OH: Hambledon Press, 1994.

A Comparison of the English and Spanish Nation: Composed by a French Gentleman against those of the League in Fraunce, which went about to perswade the king to breake his alliance with England, and to confirme it with Spaine. By occasion whereof, the nature of both Nations is liuely decyphered. Faithfully translated, out of the French, by R. A. London: John Wolfe, 1589. STC 13102, reel 304.

Coolidge, John. "Law and Love in *The Merchant of Venice.*" *Shakespeare Quarterly* 27 (1976): 243–63.

The Coppie of the Anti-Spaniard, made at Paris by a Frenchman, a Catholique, Wherein is directly proued how the Spanish King is the onely cause of all the troubles in France. Translated out of French into English. London: John Wolf, 1590. STC 684, reel 304.

Daniel, Andrew. "'I Know Not Why I Am So Sad': Melancholy and Knowledge in Early Modern English Painting, Drama, and Prose." PhD diss., University of California, Berkeley, 2006.

Danson, Lawrence. *The Harmonies of "The Merchant of Venice."* New Haven, CT: Yale University Press, 1978.

Daunce, Edward. *A Briefe Discourse of the Spanish State.* London: R. Field, 1590. STC 6291, reel 880.

Dekker, Thomas. *The Whore of Babylon.* Vol. 2 of *The Dramatic Works of Thomas Dekker*, ed. Fredson Bowers. Cambridge: Cambridge University Press, 1955.

de Sousa, Geraldo U. *Shakespeare's Cross-Cultural Encounters.* Houndmills, UK: Palgrave, 2002.

Dessen, Alan C. "The Elizabethan Stage Jew and Christian Example: Gerontus, Barabas, and Shylock." *Modern Language Quarterly* 35 (1974): 231–45.

Donne, John. "A Sermon Preached at Saint Dunstan's upon New-Years-day, 1624." In *The Sermons of John Donne*, ed. Evelyn M. Simpson and George R. Potter, 6:186–204. Berkeley and Los Angeles: University of California Press, 1953.

Duffy, Eamon. *The Stripping of the Altars: Traditional Religion in England c. 1400–c. 1580.* New Haven, CT: Yale University Press, 1992.

Edelman, Charles. Introduction to *The Merchant of Venice,* ed. Charles Edelman, 1–92. Cambridge: Cambridge University Press, 2002.

Edwards, John. *The Jews in Christian Europe, 1400–1700.* New York: Routledge, 1988.

Elukin, Jonathan M. "From Jew to Christian? Conversion and Immutability in Medieval Europe." In *Varieties of Religious Conversion in the Middle Ages,* ed. James Muldoon, 171–89. Gainesville: University Press of Florida, 1997.

Engle, Lars. "'Thrift Is Blessing': Exchange and Explanation in *The Merchant of Venice.*" *Shakespeare Quarterly* 37 (1986): 20–37.

Epp, Garrett P. J. "John Foxe and the Circumcised Stage." *Exemplaria* 9 (1997): 281–313.

———. "The Vicious Guise: Effeminacy, Sodomy, and *Mankind.*" In *Becoming Male in the Middle Ages,* ed. Jeffrey Jerome Cohen and Bonnie Wheeler, 303–20. New York: Garland Publishing, 1997.

Erasmus, Desiderius. *The Praise of Folly.* Trans. Hoyt Hopewell Hudson. Princeton, NJ: Princeton University Press, 1970.

Felsenstein, Frank. *Anti-Semitic Stereotypes: A Paradigm of Otherness in English Popular Culture, 1660–1830.* Baltimore, MD: Johns Hopkins University Press, 1995.

———. "Jews and Devils: Anti-Semitic Stereotypes of Late Medieval and Renaissance England." *Journal of Literature and Theology* 4 (1990): 15–28.

Ferber, Michael. "The Ideology of *The Merchant of Venice.*" *English Literary Renaissance* 20 (1990): 431–64.

Fiedler, Leslie A. *The Stranger in Shakespeare.* London: Croom Helm, 1972.

Fienberg, Nora. "Circumcision in *The Merchant of Venice.*" *PMLA* 113 (1998): 452.

A Fig for the Spaniard, or Spanish Spirits. London: John Wolfe, 1591. STC 1026, reel 711.

Forker, Charles R. "Webster or Shakespeare? Style, Idiom, Vocabulary, and Spelling in the Additions to *Sir Thomas More.*" In *Shakespeare and "Sir Thomas More": Essays on the Play and Its Shakespearean Interest,* ed. T. H. Howard-Hill, 151–70. Cambridge: Cambridge University Press, 1989.

Fortin, René E. "Launcelot and the Uses of Allegory in *The Merchant of Venice.*" *Studies in English Literature, 1500–1900* 14 (1974): 259–70.

Foxe, John. *The Acts and Monuments of John Foxe.* Ed. Josiah Pratt. 8 vols. London: George Seeley, 1870.

———. *A Sermon preached at the Christening of a Certaine Iew at London by Iohn Foxe. Conteining an exposition of the xi. chapter of S. Paul to the Romanes. Translated out of Latine into English by Iames Bell.* London: Christopher Barker, 1578. STC 11248, reel 543.

Franssen, Paul. "'With All My Heart': The Pound of Flesh and the Execution of Justice." In *Critical Self-Fashioning: Stephen Greenblatt and the New Historicism,* ed. Jürgen Pieters, 87–103. Frankfort: Peter Lang, 1999.

Freccero, Carla. "Cannibalism, Homophobia, Women: Montaigne's 'Des cannibales' and 'De l'amitié.'" In *Women, "Race," and Writing in the Early Modern Period,* ed. Margo Hendricks and Patricia Parker, 73–83. New York: Routledge, 1994.

Fredriksen, Paula. *From Jesus to Christ: The Origins of New Testament Images of Christ.* New Haven, CT: Yale University Press, 2000.

Freinkel, Lisa. "*The Merchant of Venice:* 'Modern' Anti-Semitism and the Veil of

Allegory." In *Shakespeare and Modernity*, ed. Hugh Grady, 122–41. New York: Routledge, 2000.

Friedman, Jerome. "Jewish Conversion, the Spanish Pure Blood Laws and Reformation: A Revisionist View of Racial and Religious Antisemitism." *Sixteenth Century Journal* 18 (1987): 3–29.

Furness, Horace Howard, ed. *A New Variorum Edition of Shakespeare: The Merchant of Venice*. Philadelphia: Lippincott, 1888.

Gabrieli, Vittorio, and Giorgio Melchiori, eds. *Sir Thomas More*. Manchester, UK: Manchester University Press, 1990.

Garber, Marjorie. *Vested Interests: Cross-Dressing and Cultural Anxiety*. New York: Routledge, 1992.

Gascoigne, George. "The Spoyle of Antwerpe." In *The Glasse of Governement, The Princely Pleasures at Kenelworth Castle, The Steele Glas and Other Poems and Prose Works*, ed. John W. Cunliffe, 590–99. Cambridge: Cambridge University Press, 1910.

The Geneva Bible: A Facsimile of the 1560 Edition. Introduction by Lloyd E. Berry. Madison: University of Wisconsin Press, 1969.

Gibbons, Nicholas. *Questions and Disputations Concerning the Holy Scripture*. London: Felix Kyngston, 1601. STC 11814, reel 1380.

Gillies, John. *Shakespeare and the Geography of Difference*. Cambridge: Cambridge University Press, 1994.

Gilman, Sander L. *Difference and Pathology: Stereotypes of Sexuality, Race, and Madness*. Ithaca, NY: Cornell University Press, 1985.

Girard, René. "'To Entrap the Wisest': A Reading of *The Merchant of Venice*." In *Literature and Society: Selected Papers from the English Institute, 1978*, ed. Edward W. Said, 100–119. Baltimore, MD: Johns Hopkins University Press, 1980.

Glassman, Bernard. *Anti-Semitic Stereotypes without Jews: Images of the Jews in England, 1290–1700*. Detroit, MI: Wayne State University Press, 1975.

Goddard, Harold. *The Meaning of Shakespeare*. Chicago: University of Chicago Press, 1951.

Goldberg, Jonathan. *Sodometries: Renaissance Texts, Modern Sexualities*. Stanford, CA: Stanford University Press, 1992.

Gollancz, Israel. *Allegory and Mysticism in Shakespeare: A Medievalist on "The Merchant of Venice."* London: George W. Jones, 1931.

Greenblatt, Stephen. *Will in the World*. New York: W. W. Norton, 2004.

Gross, John. *Shylock: Four Hundred Years in the Life of a Legend*. London: Chatto and Windus, 1992.

Gross, Kenneth. *Shylock Is Shakespeare*. Chicago: University of Chicago Press, 2006.

Gwyer, John. "The Case of Dr. Lopez." *Transactions of the Jewish Historical Society of England* 16 (1945–51): 163–84.

Hall, Kim F. "Guess Who's Coming to Dinner? Colonization and Miscegenation in *The Merchant of Venice*." *Renaissance Drama* 23 (1992): 87–111.

———. "Reading What Isn't There: 'Black' Studies in Early Modern England." *Stanford Humanities Review* 3 (1993): 23–33.

———. *Things of Darkness: Economies of Race and Gender in Early Modern England*. Ithaca, NY: Cornell University Press, 1995.

Haller, William. *Foxe's Book of Martyrs and the Elect Nation.* London: Jonathan Cape, 1963.

Halpern, Richard. *Shakespeare among the Moderns.* Ithaca, NY: Cornell University Press, 1997.

Hamilton, Donna B. "Shakespeare and Religion." In *The Shakespearean International Yearbook 1: Where Are We Now in Shakespearean Studies?* ed. W. R. Elton and John M. Muccioli, 187–202. Aldershot, UK: Ashgate, 1999.

Hammond, Paul. *Figuring Sex between Men from Shakespeare to Rochester.* Oxford: Oxford University Press, 2002.

Hannaford, Ivan. *Race: The History of an Idea in the West.* Washington, DC: Woodrow Wilson Center Press; Baltimore, MD: Johns Hopkins University Press, 1996.

Heal, Felicity. *Hospitality in Early Modern England.* Oxford: Oxford University Press, 1990.

———. "The Idea of Hospitality in Early Modern England." *Past and Present* 102 (1984): 66–93.

Helgerson, Richard. *Forms of Nationhood: The Elizabethan Writing of England.* Chicago: University of Chicago Press, 1992.

Hillgarth, J. N. *The Mirror of Spain, 1500–1700: The Formation of a Myth.* Ann Arbor: University of Michigan Press, 2000.

Hillman, David. "Visceral Knowledge: Shakespeare, Scepticism, and the Interior of the Early Modern Body." In *The Body in Parts: Fantasies of Corporeality in Early Modern Europe,* ed. David Hillman and Carla Mazzio, 80–105. New York: Routledge, 1997.

Hinely, Jan Lawson. "Bond Priorities in *The Merchant of Venice.*" *Studies in English Literature, 1500–1900* 20 (1980): 217–39.

Hobsbawm, E. J. *Nations and Nationalism since 1780: Programme, Myth, Reality.* Cambridge: Cambridge University Press, 1990.

Hockey, Dorothy C. "The Patch Is Kind Enough." *Shakespeare Quarterly* 10 (1959): 448–50.

The holie Bible. Imprinted at London: In Powles Churcheyarde by Richard Iugge, printer to the Queenes Maiestie, 1572. STC 2107, reel 1471. (The so-called Bishops' Bible.)

Holinshed, Raphael. *Holinshed's Chronicles of England, Scotland, and Ireland.* 6 vols. London: J. Johnson, 1807. This is a copy of the 1587 edition of the *Chronicles,* "Nowe newlie augmented and continued (with manifold matters of singular note and worthie memorie) to the year 1586, by John Hooker alias Vowell Gent.

Holland, Norman H. *Psychoanalysis and Shakespeare.* New York: Farrar, Straus, and Giroux, 1979.

Holmer, Joan Ozark. *The Merchant of Venice: Choice, Hazard and Consequence.* New York: St. Martin's Press, 1995.

Howard-Hill, T. H. Introduction to *Shakespeare and "Sir Thomas More": Essays on the Play and Its Shakespearean Interest,* ed. T. H. Howard-Hill. Cambridge: Cambridge University Press, 1989.

Howe, Nicholas. "An Angle on This Earth: Sense of Place in Anglo-Saxon England." *Bulletin of the John Rylands University Library of Manchester* 82 (2000): 1–25.

Hsia, R. Po-chia. *The Myth of Ritual Murder: Jews and Magic in Reformation Germany.* New Haven, CT: Yale University Press, 1988.

————. *Trent 1475: Stories of a Ritual Murder Trial.* New Haven, CT: Yale University Press, 1992.

Hunt, Maurice. *Shakespeare's Religious Allusiveness: Its Play and Tolerance.* Aldershot, UK: Ashgate, 2004.

Hunter, G. K. "The Theology of Marlowe's *The Jew of Malta.*" *Journal of the Warburg and Courtauld Institute* 27 (1964): 211–40.

Hutson, Lorna. "Emilia Lanyer." In *Dictionary of Literary Biography: Missing Persons,* ed. C. S. Nicholls, 388–89. Oxford: Oxford University Press, 1993.

Hyamson, Albert M. *The Sephardim of England: A History of the Spanish and Portuguese Community, 1492–1951.* London: Methuen, 1951.

Hyman, Lawrence W. "The Rival Lovers in *The Merchant of Venice.*" *Shakespeare Quarterly* 21 (1970): 109–16.

Iacob and Esau (A newe mery and wittie Comedie or Enterlude, newely imprinted, treating vpon the Historie of Iacob and Esau, Imprinted at London by Henrie Bynneman, 1568). Ed. John Crow and F. P. Wilson. The Malone Society Reprints. Oxford: Oxford University Press, 1956.

Japtok, Martin, and Winfried Schleiner. "Genetics and 'Race' in *The Merchant of Venice.*" *Literature and Medicine* 18 (1999): 155–72.

Johnson, Willis Harrison. "Between Christian and Jew: The Formation of Anti-Jewish Stereotypes in Medieval England." PhD diss., University of California, Berkeley, 1997.

Jones, Emrys. *The Origins of Shakespeare.* Oxford: Oxford University Press, 1977.

Josephus, Flavius. *The Antiquities of the Jews.* Book 1. Reprinted from William Whiston's 1736 translation. Peabody, MA: Hendrickson Publishers, 1987.

Kahn, Coppélia. "The Cuckoo's Note: Male Friendship and Cuckoldry in *The Merchant of Venice.*" In *Shakespeare's "Rough Magic": Renaissance Essays in Honor of C. L. Barber,* ed. Peter Erickson and Coppélia Kahn, 104–12. Newark, NJ: University of Delaware Press; London: Associated University Presses, 1985.

Kamen, Henry. *Inquisition and Society in Spain in the Sixteenth and Seventeenth Centuries.* London: Weidenfeld and Nicolson, 1985.

————. *The Spanish Inquisition: A Historical Revision.* New Haven, CT: Yale University Press, 1997.

Kaplan, M. Lindsay. "Jessica's Mother: Medieval Constructions of Jewish Race and Gender in *The Merchant of Venice.*" *Shakespeare Quarterly* 58 (2007): 1–30.

————, ed. *The Merchant of Venice: Texts and Contexts.* New York: Palgrave, 2002.

Katz, David S. *The Jews in the History of England, 1485–1850.* Oxford: Oxford University Press, 1994.

Kermode, Frank. "The Mature Comedies." In *Early Shakespeare,* ed. John Russell Brown and Bernard Harris, 211–27. Stratford-upon-Avon Studies 3. New York: St. Martin's Press, 1961.

Kermode, Lloyd Edward. "The Playwright's Prophecy: Robert Wilson's *The Three Ladies of London* and the 'Alienation' of the English." *Medieval and Renaissance Drama in England: An Annual Gathering of Research, Criticism and Reviews* 11 (1999): 60–87.

Kidd, Colin. *British Identities before Nationalism: Ethnicity and Nationhood in the Atlantic World, 1600–1800.* Cambridge: Cambridge University Press, 1999.

Kinney, Arthur F. "Text, Context, and Authorship of *The Booke of Sir Thomas Moore.*" In

Pilgrimage for Love: Essays in Early Modern Literature in Honor of Josephine A. Roberts, ed. Sigrid King, 133–60. Tempe: Arizona Center for Medieval and Renaissance Studies, 1999.

Klause, John. "Catholic and Protestant, Jesuit and Jew: Historical Religion in *The Merchant of Venice*." *Religion and the Arts* 7 (2003): 66–102.

Kleinberg, Seymour. "*The Merchant of Venice*: The Homosexual as Anti-Semite in Nascent Capitalism." In *Literary Visions of Homosexuality*, ed. Stuart Kellogg, 113–26. *Journal of Homosexuality* 8. New York: Haworth Press, 1983.

Knapp, Jeffrey. *Shakespeare's Tribe: Church, Nation, and Theater in Renaissance England*. Chicago: University of Chicago Press, 2002.

Kofman, Sarah. "Conversions: *The Merchant of Venice* under the Sign of Saturn." Trans. Shaun Whiteside. In *Literary Theory Today*, ed. Peter Collier and Helga Geyer-Ryan, 142–66. Ithaca, NY: Cornell University Press, 1990.

Lake, Peter. "Calvinism and the English Church 1570–1635." *Past and Present* 114 (1987): 32–76.

———. *Moderate Puritans and the Elizabethan Church*. Cambridge: Cambridge University Press, 1982.

Lampert, Lisa. *Gender and Jewish Difference from Paul to Shakespeare*. Philadelphia: University of Pennsylvania Press, 2004.

Lander, Jesse. "'Foxe's' *Books of Martyrs*: Printing and Popularizing the *Acts and Monuments*." In *Religion and Culture in Renaissance England*, ed. Claire McEachern and Debora Shugar, 69–92. Cambridge: Cambridge University Press, 1997.

Lawn, Brian. *The Salernitan Questions: An Introduction to the History of Medieval and Renaissance Problem Literature*. Oxford: Oxford University Press, 1963.

Lewalski, Barbara K. "Biblical Allusion and Allegory in *The Merchant of Venice*." *Shakespeare Quarterly* 13 (1962): 327–43.

Lincke, Uli. *Blood and Nation: The European Aesthetics of Race*. Philadelphia: University of Pennsylvania Press, 1999.

Lipton, Sara. *Images of Intolerance: The Representation of Jews and Judaism in the Bible moralisée*. Berkeley and Los Angeles: University of California Press, 1999.

Loades, David. "Introduction: John Foxe and the Editors." In *John Foxe and the English Reformation*, ed. David Loades, 1–11. Aldershot, UK: Scolar Press, 1997.

———. "Afterword: John Foxe in the Twenty-first Century." In *John Foxe and His World*, ed. Christopher Highley and John N. King, 277–89. Aldershot, UK: Ashgate, 2002.

Long, William B. "The Occasion of *The Book of Sir Thomas More*." In *Shakespeare and "Sir Thomas More": Essays on the Play and Its Shakespearean Interest*, ed. T. H. Howard-Hill, 45–56. Cambridge: Cambridge University Press, 1989.

Loomba, Ania. "'Delicious Traffick': Racial and Religious Difference on Early Modern Stages." In *Shakespeare and Race*, ed. Catherine M. S. Alexander and Stanley Wells, 203–24. Cambridge: Cambridge University Press, 2000.

———. "Outsiders in Shakespeare's England." In *The Cambridge Companion to Shakespeare*, ed. Margreta de Grazia and Stanley Wells, 147–66. Cambridge: Cambridge University Press, 2001.

———. "Shakespeare and the Racial Question." In *The Shakespearean International Yearbook 3: Where Are We Now in Shakespearean Studies?* ed. Graham Bradshaw,

John M. Mucciolo, Angus Fletcher, and Tom Bishop, 34–58. Aldershot, UK: Ashgate, 2003.

Lupton, Julia Reinhard. "Ethnos and Circumcision in the Pauline Tradition: A Psychoanalytic Exegesis." In *The Psychoanalysis of Race*, ed. Christopher Lane, 193–210. New York: Columbia University Press, 1998.

———. "Exegesis, Mimesis, and the Future of Humanism in *The Merchant of Venice*." *Religion and Literature* 32 (2000): 123–39.

———. "*Othello* Circumcised: Shakespeare and the Pauline Discourse of Nations." *Representations* 57 (1997): 73–89.

Luther, Martin. "On the Jews and Their Lies." In *Luther's Works*, vol. 47, ed. Franklin Sherman. Philadelphia: Fortress Press, 1971.

———. "That Jesus Christ Was Born a Jew." In *Luther's Works*, vol. 45, ed. Walther I. Brandt. Philadelphia: Muhlenberg Press, 1962.

Luxton, Thomas H. "A Second Daniel: The Jew and the 'True Jew' in *The Merchant of Venice*." *Early Modern Literary Studies* 4 (1999): 1–37.

Maitland, F. W. "The Deacon and the Jewess; or, Apostasy at Common Law." *Transactions of the Jewish Historical Society of England* 6 (1912): 260–81.

Marlowe, Christopher. *The Complete Plays of Christopher Marlowe*. Ed. Irving Ribner. New York: Odyssey Press, 1963.

Marotti, Arthur F. "Shakespeare and Catholicism." In *Theatre and Religion: Lancastrian Shakespeare*, ed. Richard Dutton, Alison Findlay, and Richard Wilson, 218–40. Manchester, UK: Manchester University Press, 2003.

Marx, Steven. *Shakespeare and the Bible*. Oxford: Oxford University Press, 2000.

Masten, Jeffrey. "*More* or Less: Editing the Collaborative." In *Shakespeare Studies*, ed. Leeds Barroll, 19:109–31. Madison, WI: Fairleigh Dickinson University Press; London: Associated University Presses, 2001.

Matchett, William. "Shylock, Iago, and *Sir Thomas More*." *PMLA* 92 (1977): 217–30.

Maus, Katharine Eisaman. *Inwardness and Theater in the English Renaissance*. Chicago: University of Chicago Press, 1995.

McEachern, Claire. Introduction to *Religion and Culture in Renaissance England*, ed. Claire McEachern and Debora Shuger, 1–12. Cambridge: Cambridge University Press, 1997.

McLean, Susan. "Prodigal Sons and Daughters: Transgression and Forgiveness in *The Merchant of Venice*." *Papers in Language and Literature* 32 (1996): 45–62.

McMillan, Scott. "*The Book of Sir Thomas More*: Dates and Acting Companies." In *Shakespeare and "Sir Thomas More": Essays on the Play and Its Shakespearean Interest*, ed. T. H. Howard-Hill, 57–76. Cambridge: Cambridge University Press, 1989.

Melchiori, Giorgio. "*The Book of Sir Thomas More*: Dramatic Unity." In *Shakespeare and "Sir Thomas More": Essays on the Play and Its Shakespearean Interest*, ed. T. H. Howard-Hill, 77–100. Cambridge: Cambridge University Press, 1989.

———. "The Master of the Revels and the Date of the Additions to *The Book of Sir Thomas More*." In *Shakespeare: Text, Language, Criticism; Essays in Honour of Marvin Spivack*, ed. Bernhard Fabian and Kurt Tertzeli von Rosador, 164–79. Hildesheim: Olms-Weidmann, 1987.

Menda, Nathanael. "The confession of faith, which Nathanael a Iewe borne, made before the Congregation in the Parish church of Alhallowes in Lombard Streete at London, whereupon he was according to his desire, receiued into the number of the faithfull and baptized the first of April, 1577." Appended to Foxe's *A Sermon preached at the Christening of a Certaine Iew.* London: Christopher Barker, 1578. STC 11248, reel 543.

Metz, G. Harold. "'Voice and Credyt': The Scholars and *Sir Thomas More.*" In *Shakespeare and "Sir Thomas More": Essays on the Play and Its Shakespearean Interest,* ed. T. H. Howard-Hill, 11–44. Cambridge: Cambridge University Press, 1989.

Metzger, Mary Janell. "'Now by My Hood, a Gentle and No Jew': Jessica, *The Merchant of Venice,* and the Discourse of Early Modern Identity." *PMLA* 113 (1998): 52–63.

Michaels, Leonard. "My Yiddish." *Threepenny Review* 95 (Fall 2003): 6–8.

Midgley, Graham. "*The Merchant of Venice:* A Reconsideration." *Essays in Criticism* 10 (1960): 119–33.

Milton, John. *Paradise Lost.* Ed. Gordon Teskey. New York: W. W. Norton, 2005.

Milward, Peter. "The Religious Implications of *The Merchant of Venice.*" In *The Medieval Dimension in Shakespeare's Plays,* 29–45. Lewiston, NY: Edwin Mellen Press, 1990.

Mithal, H. S. D., ed. *An Edition of Robert Wilson's "Three Ladies of London" and "Three Lords and Three Ladies of London."* Renaissance Imagination, vol. 36. New York: Garland Publishing, 1988.

Moisan, Thomas. "'Which Is the Merchant Here? and Which the Jew?' Subversion and Recuperation in *The Merchant of Venice.*" In *Shakespeare Reproduced: The Text in History and Ideology,* ed. Jean E. Howard and Marion F. O'Connor, 188–206. New York: Methuen, 1987.

Montanus, Reginaldus Gonsalvius. *A Discouery and Playne Declaration of Sundry Subtill practices of the Holy Inquisition of Spayne. Set forth in Latine, by Reginaldus Gonsaluius Montanus, and newly translated.* London, 1568, 1569. STC 11996, reel 297.

Moody, A. D. *Shakespeare: The Merchant of Venice.* London: Edward Arnold, 1964.

Morris, Harris. "The Judgment Theme in *The Merchant of Venice.*" *Renascence* 39 (1986): 292–311.

Morrison, Karl F. *Understanding Conversion.* Charlottesville: University Press of Virginia, 1992.

Muir, Kenneth, ed. *The Arden Shakespeare: King Lear.* London and New York: Routledge, 1972.

Munday, Anthony, et al. *Sir Thomas More: A Play by Anthony Munday and Others, Revised by Henry Chettle, Thomas Dekker, Thomas Heywood, and William Shakespeare.* Ed. Vittorio Gabrieli and Giorgio Melchiori. Manchester, UK: Manchester University Press, 1990.

Nashe, Thomas. *The Unfortunate Traveller.* In *Thomas Nashe: Selected Writings,* ed. Stanley Wells. Cambridge, MA: Harvard University Press, 1965.

Neill, Michael. *Putting History to the Question: Power, Politics, and Society in English Renaissance Drama.* New York: Columbia University Press, 2000.

Netanyahu, Benzion. *The Origins of the Inquisition in Fifteenth Century Spain.* New York: Random House, 1995.

Newall, Venetia. "The Jew as a Witch Figure." In *The Witch Figure*, ed. Venetia Newall, 95–124. London: Routledge and Kegan Paul, 1973.

Noble, Richmond. *Shakespeare's Biblical Knowledge*. London: Society for Promoting Christian Knowledge, 1935.

Normand, Lawrence. "Reading the Body in *The Merchant of Venice*." *Textual Practice* 5 (1991): 55–73.

Nugent, Teresa Lanpher. "Usury and Counterfeiting in Wilson's *The Three Ladies of London* and *The Three Lords and Three Ladies of London*, and in Shakespeare's *Measure for Measure*." In *Money and the Age of Shakespeare: Essays in New Economic Criticism*, ed. Linda Woodbridge, 201–17. New York: Palgrave Macmillan, 2003.

Nussbaum, Damian. "Whitgift's 'Book of Martyrs': Archbishop Whitgift, Timothy Bright and the Elizabethan Struggle over John Foxe's Legacy." In *John Foxe: An Historical Perspective*, ed. David Loades, 135–53. Aldershot, UK: Ashgate, 1999.

Nuttall, A. D. *A New Mimesis: Shakespeare and the Representation of Reality*. New York: Methuen, 1983.

Olsen, Palle J. "Was John Foxe a Millenarian?" *Journal of Ecclesiastical History* 45 (1994): 600–624.

Olsen, V. Norskov. *John Foxe and the Elizabethan Church*. Berkeley and Los Angeles: University of California Press, 1973.

Orgel, Stephen. "Shylock's Tribe." In *Shakespeare and the Mediterranean: The Selected Proceedings of the International Shakespeare Association World Congress, Valencia, 2001*, ed. Tom Clayton, Susan Brock, and Vicente Forés, 38–53. Newark, NJ: University of Delaware Press, 2004.

Oz, Avraham. *The Yoke of Love: Prophetic Riddles in "The Merchant of Venice."* Newark, NJ: University of Delaware Press; London: Associated University Presses, 1995.

Palmer, Daryl W. *Hospitable Performances: Dramatic Genre and Cultural Practices in Early Modern England*. West Lafayette, IN: Purdue University Press, 1992.

———. "Merchants and Miscegenation: *The Three Ladies of London, The Jew of Malta*, and *The Merchant of Venice*." In *Race, Ethnicity, and Power in the Renaissance*, ed. Joyce Green MacDonald, 36–66. Madison, WI: Fairleigh Dickinson University Press; London: Associated University Presses, 1997.

Paris, Matthew. *Monarchi Albanensis, Angli, Historia Maior*. London, 1571. EEBO.

Parker, Patricia. *Literary Fat Ladies: Rhetoric, Gender, Property*. New York: Methuen, 1987.

Parry, Glyn. "Elect Church or Elect Nation? The Reception of the *Acts and Monuments*." In *John Foxe: An Historical Perspective*, ed. David Loades, 167–81. Aldershot, UK: Ashgate, 1999.

Parsons, Mikeal C. "The Prodigal's Elder Brother: The History and Ethics of Reading Luke 15:25–32." *Perspectives in Religious Studies* 23 (1996): 147–74.

Paster, Gail Kern. *The Body Embarrassed: Drama and the Disciplines of Shame in Early Modern England*. Ithaca, NY: Cornell University Press, 1993.

Pastoor, Charles. "The Subversion of Prodigal Son Comedy in *The Merchant of Venice*." *Renascence* 53 (2000): 3–22.

Perez, Antonio. *A Treatise Paraenetical*. London: William Ponsonby, 1598. STC 19838, reel 388.

Plaut, W. Gunther, ed. *The Torah: A Modern Commentary*. New York: Union of American Hebrew Congregations, 1981.

Poliakov, Léon. *The History of Anti-Semitism from the Time of Christ to the Court Jews*. Trans. Richard Howard. New York: Vanguard Press, 1974. (Original French edition 1965.)

Pollard, Alfred W., ed. *Shakespeare's Hand in the Play of Sir Thomas More*. Cambridge: Cambridge University Press, 1923.

The Present State of Spaine. London: Richard Serger, 1594. STC 22996, reel 976.

Prior, Roger. "A Second Jewish Community in Tudor London." *Jewish Historical Studies: Transactions of the Jewish Historical Society of England* 31 (1990): 137–52.

The Problemes of Aristotle. London, 1597. STC 764, reel 167.

Pullan, Brian. *The Jews of Europe and the Inquisition of Venice, 1550–1670*. Totowa, NJ: Barnes and Noble Books, 1983.

Questier, Michael C. *Conversion, Politics and Religion in England, 1580–1625*. Cambridge: Cambridge University Press, 1996.

Rabkin, Norman. *Shakespeare and the Problem of Meaning*. Chicago: University of Chicago Press, 1981.

Ragussis, Michael. *Figures of Conversion: "The Jewish Question" and English National Identity*. Durham, NC: Duke University Press, 1995.

Resnick, Irven M. "Medieval Roots of the Myth of Jewish Male Menses." *Harvard Theological Review* 93 (2000): 241–63.

Robbins, Jill. *Prodigal Son/Elder Brother: Interpretation and Alterity in Augustine, Petrarch, Kafka, Levinas*. Chicago: University of Chicago Press, 1991.

Robinson, Benedict Scott. "John Foxe and the Anglo-Saxons." In *John Foxe and His World*, ed. Christopher Highley and John N. King, 54–72. Aldershot, UK: Ashgate, 2002.

Rockas, Leo. "'A Dish of Doves': The Merchant of Venice." *English Literary History* 40 (1973): 339–51.

Rosen, Alan. "The Rhetoric of Exclusion: Jew, Moor, and the Boundaries of Discourse in *The Merchant of Venice*." In *Race, Ethnicity, and Power in the Renaissance*, ed. Joyce Green MacDonald, 67–79. Madison, WI: Fairleigh Dickinson University Press; London: Associated University Presses, 1997.

Rosenheim, Judith. "Allegorical Commentary in *The Merchant of Venice*." *Shakespeare Studies* 24 (1996): 156–210.

Rosenshield, Gary. "Deconstructing the Christian Merchant: Antonio and *The Merchant of Venice*." *Shofar: An Interdisciplinary Journal of Jewish Studies* 20 (2002): 28–51.

Roth, Cecil. *A History of the Jews in England*. Oxford: Oxford University Press, 1941.

Rowse, A. L. *Shakespeare the Man*. New York: Harper and Row, 1973.

Ruether, Rosemary. *Faith and Fratricide: The Theological Roots of Anti-Semitism*. New York: Seabury Press, 1974.

"The Sacrifice of Isaac." In *English Miracle Plays: Moralities and Interludes*, ed. Alfred W. Pollard, 21–30. Oxford: Clarendon Press, 1927.

Shaheen, Naseeb. *Biblical References in Shakespeare's Comedies*. Newark, NJ: University of Delaware Press; London: Associated University Presses, 1993.

———. *Biblical References in Shakespeare's Tragedies*. Newark, NJ: University of
Delaware Press; London: Associated University Presses, 1987.

———. "Shakespeare's Knowledge of the Bible—How Acquired." *Shakespeare Studies* 20
(1987): 201–14.

———. "Shylock's 'Abram' in *The Merchant of Venice*." *Notes and Queries*, n.s., 38
(1991): 56–57.

Shakespeare, William. *The Arden Edition of the Works of William Shakespeare: The
Merchant of Venice*. Ed. John Russell Brown. New York: Routledge, 1988.

———. *The Complete Works of Shakespeare*. Ed. David Bevington. New York: HarperCol-
lins, 1992.

———. *The Norton Shakespeare*. Ed. Stephen Greenblatt, Walter Cohen, Jean E. Howard,
and Katharine Eisaman Maus. New York: W. W. Norton, 1997.

———. *Sir Thomas More*. See Munday, Anthony, et al.

———. *William Shakespeare: The Complete Works*. Ed. Alfred Harbage. Baltimore, MD:
Penguin Books, 1969.

Shapiro, James. *Shakespeare and the Jews*. New York: Columbia University Press, 1996.

Shell, Marc. "Marranos (Pigs), or From Coexistence to Toleration." *Critical Inquiry* 17
(1991): 306–35.

———. "The Wether and the Ewe: Verbal Usury in *The Merchant of Venice*." In *Money,
Language, and Thought: Literary and Philosophical Economies from the Medieval to
the Modern Era*, 47–83. Berkeley and Los Angeles: University of California Press,
1982.

Sinfield, Alan. *Cultural Politics—Queer Reading*. Philadelphia: University of Pennsylvania Press, 1994.

———. *Shakespeare, Authority, Sexuality: Unfinished Business in Cultural Materialism*.
London: Routledge, 2006.

Sisson, C. J. "A Colony of Jews in Shakespeare's London." In *Essays and Studies by
Members of the English Association 23*, 38–51. Oxford: Oxford University Press, 1938.

Skura, Meredith Anne. *Shakespeare the Actor and the Purposes of Playing*. Chicago:
University of Chicago Press, 1993.

Smith, Bruce R. *Homosexual Desire in Shakespeare's England*. Chicago: University of
Chicago Press, 1991.

———. "What! *You*, Will? Shakespeare and Homoeroticism." In *The Shakespearean International Yearbook 1: Where Are We Now in Shakespearean Studies?* ed. W. R. Elton
and John M. Mucciolo, 45–64. Aldershot, UK: Ashgate, 1999.

Spenser, Edmund. *Amoretti*. In *The Yale Edition of the Shorter Poems of Edmund
Spenser*, ed. William A. Oram et al. New Haven, CT: Yale University Press, 1989.

———. *The Faerie Queene*. Ed. A. C. Hamilton. Harlow: Longman, 2001.

———. "Prosopopoia: or Mother Hubberds Tale." In *The Yale Edition of the Shorter
Poems of Edmund Spenser*, ed. William A. Oram et al. New Haven, CT: Yale
University Press, 1989.

———. *A View of the Present State of Ireland*. In *The Works of Edmund Spenser (a
Variorum Edition): Spenser's Prose Works*, ed. Rudolf Gottfried. Baltimore, MD:
Johns Hopkins University Press, 1949.

Spevack, Marvin, ed. *The Harvard Concordance to Shakespeare*. Cambridge, MA: Harvard University Press, 1973.

Spiller, Elizabeth A. "From Imagination to Miscegenation: Race and Romance in Shakespeare's *The Merchant of Venice*." *Renaissance Drama* 29 (1998): 137–64.

Stacey, Robert C. "The Conversion of Jews to Christianity in Thirteenth-Century England." *Speculum* 67 (1992): 263–83.

Sternberg, Meir. "Delicate Balance in the Rape of Dinah." In *The Poetics of Biblical Narrative: Ideological Literature and the Drama of Reading*, 445–75. Bloomington: Indiana University Press, 1985.

Stevens, Scott Manning. "Sacred Heart and Secular Brain." In *The Body in Parts: Fantasies of Corporeality in Early Modern England*, ed. David Hillman and Carla Mazzio, 262–82. New York: Routledge, 1997.

Stolcke, Verena. "Invaded Women: Gender, Race, and Class in the Formation of Colonial Society." In *Women, "Race," and Writing in the Early Modern Period*, ed. Margo Hendricks and Patricia Parker, 272–86. New York: Routledge, 1994.

Strack, Hermann L. *The Jew and Human Sacrifice*. Trans. Henry Blanchamp. New York: Bloch, 1909.

Stritmatter, Roger. "By Providence Divine: Shakespeare's Awareness of Some Geneva Marginal Notes of *1 Samuel*." *Notes and Queries*, n.s., 47 (2000): 97–100.

Sundelson, David. *Shakespeare's Restorations of the Father*. New Brunswick, NJ: Rutgers University Press, 1983.

Tanner, Tony. "'Which Is the Merchant Here? And Which the Jew?' The Venice of Shakespeare's *Merchant of Venice*." In *Venetian Views, Venetian Blinds: English Fantasies of Venice*, ed. Manfred Pfister and Barbara Schaff, 45–62. Amsterdam and Atlanta, GA: Rodopi, 1999.

Taylor, Gary. *Castration: An Abbreviated History of Western Manhood*. New York: Routledge, 2002.

———. "The Date and Auspices of the Additions to *Sir Thomas More*." In *Shakespeare and "Sir Thomas More": Essays on the Play and Its Shakespearean Interest*, ed. T. H. Howard-Hill, 101–29. Cambridge: Cambridge University Press, 1989.

Tennenhouse, Leonard. "The Counterfeit Order of *The Merchant of Venice*." In *Representing Shakespeare: New Psychoanalytic Essays*, ed. Murray M. Schwartz and Coppélia Kahn, 54–69. Baltimore, MD: Johns Hopkins University Press, 1980.

Tippens, Darryl. "Shakespeare and the Prodigal Son Tradition." *Explorations in Renaissance Culture* 14 (1988): 57–77.

Trachtenberg, Joshua. *The Devil and the Jews: The Medieval Conception of the Jew and Its Relation to Modern Antisemitism*. New Haven, CT: Yale University Press, 1943; reprint, Philadelphia: Jewish Publication Society of America, 1983.

Ungerer, Gustav. "Portia and the Prince of Morocco." *Shakespeare Studies* 31 (2003): 89–126.

Vitkus, Daniel J. "Turning Turk in *Othello*: The Conversion and Damnation of the Moor." *Shakespeare Quarterly* 48 (1997): 145–74.

Wailes, Stephen L. *Medieval Allegories of Jesus' Parables*. Berkeley and Los Angeles: University of California Press, 1987.

Warner, William. *Albions England.* 1612. Hildesheim and New York: Georg Olms Verlag, 1971.

Wheeler, Richard P. "'. . . And My Loud Crying Still': The *Sonnets, The Merchant of Venice,* and *Othello.*" In *Shakespeare's 'Rough Magic': Renaissance Essays in Honor of C. L. Barber,* ed. Peter Erickson and Coppélia Kahn, 193–209. Newark, NJ: University of Delaware Press; London: Associated University Presses, 1985.

Whigham, Frank. "Ideology and Class Conduct in *The Merchant of Venice.*" *Renaissance Drama,* n.s., 10 (1979): 93–115.

William of Orange. *The Apologie or Defence, of the Most Noble Prince William.* Delft, 1581. STC 15209, reel 240.

———. *A supplication to the Kinges Maiestie of Spayne.* London, 1573. STC 25710, reel 587.

Williams, Arnold. *The Common Expositor: An Account of the Commentaries on Genesis, 1527–1633.* Chapel Hill: University of North Carolina Press, 1948.

Wilson, John Dover. *Shakespeare's Happy Comedies.* London: Farber and Farber, 1962.

Wilson, Robert. *The Three Ladies of London* and *The Three Lords and Three Ladies of London.* In *An Edition of Robert Wilson's "Three Ladies of London" and "Three Lords and Three Ladies of London,"* ed. H. S. D. Mithal. Renaissance Imagination, vol. 36. New York: Garland Publishing, 1988.

Winnicott, D. W. "Communicating and Not Communicating Leading to a Study of Certain Opposites." In *The Maturational Processes and the Facilitating Environment,* 179–92. London: Hogarth Press, 1965.

Wolf, Lucien. "Jews in Elizabethan England." *Transactions of the Jewish Historical Society of England* 11 (1928): 1–91.

———. "Jews in Tudor England." In *Essays in Jewish History,* ed. Cecil Roth, 73–90. London: Jewish Historical Society of England, 1934.

Wooden, Warren W. *John Foxe.* Boston: Twayne Publishers, 1983.

Woods, Susanne. *Lanyer: A Renaissance Woman Poet.* Oxford: Oxford University Press, 1999.

Wortheim, Albert. "The Treatment of Shylock and Thematic Integrity in *The Merchant of Venice.*" *Shakespeare Studies* 6 (1970): 75–87.

Yerushalmi, Yosef Hayim. *Assimilation and Racial Anti-Semitism: The Iberian and the German Models.* Leo Baeck Memorial Lecture 26. New York: Leo Baeck Institute, 1982.

———. *From Spanish Court to Italian Ghetto, Isaac Cardoso: A Study in Seventeenth-Century Marranism and Jewish Apologetics.* New York: Columbia University Press, 1971.

INDEX